A 100 Year Legacy

A 100 Year Legacy

JEFFREY L. RODENGEN

Edited by Christian Ramirez

Design and Layout by Cristofer Valle

Write Stuff Enterprises, LLC
1001 South Andrews Avenue
Fort Lauderdale, FL 33316
1-800-900-Book (1-800-900-2665)
(954) 462-6657
www.writestuffbooks.com

The publisher has made every effort to identify and locate the source of the photographs included
in this edition of *Henry Ford Health System: A 100 Year Legacy*. Grateful acknowledgment is made
to those who have kindly granted permission for the use of their materials in this edition.
If there are instances where proper credit was not given, the publisher will gladly make any
necessary corrections in subsequent printings.

Also by Jeffrey L. Rodengen

For a complete list, visit writestuffbooks.com

Publisher's Cataloging-In-Publication Data
(Prepared by The Donohue Group, Inc.)

Rodengen, Jeffrey L.
 Henry Ford Health System : a 100 year legacy / Jeffrey
L. Rodengen ; edited by Christian Ramirez ; design and layout
by Cristofer Valle ; foreword by William Clay Ford, Jr. &
Lynn Ford Alandt ; introduction by Nancy Schlichting.

 pages : illustrations, maps ; cm

 Includes bibliographical references and index.
 ISBN: 978-1-932022-76-6

 1. Henry Ford Health System—History. 2. Henry Ford
Hospital—History. 3. Hospitals—Michigan—Detroit—
History. 4. Medical corporations—Michigan—Detroit—
History. I. Ramirez, Christian, 1980- II. Valle, Cristofer. III.
Ford, Bill, 1957- IV. Alandt, Lynn Ford. V. Schlichting,
Nancy. VI. Title. VII. Title: 100 year legacy

RA982.D42 H46 2014
362.1/10977434   2014951777

TABLE OF CONTENTS

INTRODUCTION

IT'S HARD TO IMAGINE A MORE IMPROBABLE BEGINNING for a hospital.

Many business magnates have contributed part of their wealth to health care institutions out of gratitude for treatment they or loved ones received.

But Detroit business titan Henry Ford—who is said to have conceived the automobile assembly line after he saw the "disassembly" of chickens in a slaughterhouse and reverse-engineered the process—launched a hospital out of impatience.

Ford couldn't abide lassitude, half-measures, or inertia. After he joined others in putting up funds for the construction of what was to be called Detroit General Hospital, the project faltered. Construction stopped soon after it started, the project's planners dithered about moving forward, and, before long, Ford had had enough.

He bought out his fellow investors, put the right people in the right places, and on October 1, 1915, Henry Ford Hospital opened with 48 private beds on the site where it remains today.

Now, with almost 900 beds, 1,100 staff physicians and a sprawling campus, it's the flagship of a massive integrated health care system whose reach and service extend far beyond the central city and whose reputation for research, education, and clinical excellence is international.

The 100 year story of Henry Ford Hospital and Henry Ford Health System is one of constancy even in the face of several wars, economic depression and recession, social upheaval that left Detroit in flames, and the revolutionary health care challenges of a new millennium.

The institution was imprinted from the start with a mission that always put the patient first, fostered innovation through research that was commonly conducted in tandem with clinical treatment, educated its own and others, reached out to and became a vital part of its community, and did it all with a dedication to top quality and safety. This tone carried on down the line to the present day.

From the start, Henry Ford's aide-de-camp Ernest Liebold drew on Ford Motor Company engineering expertise to meet the needs of this singular hospital. Dr. Frank Sladen, the hospital's first physician-in-chief, and Dr. Roy McClure, its first surgeon-in-chief, supervised an ever-growing clinical staff who worked in an unusual "closed" system of salaried doctors.

Across time, clinicians and researchers made historic advances against the full range of cancers and infectious disease as well as advances in preventive care, public health, pediatrics and geriatrics, sleep disorders, sports medicine, voice care—any problems to which the human body is prey: Conrad Lam (heart surgery); D. Emerick Szilagyi (vascular surgery); Clarence Livingood (dermatology); and Edward Quinn (infectious diseases); and more recently, brain neuroregeneration by Dr. Michael Chopp and advances in treating high blood pressure by Dr. Oscar Carretero. Dr. Kimberlydawn Wisdom, the first Michigan surgeon general in state history, came from Henry Ford Hospital's medical ranks.

More recently, Henry Ford continued its international reputation for the treatment of structural heart disease by Dr. William O'Neill; became the world leader in robot-assisted minimally invasive surgical techniques, thanks to urologist Dr. Mani Menon; and created the Henry Ford Innovation Institute with Dr. Scott Dulchavsky.

The pantheon of leadership continued throughout the long history of Henry Ford Hospital, including Dr. Robin (Bob) Buerki, CEO Stan Nelson, and Dr. John Popovich, the first physician CEO of Henry Ford Hospital since Dr. Buerki more than five decades before.

And then there was Gail Warden who oversaw the health system from 1988 to 2003—a pioneering voice who put patient care ahead of business concerns and who made endless contributions to the improvement of patient safety and health care.

Through growing collaborations with leading medical schools—in the US and Canada—Henry Ford Hospital and health care system consistently replenished its own ranks and those elsewhere with first-rank practitioners educated by Ford physicians and researchers.

As *Time* magazine wrote: "The first thing to notice is that this hospital and these doctors are an example of what is right about American health care—not what is wrong. The Henry Ford Health System, which owns Henry Ford Hospital, is a well-run example of a large medical group practice."[1]

Henry Ford would no doubt take some measure of pride in *Time*'s assessment.

As in his other endeavors, Ford created something special, something unique, something generations of his family would continue to nurture with their time, creativity, and financial benevolence.

As you will read in this commemorative book, Henry Ford Hospital shared the same dark days as its city and country, meeting each challenge with courage, foresight, innovation, and the persistence to pass through its challenges with the unflagging belief that it would be better and stronger when it emerged in the light.

The founder referred to this guiding spirit as the reason for the "somewhat remarkable progression of our enterprises." He did not talk in terms of "'success,' for that word is an epitaph, and we are just starting."[2]

That remains true as Henry Ford Hospital marks its first century, a first chapter in a story without end.

Nancy Schlichting
CEO, HENRY FORD HEALTH SYSTEM

FOREWORD

OUR GREAT-GRANDFATHER, THE LEGENDARY AND iconic industrialist Henry Ford, whose name and brand are intertwined with nearly a third of Detroit's history, intended for Henry Ford Hospital to be neither a moneymaker nor a charity.

His decision 100 years ago to take ownership of a stalled general hospital project that bore Detroit's name, and get the job done under his own, put in motion a century-long story that centers on the health care needs of the city's working people. The involvement of our family in the hospital has been a constant throughout that story.

Henry Ford was not a figurehead, but a hands-on founder who dedicated his time and that of his most trusted executives to walking the halls of the nascent hospital. He spotted needs and inefficiencies and found better ways of doing what needed to be done to ensure that the people of Detroit would find quality medical care in a uniquely comfortable setting.

At the time of Henry Ford Hospital's founding, there were enough hospitals for the rich and enough for the poor, our great-grandfather said. This was to be a place where people who put their backs into their work and built a better America would be given the care and respect they deserved.

He was financially generous to the growing institution and in all ways set the standard by which we, his descendants, measure and conduct ourselves.

Henry Ford's generosity at first seems paradoxical given his belief in self-reliance, self-determination, and old-fashioned grit. Institutional, commercialized charity, he said, loses its heart and "becomes a cold and clammy thing."[1] Giving, he insisted, was most meaningful when the recipient neither asked for nor expected the gift.

Personal benevolence did not conflict with his overall philosophy. A biographer recalls that during a motor trip out East, our great-grandfather came across a farm couple who had lost their home to a storm. He gave them $200, everything he carried in his pocket.[1]

Such heartfelt personal acts of kindness were countless, most of them no doubt lost to history. But his large-scale philanthropy, including the founding and expansion of Henry Ford Hospital, was personal as he also gave away a significant percentage of his income.

Generations of Fords and our spouses have followed the leads of both our great-grandfather and our beloved great-grandmother, Clara. She made her own mark by contributing personal wealth to balance the books in the hospital's early years, pushing for the creation of its first psychiatric unit and leading the creation of both the Henry Ford School of Nursing and Hygiene and the Clara Ford Nurses Home.

Their example was followed by son Edsel Ford and his wife, Eleanor, our grandparents, who also generously supported Henry Ford Hospital. Edsel also served on its board of trustees from its opening in 1915 until his death nearly three decades later.

By then, a tradition was established and continued by Edsel and Eleanor's children, Henry II, Benson (Lynn's father), Josephine, and William Clay (Bill's father, who served on the Henry Ford Hospital board from 1950 to 1982 and then became an honorary trustee on the hospital and health system boards).

Edsel Ford II added his name and efforts to the boards of Henry Ford Health System and the Fund for Henry Ford Hospital, and Bill's mother, Martha F. Ford, as well as Lynn, served on the board of the original Henry Ford Health Care Corporation, which became Henry Ford Health System.

We were joined or followed on other system boards by many family members: Elizabeth Ford Kontulis, Sheila Ford Hamp, Elena A. Ford, Paul D. Alandt, Michael F. Hamp, Thomas C. Buhl, and Eleanor B. Ford.

Benson was a chairman of the hospital's board, and his wife, Edith McNaughton Ford, was a board member, serving for nearly 40 years. Henry II, in addition to his many personal contributions to Henry Ford Hospital's history, was instrumental in securing a major $100 million gift from the Ford Foundation, which was the genesis of the growth in medical education and research.

While the hospital continued to grow as the flagship of the ever-expanding Henry Ford Health System, yet another generation of the Ford family joined in as board members and donors to carry the multi-faceted enterprise through the 20th century and into the 21st.

Citing his own restorative treatment at Henry Ford Maplegrove Center for chemical dependency, Benson Ford, Jr., reclaimed his life and went on to serve first as an intern at the center and later on its board, as well as on those of Behavioral Health Services, the Northwest Region, and Henry Ford West Bloomfield Hospital.

The Ford name, whether that of the founder or his descendants, continued to "brand" new components added to the health system. The Edsel B. Ford Institute for Medical Research was put in place to seek and discover innovations in medical science, while scientific investigation was integrated with clinical research at the Benson Ford Education and Research Center.

The present-day Josephine Ford Cancer Institute began with a $10 million gift by our aunt after she was impressed by her husband's treatment for pancreatic cancer at the hospital. And Lynn and her husband made possible the Paul & Lynn Alandt Catheterization & Electrophysiology Center, the first of its kind in Michigan. Additionally, the Heart and Vascular Institute, a Center of Excellence, was named after Benson and Edith Ford for their donations over the years.

Through world wars, the Great Depression, near-catastrophic economic recessions, civil unrest at home and elsewhere, and even Detroit's bankruptcy—the first of any major city in the United States—Henry Ford Hospital and Health System flourished and earned a worldwide reputation for excellence.

Our family has participated in the growth of the health system since its infancy. We did so in great measure because our great-grandfather led the way by example.

Detroit and its people deserved and earned the support of our family. It never flagged. And it was always personal.

By William Clay Ford, Jr. and Lynn Ford Alandt

ACKNOWLEDGMENTS

MANY DEDICATED INDIVIDUALS ASSISTED IN the research, preparation, and publication of *Henry Ford Health System: A 100 Year Legacy*. Research Assistant Sandy Smith conducted the principal archival research for the book and Photo Research Assistant Maureen McDonald conducted research for the book's images. Senior Editor Christian Ramirez managed the editorial content, while Senior Graphic Designer and Studio Administrator Cristofer Valle brought the story to life.

The deepest of gratitude goes to the Henry Ford Health System Anniversary Book Committee: Sarah Whitehouse, Melanie Bazil, Dwight Angell, Deborah Babcock, Dr. Paul Edwards, Rose Glenn, Veronica Hall, Dr. John Popovich, Dr. Alex Shepard, Dr. Fred Whitehouse, and Gayle Williams. From the Sladen Library and the Conrad R. Lam Archives the author would like to express his sincere thanks to Melanie Bazil, Joe Escribano, JoAnn Krzeminski, Evan Benn, Barbara LeTarte, Audrey Bondar, and Gayle Williams.

Special thanks to photographers Ray Manning, John Grybas, Riva Sayegh-McCullen, David M. Griffith, and Jeff Boni, as well as Janet Dunbar from Media Resources.

The author is also grateful for assistance from Dr. David Allard, Dr. Gregory Barkley, Edith L. Eisenmann, Jennifer Harmon, Kathy Huber, Paul Kolpaski, Mary Kravutske, Dr. Margot LaPointe, Pat Pillon, Shana Reed, and Susan Schwandt.

Additionally, the efforts of Jim TerMarsch and his crew at Marsch Creative and Nardina Mein and her team at the Benson Ford Research Center at The Henry Ford are greatly appreciated.

The author would also like to thank William Clay Ford, Jr., Lynn Ford Alandt as well as the current and former employees and Trustees of Henry Ford Health System and Detroit's leaders who were interviewed for this book and whose thoughts and words added important historical context to the story, including: Dr. Marwan Abouljoud, William Alvin, Dennis Archer, Anthony Armada, Melanie Bazil, David Benfer, Dr. Michael Benninger, Dave Bing, Dr. Melvin Block, Darlene Burgess, Dr. Oscar Carretero, Dr. Robert Chapman,

Dr. Michael Chopp, Dr. C. Edward Coffey, James M. Connelly, Dr. William Conway, Dr. John Crissman, Connie Cronin, Joan Daniels, Dorothy Deremo, Dr. Donald Ditmars, Walter E. Douglas, Dr. Scott Dulchavsky, Edith L. Eisenmann, Dr. Stanton Elias, Dr. Joseph Elliott, Dr. William Eyler, Dr. Evelyn J. Fisher, Benson Ford, Jr., Kevin Frasier, Wilma Gandy, Allan Gilmour, Dr. Sidney Goldstein, Lee Gooden, Veronica Hall, Mort Harris, Dr. Christine Cole Johnson, Theresa Jones, Dr. Charles Kelly, Dr. Mark A. Kelley, Dr. Margot LaPointe, Dr. David Leach, Dr. Dennis Lemanski, Dr. Henry Lim, Dr. Frank Lewis, Madelyne Markowitz, Dr. Norman Markowitz, David McCammon, Douglas McClure, Thomas F. McNulty, Dr. Mani Menon, Dr. Benjamin Movsas, Jane Muer, Dr. Bruce Muma, Thomas S. Nantais, Stanley Nelson, Dr. William O'Neill, Dr. Theodore Parsons, Douglas Peters, Dr. Joanna Pease, Sandra Pierce, John Polanski, Dr. John Popovich, Dr. Daniel Reddy, Rondolyn Richardson, Robert G. Riney, Dr. Emanuel Rivers, Dr. Mark Rosenblum, Barbara Rossman, Dr. Thomas Roth, Dr. Thomas Royer, Vinod Sahney, Dr. Eric Scher, Dr. Susan Schooley, Nancy Schlichting, William Schramm, Dr. Richard Smith, Dr. Roger Smith, Greg Solecki, Dr. Bruce Steinhauer, Patricia Stoltz, Gary Valade, Dr. Felix Valbuena, Gerard van Grinsven, Stephen Velick, Robert Vlasic, Randy Walker, James Walworth, Gail L. Warden, Dr. W. Douglas Weaver, Dr. Teresa Wehrwein, Dr. K. M. A. Welch, Dr. Fred Whitehouse, Denise Brooks-Williams, Dr. Kimberlydawn Wisdom, Dr. Michael Workings, Dr. Kathleen Yaremchuk, and Dr. Richard Zarbo.

Finally, special thanks are extended to the staff at Write Stuff Enterprises, LLC, who worked diligently and tirelessly to produce this book: Kim Campbell, managing editor; Melinda Waldrop, senior editor; Sandy Cruz, senior vice president/creative services manager; Darcey McNiff Thompson, graphic designer; Sannie Kirschner and Nicole Sirdoreus, proofreaders; Barbara Martin and Patti Dolbow, transcriptionists; Donna Drialo, indexer; Amy Major, executive assistant to Jeffrey L. Rodengen; Marianne Roberts, president, publisher, and chief financial officer; and Norma Wolpin, marketing manager.

“ *Be ready to revise any system, scrap any method, abandon any theory, if the success of the job requires it.*”

Henry Ford
AUTOMOTIVE PIONEER, HOSPITAL FOUNDER[1]

HEALTH CARE FOR THE COMMUNITY

ETROIT WAS ON A WINNING STREAK AS THE FIRST DECADE OF THE 20TH CENTURY drew to a close. The Tigers had just completed three consecutive years of playing in the World Series from 1907 to 1909.[2] The city had cemented itself as America's captain of manufacturing. And the pharmaceutical industry, railcar production, and shipbuilding were all booming.[3] But it would be the automobile industry that would permanently tie itself to Detroit, creating a symbiotic relationship when Ransom E. Olds produced the first affordable vehicle in 1901.[4] Henry Ford built upon his own Model A (the original, sold in 1903) with the later introduction of the Model T—the Tin Lizzie— in 1908.[5] It was also the year William Crapo Durant founded General Motors.[6]

Lured by jobs that promised a steady paycheck without the uncertainty and blazing sun of an agricultural living, Detroit's population surged. In 1900, more than 285,000 people called Detroit home, making it the country's 13th largest city.[7] By 1910, the city's population

The unfinished Detroit General Hospital complex, which was purchased by Henry Ford and renamed Henry Ford Hospital, 1914. *(Detail From the Collections of The Henry Ford. ID:THF117469.)*

increased to 465,000.[8] And in 1920, Detroit's population would increase once again and leap into fourth place on the list of the nation's largest cities.[9]

Henry Ford and the Model T, Buffalo, NY, c. 1921. *(From the Collections of The Henry Ford. ID:THF112272.)*

Rapid growth strained social systems, and Detroit certainly felt the pinch. While the city focused on building industry, the construction of hospitals had fallen by the wayside; the addition of new facilities had ceased in the late 1880s.[10] The throngs of people flocking to Detroit for jobs weren't just bringing their few worldly possessions but their health and sanitary problems as well. It was a predicament created by success, and those who stood to benefit were pressured to solve the problem.

An Acute Crisis

In the early 1900s, Detroit had medical facilities with more than 1,700 beds.[11] But even that had not been enough to keep up with the population growth, and much patient care was done in the home, including surgeries.[12]

Dr. William Metcalf had worked for several years to build a new hospital facility without success. In October 1909, he convened a meeting of the city's leading industrialists, including Henry Ford, to discuss the issue.

This was a group bent on action. Just a day after its first official meeting during a dinner at the Detroit Club,[13] the group purchased a 20-acre plot of land with $90,000 in funds put up by many, including Ford; lumber tycoon David Whitney; and Frederick Alger, a former military man who served on numerous corporate boards.[14] The location—West Grand Boulevard and Hamilton Avenue—was relatively rural at the time.[15] By the end of October,

1900s

Henry Ford, the son of an Irish immigrant, begins his career as an apprentice engineer for a shipbuilding company.

1900s

Henry Ford forms the Ford Motor Company with 11 associates and only $18,000 in cash. Henry and his engineers name prototypes using the alphabet, going sequentially until they achieved the "T," the perfect car for middle class families. Henry begins producing his small, lightweight vehicle on October 1, 1908.

1900s

With the rise of the auto industry, Detroit's population increases dramatically.

the Detroit General Hospital, as the facility would be known, was officially incorporated. It would be overseen by the Detroit General Hospital Association, of which Henry Ford would serve as a trustee.

Despite the quick action on these early steps, construction of the new facility stalled numerous times during the next few years as the price tag ballooned. Nearly three years passed before the first shovel of dirt was turned. The project then stalled again. At one point, Ford—frustrated by the delays and business strategy on the project—promised not to commit any more funds unless the group had a clearly drawn-out strategy for completion.[16]

Ernest G. Liebold, a Ford associate who would later be tasked with opening the hospital, recalled how Ford preferred investing his funds, rather than his time, into such a project:

Women guests at the turning of the sod for the Detroit General Hospital, 1912. *(From the Collections of The Henry Ford. ID:THF98303.)*

In the first place, Mr. Ford never should have been on any of these committees, because he never took much of a part in them. In the second place, he wasn't interested in the details of things of that kind. He would be glad to contribute his money if he thought the people who were running it knew what they were doing and knew how to go on with it. He'd then dismiss the thing from his mind, and it would just have his support. In other words, what he did here was to lend his name and give money, to a certain extent, very liberally compared to what the others did.[17]

Dr. Frank Sladen: Henry Ford Hospital's First Physician-in-Chief

Dr. Frank J. Sladen (1882–1973) served his medical internship and residency at Johns Hopkins University from 1906 to 1912. He studied with the "father of American medicine," Sir William Osler, and performed research with Drs. Simon Flexner and Harvey Cushing on meningitis antiserum, blood coagulation, and diphtheria antiserum.

Dr. Sladen (pictured here c. 1920) brought the Johns Hopkins tradition of research and education to Henry Ford Hospital. He also endorsed the closed-group practice for the hospital. His many achievements at Ford Hospital included his recruitment of Ford's early physician staff, work with the architect Albert Wood on the original hospital design, the formation of the hospital's nursing school in 1925, establishment of the hospital's medical library, the development of the Board of Trustees, and planning for the 17-story clinic building in the 1950s. His later research included work on aging and chronic rheumatic diseases.

Dr. Sladen worked 56 years at the hospital. After his death, the hospital's library was named after him. A noted scholar and medical historian, Dr. Sladen's own manuscript collection is now preserved in the Henry Ford Health System's Lam Archives.[1]

Turning of the sod for what would later become Henry Ford Hospital, 1912. Dr. William F. Metcalf with shovel. To right of Dr. Metcalf: Henry Ford, David Whitney, and Albert Kahn. *(From the Collections of The Henry Ford. ID:THF117567.)*

Dr. Metcalf, who turned the first spade of dirt at the groundbreaking, already had much of his hospital leadership identified. While many of the initial appointments would be physicians already practicing in the Detroit area, Dr. Frank Sladen, a Johns Hopkins instructor and resident, was acknowledged as the best candidate to serve as head of the Department of Medicine.[18] Dr. Sladen and other potential chiefs were given drawings of the facility and asked for comments.

1909

Overcrowding in settlement neighborhoods, inadequate sewage systems, and rampant poverty contribute to a surge in disease. The *Detroit Journal* takes on a campaign to build more hospitals, saying Detroit has only half as many available hospital beds for its population as other cities.

1909

With the help of a team of social workers, Henry Ford saw that his workers and their families needed a clean, quality place to receive medical care. He is among the business and medical leaders who incorporate the Detroit General Hospital Association to meet the need existing hospitals cannot fulfill.

1909

Founders of the Detroit General Hospital Association include Henry Ford, Dr. William F. Metcalf, Dr. and Mrs. Harry N. Torrey, David C. Whitney, and Frederick Alger.

Henry Ford Takes Control

Moving at a slow pace was uncharacteristic for Ford. He had launched the Model T in 1908 and had moved into a new production facility just two years later. By 1913, that facility, Highland Park, would introduce the auto industry's first production line.[19] In the same amount of time that Ford had moved production into a new facility and revolutionized the way automobiles were built, the Detroit General Hospital Association had managed to create a few drawings and turned over only a few shovels of dirt. The hospital project was falling apart, though it was needed now more than ever.

In 1914, Ford offered his workers at least $5 a day—doubling what had been standard wages for factory work—and cut the typical work-day from nine hours to eight[20] in an attempt to combat high turnover at the plant. The new pay scale was part of Ford's profit-sharing plan in which employees would take half of Ford Motor Company's profits for the year—estimated at $10 million.[21] The day the announcement was carried in the morning papers, thousands of men showed up at Ford's Highland Park factory looking for work.[22]

This news made headlines around the country. The *New York Times* sent a reporter to investigate "what manner of man seems to be shoveling out money by the millions to men who were already said to be better paid than any other workmen in the automobile industry."[23] Where the early news had brought locals, this level of national attention served as a beacon of hope to those struggling to find work around the country. They packed and headed to Detroit.

Henry Ford in his office at the Ford Motor Company Highland Park plant, c. 1920. *(Detail From the Collections of The Henry Ford. ID:THF113408.)*

1909

From the Conrad R. Lam Collection, Henry Ford Health System. ID-01-016.

The physician catalyst behind the hospital is Dr. William F. Metcalf (pictured, c. 1912), a specialist in abdominal and pelvic surgery in Detroit and the former president of the Detroit Academy of Medicine, whose clients include Henry Ford's wife, Clara Bryant Ford.

1910

Judson Bradway purchases a 20-acre parcel from Lothrop Duffield Land Company. Investors Ford, Whitney, and Alger raise $90,000 and deed the land to the Detroit General Hospital Association.

1910

Streetcar access is the prime mover in the hospital association's decision to purchase the semi-rural tract at the corner of West Grand Boulevard and Hamilton Road. Mass transit lines run along Woodward, Trumbull, Fourteenth Street, and Third Avenue. The site is close enough to manu-facturing plants in Detroit and Highland Park to serve emergency patients.

Applicants at the Ford
Motor Company plant in
Highland Park, January 1914.
*(From the Collections of The
Henry Ford. ID:THF94858.)*

The booming city needed a new hospital, but the Detroit General Hospital Association was stuck in indecision. Some of the board wanted to hand any assets and properties over to the city. Ford would have none of it. Liebold recalled a conversation with Ford in which the auto magnate said: "Well, it looks as if I'll have to take over the hospital, but if I do, I don't want any strings tied to it. I want to pay back everyone who has contributed anything to it. I want the deed to the property free and clear of any obligations."[24]

Liebold was given the task of making that happen. He met with the board, presented Ford's idea, and then wrote the checks to each individual who had contributed. Henry Ford now owned the hospital—and all that went with it.

A Top Notch Facility

The proposed Detroit General Hospital had stood incomplete for more than a year, its building a shell without windows. What little work had been accomplished hadn't stood up to the weather. A week or two after the deed was handed over to Ford, Liebold asked what to do with the hospital. "He said, 'Well, I guess you better go and finish it up.'"[25]

Liebold had come to Ford Motor Company through the banking industry; his first encounters with the auto pioneer were when Ford would venture across the street from his plant to change $100 bills. Liebold didn't know anything about running a hospital. But he quickly hired new architects, and together they went through the incomplete facility. "Whenever we found that things were satisfactory, we gave them the okay to go ahead and

1912

Board members of the Detroit General Hospital Association, prominent medical leaders, and civic leaders join a groundbreaking event Dr. Metcalf calls "The Turning of the Sod."

1912

Among the ideas discussed by Dr. Metcalf and Henry Ford is free ambulance services, as the hospital is assured the gift of as many automobiles as needed. Ford ambulance (pictured, c. 1916) parked in front of Henry Ford Hospital.

finish them up: Continue the plastering and put in the work," Liebold said.[26]

The original design for Detroit General Hospital planned for 90 beds. Yet the infrastructure—power plant, service building, and kitchen—had been intended to serve a hospital of 500.[27] Liebold couldn't see a way for the hospital to operate in the black with just 90 beds. Ford told him, "Well, you better go ahead and build a building to utilize the facilities you've got."[28] But the needs of the city demanded a quicker solution.

The unfinished Patient Services Building, c. 1914. *(From the Conrad R. Lam Collection, Henry Ford Health System. ID=01-014.)*

Solving an Immediate Need

Drug use around the turn of the century was commonplace, and access was easy. Coca-Cola once contained cocaine, and Sears & Roebuck's catalog sold opium and syringes alongside the towels and tools. By the early 1910s, narcotics and alcohol each had their prohibition factions, but those who wanted to limit drugs won first. The Harrison Narcotic Act of 1914 placed stringent limits on the distribution of narcotics, even curtailing how physicians could prescribe them. Within six weeks, the law was having an effect, as reported in the *New York Medical Journal*:

> *The immediate effects of the Harrison antinarcotic law were seen in the flocking of drug habitués to hospitals and sanatoriums. Sporadic crimes of violence were reported, too, due usually to desperate efforts by addicts to obtain drugs, but occasionally to a delirious state induced by sudden withdrawal.*[29]

1913

The plans for building Detroit General Hospital are delayed by construction and business strategy issues.

1914

Henry Ford announces Ford Motor Company will pay $5 a day to workers at its Highland Park facility and shorten their work day from nine to eight hours. While this rate does not apply to all of Ford's workers, it more than doubles the average American paycheck. Thousands come to apply for 400 jobs.

1914

In the months before Henry Ford purchases the hospital outright, his Model T becomes the best-selling motor car in the country. It is only available in black, since black paint dries faster than any other color.

Ernest G. Liebold, Henry Ford's financial assistant and first administrator of Henry Ford Hospital, c. 1920. *(From the Collections of The Henry Ford. ID:THF117569.)*

Detroit was no different, except in scale, as the city increased in size. Liebold recalled:

Those fellows that came here from out of town seeking jobs and weren't able to get them here were all kinds and types of individuals. There were dope fiends, alcoholics, bums, and everything you could imagine. It sort of overtaxed the facilities of Detroit in taking care of these people at the ordinary cheap lodging houses and ordinary missions like the McGregor Mission and elsewhere. Mr. Ford said, "They're kind of blaming us for these fellows being here. You'd better see what you can do to take care of them. How long will it take you to get the hospital in shape to take care of that?"[30]

Within 48 hours, Liebold had the basement of the Private Patient Building—later known as the M-Unit—ready to go. Dr. Frank Sladen and physicians from Ford Motor Company examined patients upon their entrance to the hospital. Patients were given clean clothes, and the clothes they'd worn in were sent off to be fumigated in a steam machine created onsite. However, within days, Liebold had a near-riot on his hands. "Everybody was jumping around madder than the devil," he recalled. "I got in my car and went down as fast as I could get there. Here the pants on these fellows were about six inches short and their sleeves were halfway up their arms. They said, 'Do you expect us to go out in a suit like this?'"[31]

The steam contraption had killed the insects but shrunk the clothes. Liebold quickly dispatched someone to buy replacement suits for everyone. He then headed over to Ford Motor Company to work with researchers on determining the optimum method for killing

1914

Henry Ford tells the Detroit General Hospital Association he will buy the hospital buildings and grounds. In a letter to the board, he says if his proposition is accepted, he would "go forward with plans for a complete and credible hospital for the benefit of Detroit."

1914

After purchasing the hospital, Henry Ford chooses four medical staff administrators: Dr. John N. E. Brown, superintendent; Dr. Frank J. Sladen, physician-in-chief of the hospital; and Dr. Angus McLean of Harper Hospital, who agrees to oversee surgery assisted by Dr. James Mead, chief surgeon of the Ford Motor Company.

1914

Henry Ford places his financial assistant, Ernest G. Liebold, in charge of completing construction on the hospital. Liebold serves as the hospital's chief administrator, overseeing all hospital decisions, from the care and payments for charity patients to recruiting physicians.

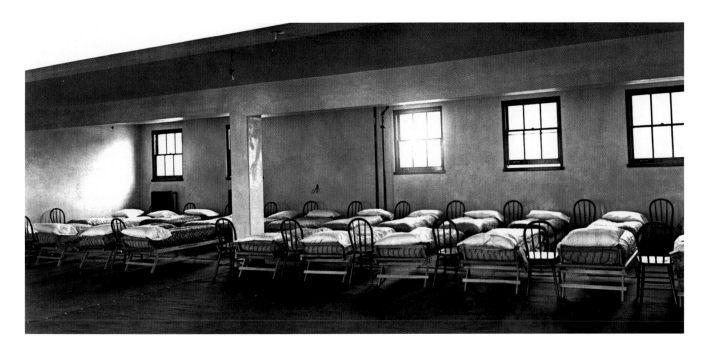

The M-Unit ward for chemical dependency at Henry Ford Hospital, the first of its kind in the country, 1914. *(Detail From the Conrad R. Lam Collection, Henry Ford Health System. ID=01-010.)*

lice and bed bugs without shrinking wool. It would be the first of many hospital problems solved working with researchers at the car company.

This was the inauspicious beginning of Henry Ford Hospital. Treating these addicts created quite a stir for the new hospital, which was not yet fully staffed. Dr. F. Janney Smith, the second physician hired at the facility in 1915, after Dr. Sladen, remembered the great lengths patients would go to just to get their fix:

They smuggled their drug supplies into the hospital, they stole from our supplies, and generally cheated us as well as themselves. Some brought their drugs into the hospital by cut-out niches in their Bibles, some hid the narcotic in a rubber container inserted in the rectum, and others put the powdered drugs between layers of a postcard.[32]

1914

As physician-in-chief, Dr. Sladen helps implement a closed hospital system whereby patients could be referred by outside doctors, yet only the appointed staff are practitioners within the hospital.

1914

Because of the closed staff policy, Dr. Angus McLean and others decide to remain in private practice but will continue to help until other physicians are recruited to Ford Hospital.

1914

The need for alcohol and drug treatment in Detroit is so great that Henry Ford Hospital staff turn the basement of the private patient building (called the M-Unit) into a ward for treating chemical dependency. The ward becomes the first of its kind in the United States.

One night, patients created a disturbance, distracted the nurses, and raided the hospital's narcotic supply. "Despite our problem, we managed to establish methods, including physical therapy, of weaning the patients away from the drugs," Dr. Smith said. "Ultimately, we were able to discharge them from the hospital, but it is my doubt that many of them were permanently cured."[33]

Henry Ford Hospital officially opened its doors to the general population on October 1, 1915, with 48 beds and a Board of Trustees comprised of Ford, Liebold, Dr. Sladen, Ford's wife Clara, and son Edsel.[34]

Influences of Outsiders

Henry Ford (left), Clara Bryant Ford, and Edsel Bryant Ford aboard ship on their European trip, 1912. *(From the Collections of The Henry Ford. ID:THF117563.)*

Deep within the lore of the Henry Ford Hospital is a notion that the closed group for physicians—one of its most revolutionary tenets—was modeled after the Mayo Clinic. According to the lore, Ford, in his frustration over the hospital that had landed in his lap, asked Dr. Mayo what to do. But it seems that idea originated much closer to Ford, as Liebold recounted:

If the hospital was to be supported by Mr. Ford and bear his name, it ought to be run differently than any other hospital. … The other hospitals to my mind were operated largely as a boarding house for the doctors' patients. While they had members of their own staff, they were men who didn't contribute actively toward the policy of the institution. It seemed the most prominent outside doctors were the ones who had the most to say in running the

---

1914

Lawmakers pass the Harrison Narcotic Act of 1914 that places stringent limits on the distribution of narcotics, even curtailing how physicians can prescribe them. Prior to this act, some soft drinks, cough drops, and toothpaste contained cocaine.

1914

Henry Ford pursues the most distinguished physicians for his hospital, commissioning Dr. Sladen and Liebold to recruit doctors. Dr. Sladen looks to his former employer—Johns Hopkins Hospital of Baltimore, Maryland—and he recruits Dr. F. Janney Smith in 1915 to be the head of cardio-respiratory diseases.

1915

Henry Ford, Clara Ford, Edsel Ford, Dr. Sladen, and Liebold sign the articles of incorporation for the new hospital. Henry Ford's signature becomes the enduring logo.

institution. That contributed largely to internal politics and things of that sort. I didn't feel
we ought to have that in any institution Mr. Ford had anything to do with.[35]

Still, there was a relationship early on between Henry Ford Hospital and Mayo Clinic.
"I used to send a good many of our doctors from the hospital up to Mayo just to observe their
operations and see how they did things, to give them a little better education or see new
ideas," Liebold said. "I always figured, if a man stays on the job and never gets around and
never sees anything else, he can never tell whether he is good or bad."[36]

While Henry Ford Hospital took some cues from the Mayo Clinic early on, its relationship with another venerable institution—Johns Hopkins—would have a more direct impact
on the early foundation of the hospital.

Dr. Frank Sladen, the former Johns Hopkins physician recruited by the Detroit General
Association, had continued in private practice in Detroit while the upheaval over the building
settled. Though Ford's contract with the board freed him from any obligations to those who
had been hired, he opted to keep Dr. Sladen on—the only physician whose job survived the
tumult during the hospital's construction. With the hospital now open, Sladen
assumed the position of physician-in-chief and brought his clinical practice
along with him.

Dr. Sladen's first hire would be another colleague from Johns Hopkins,
Dr. F. Janney Smith.

Dr. Smith arrived in Detroit October 11, 1915, and by 1919, he established
the hospital's first inpatient unit for cardio-respiratory disease.[37] He had
heard much about the hospital from Dr. Sladen through the years and found
the setup intriguing. "The type of practice, the opportunities of teaching
and research, appealed to me," said Dr. Smith. "Then, too, obviating the

Dr. Roy D. McClure, first
surgeon-in-chief at Henry
Ford Hospital, c. 1920.
(From the Conrad R. Lam
Collection, Henry Ford
Health System. ID=01-012.)

Dr. Roy McClure: First Surgeon-in-Chief

A fourth-generation physician, Dr. Roy
McClure had the practice of medicine in his
blood. After graduating medical school at
Johns Hopkins, he trained under Dr. William
S. Halsted—a father of American surgery—
and served as his chief resident.

"He was naturally strict, requiring excellence in surgical judgment and technique.
He worked tirelessly in his vital interest in the

development of the Henry Ford Hospital,"
said Dr. F. Janney Smith, who knew
Dr. McClure at Johns Hopkins and preceded
him at Henry Ford Hospital.[1]

As adept at research as he was skilled in
surgery, Dr. McClure led development of
transfusion processes. Later, with Dr. Frank
Hartman, he advanced research into the
preservation and storage of blood.[2]

Dr. F. Janney Smith, c. 1918.
(From the Conrad R. Lam Collection, Henry Ford Health System. ID=01-020.)

problems of establishing an office, having to buy equipment, and not needing to be concerned with collecting fees appeared as additional advantages."[38]

Dr. Roy D. McClure was not such an easy sell. Liebold traveled to Baltimore and interviewed him, along with two other candidates. When Liebold offered the job to Dr. McClure, "he didn't seem to be very enthusiastic about coming out here," Liebold said. "I told him about the closed hospital idea. They were all ideas that were foreign to him. He was just a little hesitant about whether he wanted to do a thing of that kind."[39]

But Drs. Sladen and Smith were eager for Dr. McClure to join the Henry Ford Hospital staff. "Naturally, he was an optimal choice as far as Dr. Sladen and I were concerned," Dr. Smith said. "We knew him well, admired him, and respected his surgical abilities; and we knew that he was conscientious and industrious."[40] Dr. McClure had trained under Dr. William S. Halsted, considered the father of American surgery.[41]

Hoping to sell the young surgeon on Henry Ford Hospital's growing potential, Liebold invited Dr. McClure to the city for a visit. He took Liebold up on his offer to come to Detroit. There, he accepted the job on the spot in February 1916. Those three successful Hopkins hires—Drs. Sladen, Smith, and McClure—opened the door for others to follow.

"We had quite a few Johns Hopkins graduates at the hospital," Liebold said. "After Dr. McClure came here, and Dr. F. Janney Smith came on the staff, I think word got back to Johns Hopkins that these men were doing very well, and we had a very fine institution. I think that when these fellows graduated down there in the medical work and served their internship, or a portion of it, they wanted to come out to the Ford Hospital. Of course, if they came from Johns Hopkins, we gave them preference."[42]

1915

The first board meeting of the incorporated Henry Ford Hospital includes Henry Ford, Clara Ford, Edsel Ford, Dr. Frank Sladen, and Ernest Liebold.

1915

Henry Ford Hospital's first documented patient admission occurs on July 13, 1915. The 48-bed hospital officially opens to the public on October 1, 1915.

Detail From the Conrad R. Lam Collection, Henry Ford Health System. ID=01-019.

1915

The first five departments of the hospital to be developed are medicine, surgery, urology, cardio-respiratory, and gynecology.

Building A World-Class Staff

In 1916, Drs. Sladen and McClure began to build the core of leadership for Henry Ford Hospital; those leaders were charged with developing departments within the hospital. "When Dr. McClure accepted his position at the hospital, he interested some other young surgeons in joining the staff with him," Dr. Smith said. "Dr. Charles Watt and Dr. John Ormond came to the hospital shortly after Dr. McClure's arrival."[43]

Dr. Ormond ultimately became the surgeon-in-charge of the Urology Department, while Dr. Jean Paul Pratt was charged with creating the Obstetrics & Gynecology Department. Dr. Ralph Major was recruited to work in metabolic diseases. Like the others, Drs. Pratt and Major were Hopkins alumni.

Dr. Russell Haden was in charge of setting up the hospital's laboratories, an early commitment to medical research where all physicians on staff were expected to continue their education—a philosophy that Dr. Sladen had learned at Hopkins under his mentor, Sir William Osler, "the father of modern medicine." Though Dr. Haden's term would be brief—he and Dr. Major left in 1921—"he did not need much time to soundly establish our laboratory service," Dr. Smith said.

The hospital also recruited interns, many of whom would devote significant portions of their careers to Henry Ford Hospital and would later be counted among its leaders. Dr. Smith recalled the first group of interns: "Among them was an outstanding man, Dr. David Murchison. He had considerable spirit as well as talent, making him an excellent house officer. … He was a great help to us in many ways, particularly as he organized the nursing service for patient care."[44]

The first Henry Ford Hospital staff. From left, first row (both shoes visible): Dr. Charles H. Watt, Dr. Frank J. Sladen, Dr. Roy D. McClure, Ernest G. Liebold, John N. E. Brown, and Dr. F. Janney Smith. Back row: Dr. John K. Ormond, unknown, Dr. Russell Haden, Dr. David R. Murchison, and Dr. Irvin L. Barclay, 1916. *(Detail From the Conrad R. Lam Collection, Henry Ford Health System. ID=01-011.)*

1915

Henry Ford works with scientist George Washington Carver to develop industrial and commercial uses for the soybean. Ford is so impressed with the taste and promise of soy milk that he builds a plant that produces 150 gallons a day and supplies bottles to Henry Ford Hospital.

1915

Isabella Napper, R.N., becomes the first Henry Ford Hospital nursing supervisor, overseeing 20 nursing positions. She works in the M-Unit building.

1916

Dr. F. Janney Smith establishes one of the first cardiology units in the country at Henry Ford Hospital. He is assisted by Drs. Leslie T. Colvin and Ray E. Logan.

Later classes of interns in these early years would continue to grow. Dr. Frank Menagh and Dr. John Montgomery would begin their careers as interns before going on to found Dermatology and Pediatrics, respectively.[45] Dr. Clyde Allen, a one-time Ford Hospital intern, would later work alongside Dr. McClure in overseeing intern training.

Nurses had key leadership as well. When the facility opened in 1915, there were 20 available nursing positions. Most of these were introduced to the hospital by Olive Day, Sladen's assistant. While the medical end of nursing care for patients was left to the doctor's supervision, Day supervised the nurses' work to ensure consistency throughout the hospital.[46] "In their administrative work and in the manner in which they conducted themselves and how they responded to patients, that was an activity that I thought should come under another person's jurisdiction," Liebold explained. "Miss Day built up a very fine group of women around here."[47]

Within the first few years of the hospital's opening, it had put in place capable leaders, many of whom would serve Henry Ford Hospital for the remainder of their careers. Drs. Sladen and McClure—the physician-in-chief and the surgeon-in-chief, respectively—would work together for 35 years, cementing the hospital's commitment to education, research, and outstanding patient care into Henry Ford Hospital's mission.

Proving Themselves Time and Again

Under Drs. Sladen and McClure, the hospital had built a top-notch staff, one that would make a tremendous impact in Detroit's medical community. However, Henry Ford Hospital's closed staff arrangement with its physicians was not widely accepted in the broader medical community. At one point, the Wayne County Medical Association would not admit Henry Ford Hospital physicians into its ranks.[48] Dr. McClure resigned from the Detroit Academy of Surgery after the

1916

Dr. Roy McClure becomes Henry Ford Hospital's first surgeon-in-chief. Dr. McClure will work with physician-in-chief Dr. Frank Sladen for the next several decades to develop the clinical, education, and research mission of the hospital.

1916

The first interns accepted at Henry Ford Hospital are Dr. David Murchison in general medicine and Dr. Irvin Barclay in surgery. Other new interns are Dr. Frank Menagh and Dr. John Montgomery, who would later establish dermatology and pediatrics, respectively.

1916

Dr. Jean Paul Pratt (pictured, c. 1925) joins the Department of General Surgery working in anesthesiology, orthopedics, and abdominal surgery. He later establishes obstetrics and gynecology.

From the Conrad R. Lam Collection, Henry Ford Health System. ID=01-023. Credit: Joseph Merante, NYC.

organization refused to hold its meeting at the hospital in 1924.[49] His national prominence was well-established then, enough that the resignation drew attention.

The hospital's closed relationship was just one of many unusual policies in place at Henry Ford Hospital—arrangements that might not look so atypical today. But not every idea was successful. With his business background, Liebold often instituted policies that were outside the mainstream of modern medicine. He had a rule that if a patient waited 30 minutes for service, he expected a memo explaining who the patient was and what caused the delay. "Of course, sometimes things will happen, and you can't avoid them," he said. "Sometimes people stay longer than you expect. Sometimes they have other things wrong with them that the doctors want to discuss with them. You can't always blame the doctor for that, but when it gets to be constant, and a habit, then of course something has to be done about it."[50]

The architect Albert Wood (far left) with other dignitaries at the cornerstone laying for Henry Ford Hospital in 1917. *(From the Conrad R. Lam Collection, Henry Ford Health System. ID=1-015.)*

Not all challenges of a hospital could be solved with factory solutions. Liebold once suggested that surgeons schedule their work with efficiency, choosing to operate on hernias on Mondays, appendices on Tuesdays, gallbladders on Wednesdays, hysterectomies on Thursdays, and prostatic surgery on Fridays.[51] Surgeons ignored that impractical mandate.

Though the hospital bore his name, Henry Ford himself was not a routine presence in its halls. But his legacy clearly clung to every inch. Creativity and a willingness to try new methods—to revolutionize modern medicine—were evident.

1917

Dr. Russell Haden becomes the hospital's first pathologist, charged with setting up the pathology laboratories (pictured, 1922).

From the Collections of The Henry Ford. ID:THF117470.

TWO

" *We believed in the principles of a full-time salaried staff organized on a nonprofit basis. We were convinced that it was an epoch-making approach to the practice of medicine. On the other hand, we all faced the problem of growth, lack of space, the demand for medical service, the need of graduate medical education, and the command to medical research and progress. It has been difficult to plan the organization that could reach out to these principles and be unified sufficiently to meet them, yet be loosely enough organized to cope with the needed flexibility required by the medical public.*"

Dr. F. Janney Smith
HENRY FORD HOSPITAL CARDIOLOGIST[1]

BUILDING A FOUNDATION ON WHICH TO GROW

**1918
1926**

Henry Ford Hospital, 1919.
*(Detail From the Collections of
The Henry Ford. ID:THF117659.)*

T HE HOSPITAL'S FORMATIVE YEARS HAD BEEN DIFFICULT, TO SAY THE LEAST. The doors opening did not put an end to the challenges. While administrator Ernest Liebold continued shaping the 48-room hospital into the new plan for 500 beds, outside forces intervened, delaying the expansion for years.

At the time, the United States was entering the Great War. Many doctors from Henry Ford Hospital joined the fight, and for a time, the hospital was better known as US Army General Hospital No. 36.

When the war ended, the hospital moved into a remarkable time of growth, opening the expansion and adding key personnel. Both Henry and Clara Ford referred friends and employees for treatment and ensured that the staff had virtually everything it could possibly need.

An Ideal Room

When Henry Ford Hospital opened, it had inherited a small building that had taken years to design and construct. When it came time to expand, creativity and attention to detail were in order. Liebold opted to start by building the best hospital room, then creating the hospital itself. He noted:

Patient room, Henry Ford Hospital, 1915. *(From the Conrad R. Lam Collection, Henry Ford Health System. ID=01-009.)*

We spent a couple of months up in the service building. We built a room of ordinary beaverboard they used in those days. We put up walls. We moved them here and moved them there and changed them around. We decided to put a bathroom in every room, and then we decided the bathroom would adjoin two rooms. We changed that around. We then provided for a ventilating duct in back of the bathroom so we could get at all the plumbing.[2]

The formation of the hospital wards came next, with each of the units a duplicate of the others. "The end units were designed so they could be cut off from the rest of the hospital in case of an epidemic like smallpox or influenza," Liebold said. "They had their own equipment and everything to operate without being dependent on the other part of the hospital."[3]

The design team also opted to improve the patient experience with a ventilation system that helped eliminate odors, as well as a nurse's signal system designed for easy repair. "In those days, they had a relay that was built into the wall," Liebold said. "When you pressed the button, it would activate the relay and light the signal

1918

Dr. F. Janney Smith (pictured, c. 1918) and other doctors from Henry Ford Hospital join the many Americans who enlist to fight in World War I.

1918

Henry Ford Hospital is transferred to the US Army Hospital No. 36, helping more than 2,000 wounded soldiers over the next year.

outside the room. The nurse had to come back and push the button and release the release to turn the light off. Sometimes those relays would get out of order, and then the electrician would have to come up in the room and pull them out. He would have to fuss around and even pull the bed aside."[4]

Liebold worked with the Chicago Signal Company to design a relay button that plugged into the wall, so that when one failed, electricians only needed to quickly replace it without bothering the patients.

A Wartime Hospital

World War I put a stop to Henry Ford Hospital's expansion. As the call went out for doctors and nurses to join the war effort, the hospital lost much of its staff, making it difficult to continue operating. In his unpublished memoir, Dr. Frank Sladen wrote about Dr. McClure's turn as a commanding officer during the war and the medical team from Henry Ford Hospital that followed his lead:

The Henry Ford Hospital early ambulance garage, c. 1917. *(From the Collections of The Henry Ford. ID:THF117448.)*

The patriotic spirit of the staff was quite apparent. All the men did not wait to be

drafted. … A certain group of the staff men were sent overseas as a team under Major

[Roy] McClure's leadership. Others were assigned as individuals to military groups

1918

Many wounded soldiers are in need of therapy to recover. Fifty-four teachers and administrators from the hospital offer skill-building, from arts and crafts to mechanical labor. In the mess hall, 13 cooks and 75 assistants prepare meals for 1,300 people daily.

1919

Armistice Day, on November 11, celebrates an end to the war.

1919

The US Army returns the hospital to civilian use as Henry Ford Hospital. Administrators send word to each staff member encouraging them to return to work, including those affected by war injuries.

stationed in this country. Some were at training camps. The government had no intention
or desire to take the staff as it was, other than Dr. McClure's unit, in the capacities and
relationships already established. In the company that went with Dr. McClure, the
advantage of previous assignments and specialties were not recognized or designated unless
it was successfully obtained by the endeavor of the man himself.[5]

Ford himself had done everything he could to stave off the war, including sailing to Copenhagen, Denmark, in 1915 on what he called the Peace Ship. He discussed the idea with Henry Ford Hospital physicians one day, as Dr. F. Janney Smith recalled:

> *One afternoon, Mr. Ford joined Dr. Sladen and me at the hospital. We found an*
> *empty room, and Mr. Ford relaxed on the bed. As he studied the ceiling, hands behind*
> *his head, he finally avowed, "Well we've got to get those boys out of the trenches, and*
> *I'm going to see what I can do to get them home."[6]*

After the failure of the Peace Ship effort, Ford committed significant resources to the war. Production lines were turned over to military needs, and build-

No Smoking, Please

Henry Ford and Thomas Edison not only traded ideas about inventions, but about health. Neither liked smoking. In 1916, Ford published *The Little White Slaver*, a book intended to discourage the deed.

It's no surprise, then, that Ford banned smoking at the hospital for staff and patients. That did not stop staff from breaking the rule. Dr. F. Janney Smith, a cardiologist; and Dr. David Murchison, an intern, were once caught next to a pile of cigarette butts that had accumulated beneath the window of their rooms in the staff quarters.[1] Whenever Ford was at the facility, a quick code went out among the staff to extinguish all cigarettes.

The Henry Ford Hospital smoking policies were eased in the 1950s, but medicine eventually caught up with Ford's beliefs, and the hospital again took a leadership role in anti-smoking efforts. Dr. Ron Davis became the director of the Center for Health Promotion and Disease Prevention at Henry Ford Health System in 1995[2] and was a strong anti-tobacco advocate, leading the health system to again become a smoke-free zone. Much of Dr. Davis' research was dedicated to tobacco control and treatment of nicotine addiction. He went on to serve as president of the American Medical Association.

After Dr. Davis' death in 2008, Michigan Governor Jennifer Granholm signed the Dr. Ron Davis Smoke-Free Air Law, which banned smoking in public places.[3]

ings, including the hospital, were loaned to the government. Liebold told Colonel A. B. Cooper the staff had been notified that the government may not have jobs for all of the workers. "The colonel replied, 'I'm not going to replace anybody. I want your organization, and I want you, too. We expect you to be a lot of help to us down here.'"[7]

On October 26, 1918, the hospital facility was turned over to the US Army in an official ceremony. Weeks later, the war officially ended, as Germany surrendered on November 11. But for those wounded in the war, treatment continued. Henry Ford Hospital operated under the Army's orders throughout most of 1919.

Open for Business, Again

By November 1919, Henry Ford Hospital had returned to being a civilian endeavor. Yet the effects of the war would bring another challenge. Many of the returning soldiers had contracted a strain of influenza, which they then brought home. The Spanish Flu pandemic of 1918 had swept the world, costing millions of lives. In 1919, another flu epidemic arrived with the soldiers, and Detroit was hard-hit. Liebold observed the dire circumstances at the hospital:

The Henry Ford Hospital ambulance driver, John Burkmyre, with the hospital ambulance in 1923. *(From the Conrad R. Lam Collection, Henry Ford Health System. ID=02-002.)*

They were dragging people in there, and they weren't there 15 minutes and they would die. The first thing I did was stop them from bringing people in. I had some cars sent over from the Ford Motor Company, and I sent doctors out to see people,

1919

1919

From the Conrad R. Lam Collection, Henry Ford Health System. ID=02-028.

D. H. Moats is the first hospital pharmacist hired post-war. Prior to Moats' arrival, all medication purchases were made by Ernest Liebold, the Ford Hospital administrator. Photo: Henry Ford Hospital pharmacy, 1916.

An influenza epidemic hits Detroit, and beds spill into the hallways of Henry Ford Hospital.

Detail From the Conrad R. Lam Collection, Henry Ford Health System. ID=02-004.

check up on them, and see if they were all right to bring to the hospital. They would okay them, and we would send the ambulance for them to be brought in for treatment.[8]

The intensity of the pandemic went just as quickly as it came; Liebold remembers four or five days passed before it began to subside. But for some patients, the effects lingered for months, recalled Dr. Smith, who had just returned from Army service when the flu struck:

> *The influenza patient was terrifying; most of them were seriously ill, many of them dying. Even some of the survivors were plagued with secondary hemolytic streptococcus, developing empyema. The treatment of the empyema of about 25 or 30 of these patients took our attention for many months. Experimentally, we tried to treat a series of them by conservative chemotherapy. In general, it was unsuccessful, and we had to surgically drain most of them.*[9]

Creative Problem Solving

The completion of Henry Ford Hospital's expansion would be delayed until 1921, creating a crunch in the immediate post-war years. Dr. Smith recalled how physicians made do:

> *Badly in need of an Outpatient Department while awaiting the final construction, we had temporary beaverboard partitioned offices set up on the second floor of the Laboratories Building. Anyone of resonant voice could be heard from one end of the offices to the other. Notable among the resonant voices was Dr. Menagh's, whose confidential comments with venereal disease patients became common knowledge.*[10]

1920

From the Conrad R. Lam Collection,
Henry Ford Health System. ID=02-029.

Construction resumes on Henry Ford Hospital. Ernest Liebold, administrator; Albert Wood, architect; and Drs. McClure and Sladen work with the Albrecht Company to transform a steel and masonry shell into what Henry Ford envisions as "a hotel for sick people."

1920

From the Conrad R. Lam Collection,
Henry Ford Health System. ID=02-009.

Anesthesiology equipment for surgery, Henry Ford Hospital, c. 1920.

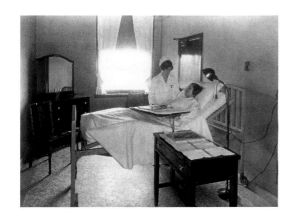

But when the expansion was completed, it proved to be worth the wait. The hospital boasted a number of enhancements to improve the patient's stay. Some were created when Liebold and his team fashioned the ideal patient room. Another was born at Ford's engineering lab—a hospital bed in which both the head and feet could be raised.

According to the patent paperwork filed by Ford in July 1921 and granted in December 1924, Ford's objective was to "furnish a bed with an adjustable framework, including back and leg supports that may be placed at an inclination relative to the bed to safely support a patient in a lounging or reclining posture relative to the bed, and provision is made for adjusting the body and leg supports while being occupied."[11]

The patent paperwork also included discussion of a "lounging attachment," which allowed the occupant to adjust the bed; a novel reduction gear that locked to prevent collapses or accidental movement; and "a tiltable attachment for hospital beds wherein the parts are constructed so as to be applicable to an ordinary iron bed or cot, easy to install and adjust, and highly efficient as a comfortable support for a patient or invalid."[12]

Whether created or purchased, Henry Ford Hospital would have the latest technology. The electrocardiogram machine, which Dr. Smith recalled was purchased around the time of the opening of the addition, was still a relatively new invention. Though some form of measurement of the

Left: The early adjustable hospital bed in the patient room in 1927. *(Detail From the Collections of The Henry Ford. ID:THF117487.)*

Below: The early electro-cardiogram machine at Henry Ford Hospital, c. 1920. *(Detail From the Conrad R. Lam Collection, Henry Ford Health System. ID=02-023.)*

1921

Liebold returns to his duties at the Ford Motor Company. Henry Ford appoints William L. Graham from the Ford Motor Company's treasurer's office as hospital superintendent and assistant treasurer of the Board of Trustees. Hospital staff grows to 100 doctors, 137 nurses, and 100 clerical staff.

1921

The new, four-story section of Henry Ford Hospital is 50,000 square feet, with 40 porches with steel railings extending over the length of the building.

heart had been around since the 18th century, Willem Einthoven, the machine's inventor, had continued to improve its capabilities. Previous iterations were hulking, weighing some 600 pounds and occupying two rooms. Soon after World War I, the machine had been refined to a size that could be rolled to a patient's bedside. Einthoven won the Nobel Prize in Physiology or Medicine for his developments in 1924.[13] By then, the machine was already in use at Henry Ford Hospital.

The Henry Ford Hospital Power Plant, c. 1920. *(Detail From the Collections of The Henry Ford. ID:THF117463.)*

When Ford visited the hospital, he took time to ensure that the staff had everything it needed. If a need was expressed, it often was quickly met. Dr. William Eyler, current Chairman Emeritus of Radiology, relayed a story told to him by Dr. Howard Doub, who joined the hospital in its rapid 1920s expansion. The hospital, which had its own power plant onsite, operated on direct current. Dr. Doub mentioned to Ford that The Newark Company, a Chicago electronics distribution company, preferred alternating current instead. "A very few days later, we had AC in the department. Just like that."[14]

Staff Development

Staff capabilities had grown during this time period as well, with a number of new specialties developed and key physicians coming on board. Many of the hospital's young physicians would spend the majority of their careers at Henry Ford Hospital, with some rising to major leadership positions. A Johns Hopkins alumnus, Dr. John G. Mateer, joined Henry Ford

1921

Henry Ford Hospital purchases a relatively new invention to monitor heart health of patients: the electrocardiogram machine, invented by Willem Einthoven.

1921

Ford Motor Company's experimental staff develops a hospital bed with devices to elevate or lower the head and foot of the bed to make patients as comfortable as possible.

1922

Dr. Robert H. Durham becomes an intern at the hospital. He serves as physician-in-charge of general medical patients from 1927 to 1966 and writes *Encyclopedia of Medical Syndromes* based on his clinical experience.

Hospital in 1920 as physician-in-charge of the Divison of Gastroenterology. He would remain for 40 years, including a term as chief of Internal Medicine. Dr. Charles Peabody, who trained at Massachusetts General Hospital, joined Henry Ford Hospital in 1922, creating the orthopedic surgery department.[15] Dr. Arthur McGraw joined in 1922 and later became the surgeon-in-charge of the tumor clinic.[16] Dr. Clarke McColl began as a resident in gastroenterology in 1923. From 1963 to 1966, he served as the hospital's chair of the Department of Medicine.[17] Dr. Dwight Ensign joined as an intern in 1924, beginning a 58-year term as a physician at Henry Ford Hospital. In 1942, he founded the Division of Rheumatology and served as its chief until 1966.[18] Dr. Laurence Fallis, one of the hospital's first surgical interns, would rise to the position of surgeon-in-chief many years later.[19] And in 1926, Dr. Albert Crawford established the Division of Neurological Surgery.[20]

The hospital's emphasis on metabolic diseases, including diabetes, grew tremendously during this time. Dr. Daniel Foster was the first chief of this division, which was housed within the Department of Medicine.[21] Dr. William Lowrie also joined in 1922, becoming head of the Metabolic Diseases Division in 1924, a position he held until 1962.[22]

Dr. Howard P. Doub, a Johns Hopkins alum, became radiologist-in-chief at the hospital in 1923, coming from private practice. Dr. Doub helped raise

Left: The first fluoroscopic unit in the Department of Roentgenology in 1918. *(From the Conrad R. Lam Collection, Henry Ford Health System. ID=02-003.)*

Below: Dr. Howard P. Doub, the first chair of the Department of Roentgenology (later called Radiology), in 1954. *(From the Conrad R. Lam Collection, Henry Ford Health System. ID=02-031.)*

1922

New hires to Henry Ford Hospital include Dr. Arthur B. McGraw, junior surgeon; Drs. William L. Lowrie and Daniel P. Foster, metabolism; and Dr. Frank Hartman, who would stay at the hospital for 34 years in pathology and clinical testing.

1922

The first baby is delivered at Henry Ford Hospital by Drs. Roger S. Siddall (pictured, c. 1925) and William B. Thompson.

the stature of Henry Ford Hospital throughout the medical community. During the course of his career, he served as president of the Radiological Society of North America and edited the journal *Radiology* for 25 years. His impact on the hospital was just as keen. After his death in 1975, *Radiology* recapped his career: "When he went to the Ford Hospital, the radiology department was one man, one room, one machine; when he left 47 years later, it was a large and well-known department."[23]

Though the tenure of most physicians was long, there was occasional turnover. When Dr. Russell Haden, who had founded the Department of Pathology, departed, Dr. Frank Hartman was named as his replacement. Dr. Hartman went on to serve as the first president of the College of American Pathology; the specialty society has given an award in honor of Dr. Hartman annually since 1977.[24]

Dr. Wendell Garretson, an ear, nose, and throat specialist who had trained in Scotland under one of the foremost experts in the specialty, joined the hospital after serving with the American Red Cross during the war. After establishing the department, Dr. Garretson died suddenly; Dr. Elmer L. Whitney replaced him.[25]

In the midst of growth and rapid expansion, gaining perspective on the hospital's stature was difficult. For Dr. Smith, it took a trip to other clinical facilities in 1924, including those in Boston, New York, Philadelphia, Baltimore, and Washington, DC. "I came back with a considerable respect for the type of work we were doing at the Henry Ford Hospital and with renewed confidence that we were going along the right road. Meanwhile, the teaching program became

A surgical pavilion suite at Henry Ford Hospital, c. 1920. *(From the Conrad R. Lam Collection, Henry Ford Health System. ID=02-010.)*

1923

Henry Ford Hospital's ambulance driver John Burkmyre is one of the first to drive the Lincoln-Guilder-Sweetland ambulances, which were produced in Detroit.

1923

Dr. Thomas J. Heldt, a Johns Hopkins student under Dr. Adolf Meyer, establishes the Division of Neuropsychiatry at the hospital. He comes to Detroit to begin a new type of treatment that integrates psychiatry with general medicine. He is known for not using patient restraints and for creating one of the first open psychiatric wards in the country.

1923

Dr. Harry O. Davidson comes to Henry Ford Hospital as an intern and remains in the Department of Pediatrics for more than 50 years. The department was founded by Dr. Irvine P. McQuarrie (pictured).

From the Conrad R. Lam Collection, Henry Ford Health System. ID=02-033.

amplified at the hospital to include clinical and pathological conferences, regular ward rounds, medical clinics, and hospital medical society meetings. Our men began to make themselves heard in some of the local and national meetings."[26]

But for every step forward in gaining an appreciation for the skilled staff in place, Henry Ford Hospital physicians continued to have to prove themselves time and again with their local peers. Soon after the expansion was complete, the hospital's reputation took a step back as Liebold invited reporters in to view the changes. As Dr. Smith recalled, Liebold boasted too much and placed blame on reporters who overheard doctors talking about future plans that hadn't yet been approved. Regardless of the source of information, the exaggerated press

Henry Ford Hospital, West Grand Boulevard view, 1923. *(Detail From the Collections of The Henry Ford. ID:THF117472.)*

1923

Dr. Howard P. Doub, a Johns Hopkins alum, establishes the roentgenology department and pioneers the use of the roentgen ray. The hospital invests in state-of-the-art medical equipment, such as the fluoroscopic unit to support the early diagnosis of disease. In 1925, the department is recognized by the AMA for its medical and scientific presentations.

1923

A maternity ward and nursery opens with 24 bassinettes. Dr. Everett D. Plass heads obstetrics from 1922 to 1926. Obstetrics is later merged with the Department of Gynecology under Dr. Jean Paul Pratt.

1923

At the inception of the hospital, Henry Ford issued an edict that smoking was banned throughout the buildings and its grounds. Katherine Kimmick, R.N., appointed in 1923 as head of the Department of Nursing, resigned three years later after a smoking scandal on the premises.

Clara Ford: Henry's 'Great Believer'

While Henry Ford Hospital bears the name of the auto magnate, his wife Clara certainly had a significant influence on the project, as she did with most of his other business ventures.

"She advised him to do or not do a lot of things," recalled Mrs. Clarence Davis, a distant relative and close friend of the Fords. "She certainly must have had sound advice."[1]

The Fords (pictured above in 1938) were always in sync on charitable matters, though most were handled quietly. With few exceptions—the hospital being one—the Fords often worked with individuals rather than large endeavors.

"I don't think anybody will know what Mr. and Mrs. Ford did to help people out," Mrs. Davis' husband, Clarence, said. "I think that was kept very quiet."[2]

coverage drew a backlash from other physicians in the area, who felt that Henry Ford Hospital was advertising its medical facilities—something that was frowned upon at the time.

"Needless to say, our relationship with the city's doctors went completely awry and left us floundering on the rocks of competitive medicine," Dr. Smith recalled. "The publication, however, brought an avalanche of patients to the hospital, and in doing so served to emphasize the accusation of competition. We couldn't handle the patient load, so we took names, addresses, and a short medical note only to later phone them with an appointment."[27]

Soon after, Liebold was recalled to Ford headquarters, where he began working on the Detroit, Toledo and Ironton Railroad, which Ford Motor Company had purchased in 1920 for $5 million.[28] William L. Graham of the Ford Motor Company transferred into the hospital's superintendent role.

"This gave us all a great measure of relief, since Mr. Graham was a man of refinement, sensibility, and justice," Dr. Smith said. "He remained at the hospital only a few years, but in the main did a very good job."[29]

Graham was replaced in 1926 by another Ford Motor employee, Israel R. Peters, who stayed until 1952 and worked closely with Dr. Sladen and Dr. McClure on management of the hospital. "He was a capable accountant and business administrator, but, having a vested authority, he was in a position to block medical progress and to accentuate differences of opinion between medical and surgical chiefs," Dr. Smith said.[30]

1923

Annual hospital revenues reach $2 million, but Henry Ford makes up a deficit of $300,000. Both Henry and his wife Clara Ford continue to balance the finances of the hospital with their personal funds.

Hospital Adds Psychiatric Unit

Henry Ford Hospital was on the forefront of mental health practices since its first chemical dependence ward in the M-Unit in 1914. In 1923, a psychiatric unit was added within the main hospital. Dr. Thomas J. Heldt was in charge of the Neuropsychiatry division. Liebold said the idea for the unit had the support of Clara Ford.[31]

Dr. Heldt graduated Johns Hopkins and served as a clinical assistant in psychiatry at Ward's Island facility in New York before a time in the army as a lieutenant in the medical corps.[32]

A psychiatric unit was set in the hospital after "we judged it best to review unostentatiously the hospital's needs and to fit unobtrusively into its existing organization," Dr. Heldt told peers at a meeting of the American Psychiatric Association in 1927. "This is not because neuropsychiatry need offer any apology for its presence in a general hospital—nor for its methods of examination, study, or treatment—but because there is still altogether too much evidence of those traditional barriers that lie in segregation, institutionalization, hoary court proceedings, and all that they imply. Assignment to institutional care is still too much a matter of habit and too little a matter of last resort."[33]

While the idea was novel at the time, within just a few years, newspapers carried reports of Dr. Heldt's work, proclaiming, "the experiment of caring for mental patients in the general hospital has been tried and found successful, and this method of care has many advantages."[34]

Dr. Heldt spent 29 years as head of the division before retiring in 1952; he remained as senior consultant. His advances in psychiatric understanding, as well as his treatment of patients with dignity, was heralded.[35] At his death in 1972, Dr. Heldt was credited with creating the first neuropsychiatry division in a general hospital that did not use restraints, did not isolate its patients, and did not separate men and women.[36]

1923

Among the Henry Ford Hospital staff (pictured) is Dr. Dwight C. Ensign. He arrives as an intern, founds the Division of Rheumatology in 1942, and works at the hospital for 58 years.

From the Conrad R. Lam Collection, Henry Ford Health System. ID=02-001.

1924

Dr. Roy D. McClure, one of the pioneering physicians of Henry Ford Hospital, submits his resignation to the Detroit Academy of Surgery after the organization cancels a meeting at the hospital in criticism of its closed-practice system. His resignation receives national attention. Photo: Dr. McClure (left foreground) in Ford Hospital's operating room, c. 1920s.

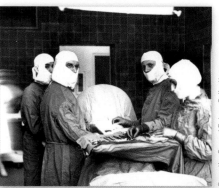

From the Conrad R. Lam Collection, Henry Ford Health System. ID=02-030.

CLARA FORD NURSES HOME

1924

1925

Dr. Laurence S. Fallis, a young Canadian who had trained in London and Edinburgh, begins working with Dr. Roy McClure in the Department of General Surgery.

The Henry Ford Hospital dietary staff in the kitchen, c. 1925.

From the Collections of The Henry Ford. ID:THF117436.

A School and Home for Nurses

If the psychiatric unit had come to fruition because of Clara Ford's support, another idea would also have her hearty input. In 1925, both the Henry Ford Hospital School of Nursing and Hygiene and the Clara Ford Nurses Home opened. Nurse Katherine G. Kimmick, a graduate of the Rochester General Hospital in Rochester, New York, and of the Columbia University Teachers' College in New York City, was named director of the new tuition-free school.[37] She was said to be the highest-paid nurse in the country, with a yearly salary of $7,200.[38]

Courses covered 28 months, with a four-month preparatory period and then a first and second year. Two classes would be admitted—one in January and one in September, with the class size limited to 100.[39]

The hospital's reputation surely was a draw for nursing students. But the Clara Ford Nurses Home could not help but seal the deal. Drs. Sladen and McClure had pushed Ford for years to open a nurses' training program. When Ford finally agreed, Clara worked with noted architect Albert Kahn, who had built many of the factories and buildings in Detroit,

1925

Cancer research begins
with the collaboration of
Drs. Sladen and McClure.
They both speak in public
lectures and with the
American Cancer Society
on the danger of smoking.

1925

The Clara Ford Nurses Home features
326 private rooms and a luxurious
environment for formal events.

From the Collections of The Henry Ford. ID:THF117493.

1925

The Education Building
of the new nurses quar-
ters feature classrooms,
a pool, squash courts,
and a gymnasium with a
stage for special events.

The Henry Ford Hospital Education Building in 1925. *(From the Collections of The Henry Ford. ID:THF117481.)*

including several for Ford Motor Company. She also worked closely with a designer to ensure that both the private rooms and common areas were outfitted with precision.

"Every room in the home had a private bath, and there were beautiful reception rooms and furnishings," Dr. Smith recalled. "Despite his advisors arguing with Mr. Ford that all these furnishings were unnecessary, he insisted upon them in construction. Many of the older graduates of other nursing schools expressed the desire to return to training just to live in these luxurious surroundings."[40]

By 1926, Kimmick had resigned and Mabel McNeel, R.N., was named director of the nursing school and the director of nurses at the hospital.

Taking a Personal Interest

While Henry and Clara Ford's commitment to the hospital ran deep, they expected top care because they referred so many of their friends and employees there. The Ford Motor Company had established a sociological department soon after Ford implemented the $5 workday in 1914. Workers in the department routinely visited Ford workers' homes, assessing how they could help. Those in need could seek out assistance from the department for guidance. Many of those were referred to Henry Ford Hospital. But outside the formal program, the assistance often came at the direction of Henry and Clara Ford.

Ford Motor Company engineer E. J. Farkas recounted a story that many Ford employees could tell of how the Fords helped in a time of crisis. In 1925, Farkas and his son Louis were traveling near West Branch in an open car when Farkas lost control, and the vehicle

1925

The Henry Ford Hospital School of Nursing and Hygiene admits its first class of 93 student nurses. The 28-month, tuition-free program includes science, medicine, and training rounds.

1926

The book, *Collected Papers by the Staff of the Henry Ford Hospital 1915–1925*, is published and illustrates the early departments and research at the hospital. The book is dedicated to founder Henry Ford.

1926

Nurse Mabel McNeel becomes the director of the School of Nursing and Hygiene. She serves for eight years, leaving in 1934.

flipped. When passersby stopped to help, Farkas sent his son on to the doctor to be seen. "I didn't realize how serious he was hurt because he was still talking and asking for water," Farkas said.[41] The nearest hospital was in Bay City, and the doctor was concerned that the 8-year-old might not survive the trip. Bringing him all the way to Detroit was out of the question.

The next day, Ford called Farkas to inquire about his son. Farkas told Ford the boy had a collapsed lung. Immediately, Ford sent Dr. Roy McClure to Bay City, to oversee the boy's care until he was stable enough to transfer to Henry Ford Hospital. "So Dr. McClure came up pretty quick. That's about 115 miles from Detroit, but they were there that morning in a Lincoln car."[42]

The Henry Ford Hospital Pediatrics ward in 1928. *(Detail From the Collections of The Henry Ford. ID:THF117490.)*

Dr. McClure brought an orthopedic specialist with him. Farkas didn't recall his name, but that physician "took charge of the case. He attended to the details. He straightened out his arm. It was broken at the shoulder."[43] Dr. McClure returned to Detroit and then back to Bay City a few days later when the X-rays were developed. The doctors counted 13 fractures. Within a week, Louis was well enough to be transferred to Detroit to recover at Henry Ford Hospital. "Mr. Ford did a whole lot in making us comfortable. Later, he visited Louis, and, eventually, so did Mrs. Ford. She even brought some flowers from her own garden."[44]

Stories like this were not uncommon at Henry Ford Hospital. The Fords had built a premier hospital and were confident that the physicians, nurses, and staff there could provide the absolute best care. The hospital's leadership had built a staff worthy of the Fords' belief.

1926

Israel R. Peters becomes the hospital superintendent and holds the position until 1952. He works in concert with Drs. Sladen and McClure.

1926

Dr John K. Ormond, on staff since 1916, officially establishes the Department of Urology.

1926

Dr. Albert S. Crawford establishes the Division of Neurological Surgery. He heads this area for 27 years and fosters innovation in surgical equipment and research.

Three

"*The responsibilities of this hospital were placed upon younger men whose loyalty meant a sacrifice of ambitions to the accomplishment of a greater understanding in which they must submerge themselves.*"

Dr. Frank Sladen
PHYSICIAN-IN-CHIEF[1]

EXCELLENT WORK, TRYING TIMES

**1927
1940**

T HE ROARING TWENTIES SENT THE MESSAGE THAT ANYTHING WAS POSSIBLE. Building upon the work of the great inventors of the early 20th century, innovation appeared at every turn. Henry Ford Hospital was no different.

Many of the young physicians who had joined the hospital in its earliest days had matured into leaders in their respective fields. Research was expected, and exploring the unknown led to key breakthroughs.

Despite the breakthrough medicine practiced within its halls, the hospital was beset by financial struggles. Henry Ford had a policy that his hospital would never turn anyone away for an inability to pay. While the Fords were able—and willing—to write a check to cover the shortfalls that occurred almost monthly, the hospital and the community were about to enter a time of unprecedented financial challenge. But mere money woes—whether happening within the hospital or in the nation—would not stop Henry Ford Hospital from remarkable growth.

The Henry Ford Hospital Department of Eye, Ear, Nose and Throat, 1939. *(Detail From the Collections of The Henry Ford. ID:THF117511.)*

Above: Henry Ford Hospital, c. 1931. *(Detail From the Collections of The Henry Ford. ID:THF117539.)*

Above right: The Henry Ford Hospital main lobby, c. 1931. *(From the Collections of The Henry Ford. ID:THF117430.)*

Increased Recognition

Detroit's medical community had not always embraced Henry Ford Hospital and its physicians. But when the 1927 Clinical Congress of the American College of Surgeons came to Detroit—and to Henry Ford Hospital in particular—there was no denying that the hospital was among the top facilities in the country.

Having the Congress in town was quite a coup for Detroit as well. Since the first Congress in 1910, the annual meeting had rotated through just six cities: Chicago, Philadelphia, New York, London, Boston, and Montreal.[2] The annual Congress provided a prime opportunity for surgeons and other physicians and researchers at Henry Ford Hospital to showcase the innovative spirit that was creating new ideas, techniques, and equipment. In all, some 1,600 visitors attended clinics, demonstrations, and exhibits during the five days.[3]

1927

1927

Henry Ford purchases a parcel of land twice the size of Delaware in the Brazilian Amazon to grow rubber for tires. The property is called Fordlandia. The hospital sends Dr. Laurence Fallis in 1928 to serve as physician-in-chief. He is followed by Dr. Colin Beaton and later Dr. D. Emerick Szilagyi (pictured), also of the Department of Surgery.

Henry Ford Hospital receives international acclaim when the annual five-day Clinical Congress of the American College of Surgeons is held in Detroit with 1,600 attendees. Numerous clinics within the hospital showcase their technologies.

That the prestigious American College of Surgeons chose Detroit and Henry Ford Hospital for its annual Congress still resonates decades later. "That's a big deal," said Dr. Scott Dulchavsky, who joined Henry Ford Hospital in 2003 as chief of the Department of Surgery. "We've placed many of the physicians in the Henry Ford Medical Group in national leadership roles, and we do today: the American Medical Association, the American College of Cardiology, a wide variety of others. That doesn't come by accident. It's by having these visionary leaders."[4]

Expanding the Reach

In the early 1920s, Henry Ford intended for his automotive company to become self-sufficient. He purchased more than 300,000 acres of forest and two iron mines in the Upper Peninsula of Michigan[5] near an area where he and son Edsel had camped years earlier.[6]

Out of that purchase grew the Iron Mountain facility, which began distilling charcoal from the wood waste. Ford Charcoal was later renamed Kingsford Charcoal (after a Ford relative in charge of the Iron Mountain operations), and another iconic American brand was born.[7]

Elizabeth Moran, R.N. (center), with Dr. Frank Sladen (right) and Dr. Roy McClure (far right), c. 1947. *(Detail From the Collections of The Henry Ford. ID:THF117557.)*

Elizabeth Moran: A Leader with Exacting Standards

In 1934, Elizabeth Moran, R.N., took on the position of director of the Department of Nursing. A Johns Hopkins graduate, Moran would lead Henry Ford Hospital into a new era of respect in the nursing profession.

Outside the hospital, she led the Michigan Nurses Center Association[1] and served the state on the Michigan Joint Legislative Committee on Reorganization of State Government: Michigan's Health Agencies. At the national level, she was president of the American Nurses Association and had a number of papers published in the *American Journal of Nursing* on business practices in the nursing department.

Perhaps more profound was her impact on the School of Nursing and the hospital itself. Her passion for nursing education was apparent: "There is no group more interested in you than your faculty, because your instructors, supervisors, and head nurses see in you the product of their efforts," Moran wrote in the *1937 School of Nursing Yearbook*. "Whether you stand or fall as students, whether or not you succeed as graduate nurses, we ask ourselves, 'Wherein have we been a part of your achievement?'"[2]

"She held her charges to the highest standards," said Wilma Gandy, who joined the hospital as a ward clerk in 1955. "The greatest director that we ever had at the hospital was Miss Moran, and she was tough. But I loved her toughness. She was about your dress code. She would tell you, 'Well, before you go on duty tomorrow, you stop by my office. ... I want shoes polished, and the shoe strings, you wash 'em.' She was really strict, but she was just as strict on the doctors as she was on the housekeeper."[3]

The Henry Ford Hospital School of Nursing Graduation in 1937. *(From the Collections of The Henry Ford. ID:THF117715.)*

With the charcoal plant, iron mines, and forestry operations—all dangerous lines of work—Ford wanted to develop his own hospital at Iron Mountain. Dr. W. H. Alexander, a protégé of Dr. Roy McClure's at Henry Ford Hospital, was tapped to open the facility.

"Apropos of the little antagonistic feeling that existed between the Medical and Surgical Departments, Dr. McClure wanted me in on the ground floor at the hospital at Iron Mountain," Dr. Alexander recalled. "He figured if I was here when the hospital was built, I would step in and rule the roost."[8]

Albert Kahn, who had designed the Clara Ford Nurses Home, also drew up plans for the Iron Mountain hospital. The estimated price tag was $350,000. "They thought this was a little too much for a 50-bed hospital at the time, so they knocked off some of the pillars from in front. … They skimped in a few other ways, and the cost was down to $300,000," Dr. Alexander said. By 1925, that plan had been scuttled; Dr. Alexander remained to run a hospital out of a converted house. "So much equipment was put in there that I was afraid it was going to squash it down flat."[9]

Henry Ford, though, was intent on making sure his workers had access to medical care, no matter where they worked. He and Clara Ford financially supported a clinic close to their Richmond Hill Plantation near Savannah, Georgia.[10] But it was a hospital facility in Brazil, near Ford's rubber plantation, that would maintain the closest affiliation to Henry Ford Hospital.

From the Collections of The Henry Ford. ID:THF117712.

Edsel and Eleanor Ford: The Second Generation of Commitment to the Hospital

As Henry and Clara Ford's only child, Edsel Ford (pictured with his wife Eleanor, 1938) was involved in many of his parents' projects. Working alongside his father at the Ford Motor Company, Edsel Ford also joined the Henry Ford Hospital Board of Trustees at its inception.

"Edsel Ford was valued by every member of the early professional staff as the best friend of each one, and of the hospital," Dr. Frank Sladen wrote in an unpublished memoir. "With his spirit, his understanding, and encouragement, he exerted a big influence on the decisions."[1]

Edsel Ford's wife, Eleanor, was equally devoted to the hospital and to raising the couple's four children. After Edsel's death in 1943 from cancer at age 49, his children funded the Edsel B. Ford Institute for Medical Research at the hospital.[2]

Eleanor became more actively involved in the hospital and was key to ensuring Ford family support after Edsel's death and the subsequent deaths of Henry and Clara, said Dr. F. Janney Smith, a longtime cardiologist at the hospital. "I feel that her sincere interest in the hospital's welfare has been of inestimable value to its present affairs and its future development. She has supplied the bridge of strength that has carried the affairs of the Ford Motor Company into the hands of the younger members of the Ford family. The characters of her children so easily bear me out in this contention."[3]

Fordlandia

Rubber was native to Brazil, but in 1876, explorers had taken seeds for rubber trees to the East Indies. By the start of the 20th century, the East Indies was the leading producer of rubber, dominating the market and resulting in high prices. The US government launched a study to develop alternative sources of rubber and deemed the Amazon a suitable location.[11] Ford followed up with his own study, identifying the Tapajos River Valley as the ideal place for a Ford rubber plantation known as Fordlandia.

In 1927, the Brazilian government provided Ford with 2.5 million acres of land along the Tapajos River Valley in exchange for a percentage of Fordlandia's profits.[12] Once the plantation was built, Ford sent key executives from Detroit to launch the facility, though many of the workers would be locals. Dr. Laurence Fallis, who had begun his career as an intern at Henry Ford Hospital, was sent to operate the health facilities.

The patient ward at Fordlandia, the Ford Motor Company rubber plantation factory hospital in Brazil, 1931. *(Detail From the Collections of The Henry Ford. ID:THF115477.)*

1927

1928

Margaret L. King (pictured) is one of Henry Ford Hospital's first dietitians.

From the Conrad R. Lam Collection, Henry Ford Health System. ID=03-033.

The newly established National Institutes of Health gives funds to Henry Ford Hospital for research activities.

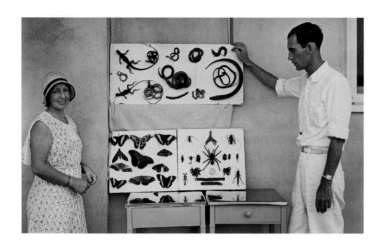

Dr. and Mrs. Claude Smith at The Ford Motor Company Fordlandia hospital in 1931 showing their collection of specimens. *(Detail From the Collections of The Henry Ford. ID:THF117671.)*

In the Amazon, providing health care was not just a way to ensure employee happiness—it was a necessity. Native diseases such as malaria and hookworm were a challenge, and doctors had to institute policies that required employees to wear shoes and follow sanitary processes.[13]

Fordlandia struggled almost from the beginning. Heavy rains made planting rubber trees difficult, and local workers rebelled against the paternalistic requirements of a Midwestern US diet and social dances.[14]

By 1933, Ford Motor Company had developed a new location—Belterra—about 80 miles from Fordlandia. It was considered a more ideal location for the agricultural aspects of rubber growth. It also provided a fresh start. Ford had learned a few lessons at Fordlandia and eased the cultural aspects of employment, but health issues remained a concern during the years.

Dr. Colin Beaton, another Ford Hospital physician, succeeded Dr. Fallis and took a heavy hand in enforcing sanitation standards to eradicate disease. Under his direction, medical teams routinely dismantled potential mosquito breeding grounds, inspected food storage inside the homes, and fined families if their pig and chicken coops were not clean.[15]

Dr. D. Emerick Szilagyi, a Henry Ford Hospital surgical intern in 1939, served as medical director at Fordlandia. As Dr. Fallis had to confront issues that were not common in Detroit, Dr. Szilagyi also learned on the job in Brazil.

"There were a lot of people who were blind in both eyes, and so he told the story that he had been on ophthalmology for two weeks as a resident, but had traded off," said Dr. Joseph P. Elliott Jr., who later worked alongside Dr. Szilagyi at Henry Ford Hospital and served

1928

Dr. Clyde I. Allen, head of industrial surgery, coordinates emergency calls to surrounding factories using a fleet of custom ambulances with doctors who ride on board to help. Those needing surgery are brought back to the hospital.

1928

Dr. Oliver H. Gaebler is hired as a research assistant in chemistry within the Department of Pathology. Pictured are Dr. Gaebler (right) and technician Irma Hill in 1931.

From the Collections of The Henry Ford. ID:THF117457.

1929

The stock market crashes, causing a run on the banks and an uproar in the economy. Within the next few years, the hospital would be forced to lay off staff temporarily.

as Division Head of Vascular Surgery in the 1980s. "He wrote back to the Ophthalmology Department and got several letters on how to do cataract surgery. He got instruments sent to him, and besides doing general surgery and taking care of everybody, he practiced on bulls' eyes, and then took out cataracts, and had some standard glasses that he gave people, and he only operated on one eye. But he had people who were very thankful that they could see enough to get around and do things."[16]

Cultural differences remained. Medical staff had tried to enforce a ban on home births among workers at the plantation. "There was so much resistance that half the people didn't obey it," Dr. Szilagyi said, "so I lifted the rule and made it voluntary."[17]

When Dr. Szilagyi returned to Detroit in 1945, he had planned to discuss the Brazilian work with Henry Ford II, Edsel's son, who had just been named Ford Motor Company chair. "I would have told him that Fordlandia should be abandoned. It was a very picturesque place and would have been a wonderful hideaway for Ford executives—like a little Switzerland for fishing and hunting—but it was not appropriate for a plantation. For Belterra, if I had had a chance, I would have told him to keep going. They shouldn't have given it up."[18]

Left to right: Edsel Bryant Ford, Eleanor Clay Ford, Henry Ford II, Benson Ford, Josephine Clay Ford, and William Clay Ford outside their home at Gaukler Pointe, Grosse Pointe Shores, Michigan, 1938. *(From the Collections of The Henry Ford. ID:THF99953.)*

That meeting was cancelled and never rescheduled. But Ford gave up control of both plants in the years after World War II as worldwide supplies stabilized.

1930

1930

From the Collections of The Henry Ford. ID:THF117514.

Early Henry Ford Hospital brochures advertised the cleanliness of the facilities, including the kitchen (pictured c. 1930).

From the Collections of The Henry Ford. ID:THF117542.

The Henry Ford Hospital main lobby pharmacy, c. 1930.

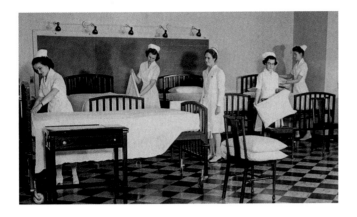

Above: Cleo Stewart (center) shows student nurses how to make a hospital bed in 1946. *(Detail From the Collections of The Henry Ford. ID:THF117724.)*

Opposite: The Surgical Pavilion operating room, 1939. *(From the Collections of The Henry Ford. ID:THF117508.)*

Financial Challenges

By the late 1920s, Henry Ford Hospital's reach and acclaim were worldwide. The hospital's unique set-up, in which physicians were employees—the "closed" system—meant they were free to focus on medical excellence without the worries of running a separate practice. But the business end of operations suffered. Rates for treatment had not changed since the hospital opened its doors more than a decade before.

Henry and Clara Ford—who were fond of sending friends and employees to the hospital for free treatment—continued to donate significant sums to keep the hospital in the black. But even their wealth and philanthropy were about to be stretched as the United States, Detroit, and Henry Ford Hospital encountered unprecedented financial difficulties.

When the stock market crashed in October 1929, Detroit was hit hard. Having built the auto industry in the preceding two decades, the city found that its reliance on manufacturing left it vulnerable. In 1929, more than 5.3 million vehicles rolled off Detroit assembly lines. By 1930, 2 million fewer vehicles were produced, and a year later, that total shrank to just 1.32 million.[19]

Not surprisingly, the drop in vehicle sales brought a related reduction in employment. Ford laid off more than two thirds of its workforce.[20] Those workers who remained saw their hours cut. Ford's auto interest struggled again with the Ford Hunger March in 1932. Demonstrators—some 3,000 strong—gathered in Detroit, intending to march to Dearborn and demand Henry Ford recognize union representation and provide longer working hours for his employees. The march was met with violence; several demonstrators were killed and many injured.[21]

1931

With the rise in factory injuries and the upcoming Crippled Children's Act, Henry Ford Hospital forms the Division of Orthopedics with Dr. Carl E. Badgley as chief. He implemented use of occupational therapy for industrial cases.

1931

Cleo Stewart enters the School of Nursing and Hygiene and stays at the hospital until her retirement in 1974. She served as associate director of the School of Nursing from 1948 to 1966 and assistant director from 1966 to 1974. She is known for her hands-on teaching style.

1932

Dr. Conrad R. Lam begins his internship and residency under Dr. McClure. He becomes known for his innovative work in cardiac surgery.

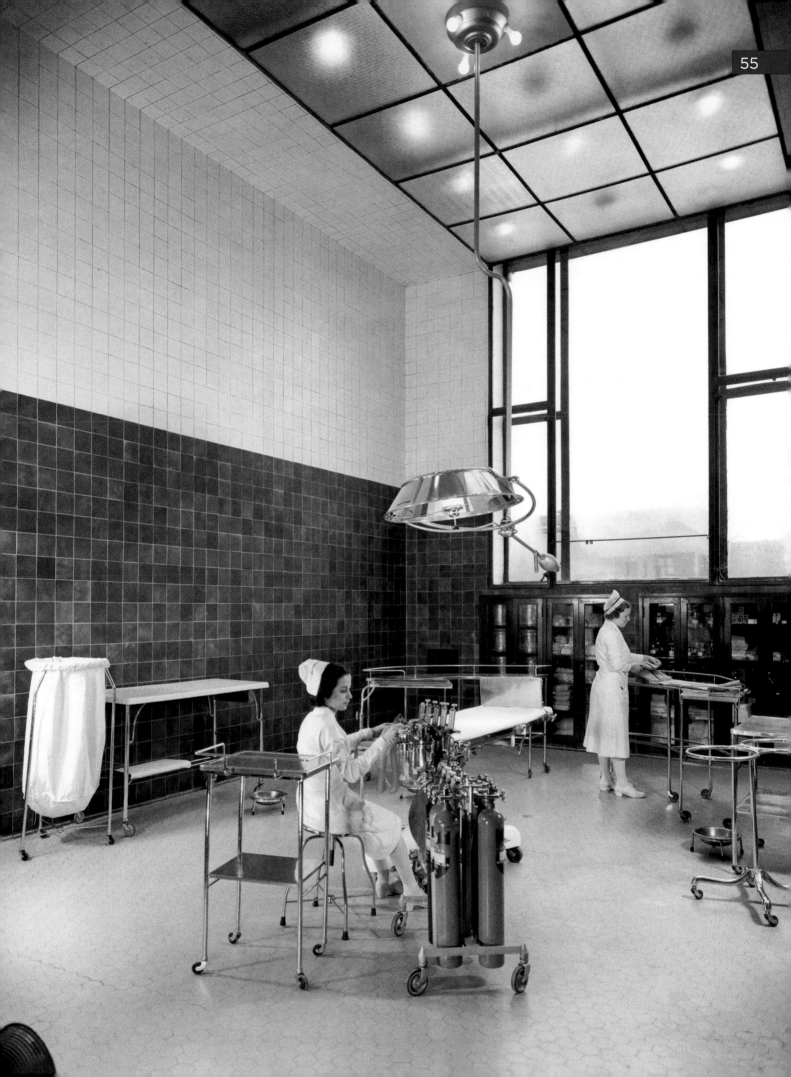

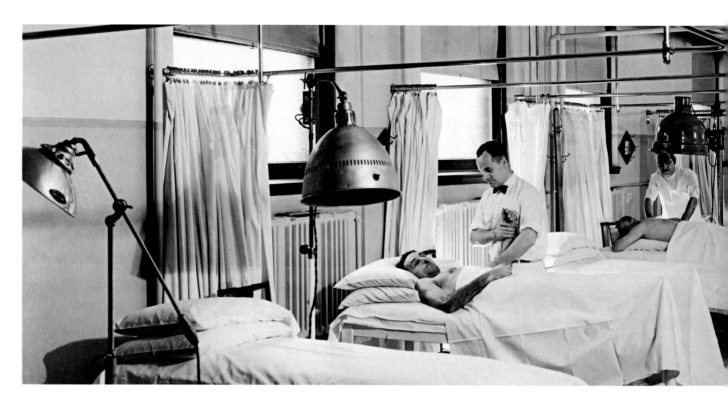

The Henry Ford Hospital
Physical Therapy Department
in 1939. *(Detail From
the Collections of The
Henry Ford. ID:THF117499.)*

Henry Ford Hospital was not immune to what was occurring in its community. Hospital census counts dropped, and, in 1934, the hospital only treated an average of 309 patients per day.[22] Units were shuttered, and work weeks were cut back. Patient charges were also cut—a reflection of the community's economic realities, not decreasing costs.

Famous Patients

On November 16, 1933, Henry Ford Hospital admitted its most famous patient: the man whose name was on its doors. Newspapers breathlessly carried details of "the first serious

1932

1932

Edsel Ford commissions world-renowned muralist Diego Rivera to paint a mural of the Ford Rouge Plant on four walls of the Detroit Institute of Arts in honor of Detroit's largest industry. While Rivera and his wife, Frida Kahlo, are in Detroit, she suffers a miscarriage and is taken to Henry Ford Hospital to recover. She paints "The Flying Bed" (pictured).

Dr. Elizabeth M. Yagle, a noted serologist and immunologist, is hired by Dr. Hartman to head the serology lab.

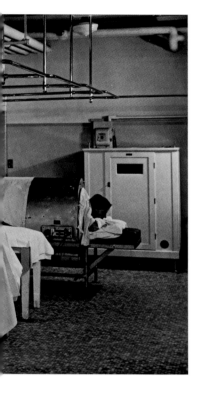

illness of his 69 years," reporting that Henry Ford was brought into surgery for a strangulated hernia and an inflamed appendix at 5 p.m. Just a few hours later, "his pulse and temperature were normal, and he was resting well."[23] Clara Ford stayed in a suite next to his hospital room. Doctors planned to keep Ford in the hospital for two weeks, newspapers reported.[24]

Though the media reported Ford was making "normal" progress, it was anything but. The auto magnate had his own ideas about good health. Just a few hours after the operation—serious abdominal surgery no less—he wanted to be up and around. Doctors urged him to stay in bed, but he would not consider it. He continued to make rapid progress, especially for a man of his age, though early ambulation was not the prevailing attitude of the time. In fact, when Henry Ford Hospital physicians discussed the idea at professional meetings, they were met with derision.[25]

The preliminary physical examination, 1939. (*Detail From the Collections of The Henry Ford. ID:THF117647.*)

The strangulated hernia may have been the first time Ford stayed at the hospital, but it was far from his only encounter with the medical staff there. "His ideas on health and medicine were certainly bizarre, but there was one constant feature," said Dr. F. Janney Smith, a cardiologist at the hospital in its early years. "He firmly believed that the road to health was chiefly a matter of diet and nutrition. It soon became apparent that Mr. Ford expected the hospital to come up with some

1933

Henry Ford requires emergency abdominal surgery for a strangulated hernia. A few hours later, Ford insists on getting up and moving about. The quandary over early ambulation leads to studies on the topic and sweeping changes in post-surgical care.

1934

Elizabeth S. Moran, R.N, (pictured in 1934), one of the most academic-principled nurses at Henry Ford Hospital, comes on board. She later succeeds Mabel McNeel, R.N., as director of the Department of Nursing and stays in leadership until 1960.

major scientific proof for his contentions. It's also apparent that we disappointed him in this regard."[26]

Treating Ford for a serious bout of bronchitis, Dr. Smith found him to be "a most difficult patient. He did not accede to my advice of bed rest, and he was overly suspicious of the medicines I offered because I could not describe the manufacturing process on the spur of the moment."[27]

For a man who had built a world-class medical facility, Ford was known to hold firmly to his own beliefs in spite of medical advice, Dr. Smith said. "On more than one occasion, he visited patients of mine who were friends of his. Despite the fact that they were all heart patients, he would tell them, 'Pay no attention to that doctor. All you have to do is get out of bed and lie on the floor for half an hour twice a day and eat celery and carrots, and then you'll be all right.'"[28]

The cast room in the Department of Orthopedics, c. 1935. *(Detail From the Collections of The Henry Ford. ID:THF117551.)*

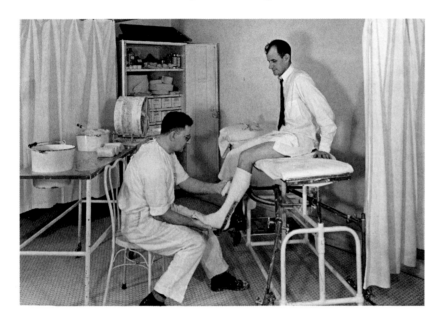

Other celebrities who had accessed the hospital included Detroit Tigers manager and player Gordon (Mickey) Cochrane, a patient of Dr. McClure's. He had been treated at the hospital for an illness in 1936 after the Tigers' two consecutive World Series titles in 1934 and 1935.[29]

In 1937, Cochrane's playing career ended when he was hit in the head by a ball thrown by Yankees pitcher Irving (Bump) Hadley. When the ball hit Cochrane on the left temple, he collapsed at the plate. As soon as he was stable enough to do so, he left New York

1935

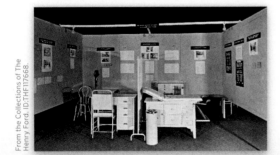

From the Collections of The Henry Ford. ID:THF117668.

A display at the Henry Ford Hospital Education Building on the hospital examination room, c. 1935.

1936

The Department of Eye, Ear, Nose, and Throat separates under Dr. Elmer Whitney and forms the two departments of Otolaryngology and Ophthalmology.

1937

Henry Ford Hospital and the University of Michigan form an education partnership. The hospital is designated as a center for graduate study work, and work conducted by surgical fellows in the laboratories is credited toward a Masters of Science degree from the University of Michigan.

and checked in to Henry Ford Hospital. The future Baseball Hall-of-Famer even accompanied Dr. McClure on a trip to Europe. Though the newspapers at the time reported that Dr. McClure was traveling along with the player as part of his convalescence,[30] it was Cochrane who accompanied Dr. McClure. The physician was to receive a prestigious award in France.[31]

Boxer Jimmy Adamick had survived more than 60 professional bouts without being knocked out—until he encountered Roscoe Toles in Detroit. In the fight's second round, Toles delivered a blow that left Adamick unconscious for 11 hours.[32] He was brought to Henry Ford Hospital, where neurosurgeon Dr. Albert Crawford treated his concussion with an oxygen tent to prevent pneumonia and a blood transfusion to speed recovery.[33]

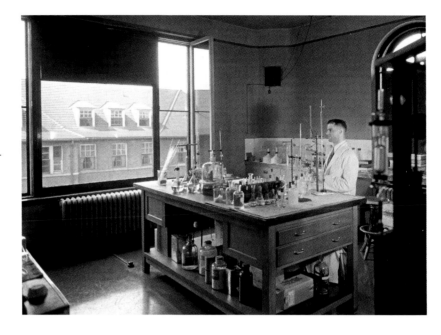

Important Medical Breakthroughs

Henry Ford Hospital had earned its reputation for innovative treatments, whether the patient was rich and famous or penniless and unknown. The hospital had continued to invest in research and even explored the idea of creating a Department of Experimental Surgery.[34] Though the department never materialized, that did not prevent experiments of all sorts, leading to key medical breakthroughs.

Dr. McClure's European trip—the one overshadowed by the baseball player—had come as a result of his work in advancing understanding of treatment for burn patients. Dr. Edward

Dr. Victor Schelling in the chemistry laboratory in 1931. *(From the Collections of The Henry Ford. ID:THF117451.)*

1938

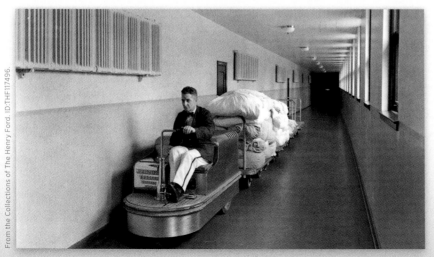

A laundry maintenance staff member in a Mercury truck transporting hospital laundry in Henry Ford Hospital.

Davidson had developed a tannic acid ointment for burn patients; after Dr. Davidson's death, Dr. McClure and Dr. Conrad Lam continued to advance the treatment.[35]

Dr. Lam joined Henry Ford Hospital in 1932 as a surgical resident under Dr. McClure. By 1938, he became a member of the staff. In addition to his work with Dr. McClure on the tannic acid treatment, Dr. Lam became the first physician to administer the anti-clotting agent heparin in patients. Publishing his findings in *Annals of Surgery* in 1941, Dr. Lam concluded: "Heparin is of great value in the treatment of thrombo-embolic manifestations and in arterial surgery."[36]

Dr. McClure also researched the effect of iodine on goiters, publishing his findings in *Science* in October 1935. Iodine was added to salt in Michigan—part of North America's so-called "goiter belt"—in 1924.[37] Dr. McClure's study only reinforced the idea that the simple food additive might have significant benefits; the addition of iodine in salt is routine today.

Scientist Dr. Elizabeth Yagle in her office at Henry Ford Hospital, c. 1945.
(From the Conrad R. Lam Collection, Henry Ford Health System. ID=03-006.)

Groundbreaking research no doubt added to the hospital's ability to attract top-notch staff. Dr. Frank Hartman hired scientist Dr. Elizabeth Yagle in 1932 as head of the serology laboratory. Dr. Yagle was noted for her collaborative spirit and willingness to participate in various research projects. That idea was deeply ingrained throughout Henry Ford Hospital, with physicians all engaged in the pursuit of knowledge and advancement.[38]

1938

1939

Dr. Brock Brush comes to Henry Ford Hospital for training in the Department of Medicine and transfers to the Department of Surgery. He becomes chief of surgery and receives Henry Ford Hospital's Distinguished Career Award in 1985. Photo: c. 1965.

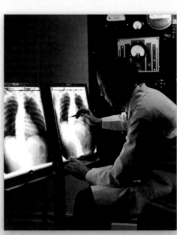

X-rays being read in Radiology, 1939.

The hospital also experimented broadly in the financial side of medicine, joining the Michigan Society for Group Hospitalization in 1939. Affordable prepaid insurance plans had been developed in the 1920s in Texas. By 1939, these plans were widely accepted around the country. The Michigan Society for Group Hospitalization and its companion, the Michigan Medical Service for physicians, later became known as Michigan Blue Cross Blue Shield. By the end of 1940, more than 52,000 Ford Motor Company employees—175,000 employees all together—had enrolled.[39]

The hospital marked its 25th anniversary in 1940. In his speech commemorating the occasion, Dr. Frank Sladen, the hospital's physician-in-chief, praised those who had forsaken their own ambitions for the greater good and dedicated their careers to increase medical understanding. "They have lived in close association, bringing to individual patients a concentrated teamwork of service, and the hospital itself a personality which has proved its greatest asset. I close by paying tribute to these leaders in their various fields and their associates for their unselfish devotion to a hard master: work—the reason for the recognized success of Henry Ford Hospital."[40]

The hospital leadership could not be faulted for its optimism. It had survived a war, an epidemic, and the Great Depression, all while creating innovative research and transforming the standard hospital/physician agreement. Unfortunately for Henry Ford Hospital, just as it paused to celebrate this significant milestone, a tragic event occurring half a world away in the Pacific would thrust the United States into war once again.

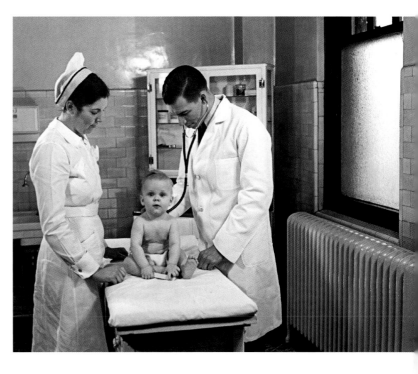

A physical examination in the pediatric department, 1939.
(From the Collections of The Henry Ford. ID:THF117517.)

1939

Research begins on the oxyhemograph developed by Drs. Frank Hartman (pictured, left, in 1949), Vivian G. Behrmann, and Roy McClure. The device records oxygen content of blood during surgery.

From the Conrad R. Lam Collection, Henry Ford Health System. ID=03-036. Credit: *Detroit Times.*

1939

Detroit boxer Jimmy Adamick, with 60 victories to his name, receives a blow from Roscoe Toles that leaves him unconscious for 11 hours. He is rushed to Henry Ford Hospital, where Dr. Albert Crawford treats his concussion with an oxygen tent to prevent pneumonia and a blood transfusion to speed recovery.

Four

> *Our nurses at Henry Ford are caring, compassionate, and collaborative. They are critical thinkers dedicated to providing the highest quality and safest care possible to patients through evidence-based practice. Henry Ford nurses are relentless learners—they are committed to continuous learning and discovery to improve patient outcomes and the delivery of care. Health systems nationwide recognize our nurses because we have a longstanding reputation for clinical competency and ability to care for a diverse patient population with very complex medical conditions."*

Veronica (Ronnie) Hall
CHIEF NURSING OFFICER, HENRY FORD HEALTH SYSTEM
AND CHIEF OPERATING OFFICER, HENRY FORD HOSPITAL[1]

CAN-DO ATTITUDE

WHEN JAPAN ATTACKED THE UNITED STATES ON DECEMBER 7, 1941, THE REVER-berations were felt acutely in Detroit. The war would permanently change the city, which would thereafter be known as part of the country's and the state's "Arsenal of Democracy." The US government called on the automotive industry, including the Ford Motor Company, to equip the armed services with tanks, aircraft, and other war-related machinery.

Henry Ford Hospital again felt the call to duty, sending its young physicians to battlefields and posts around the world. At home, it prepared its existing staff for any uncertainty that war might bring, whether a mass trauma in the city or an attack on the hospital itself. But war brought innovations, too. Some were born of necessity, others by the post-war "anything is possible" attitude that swept the nation.

As soldiers returned from battle, they found jobs, got married, started families, and bought cars and houses. Detroit was in its heyday; its population swelled to nearly 1.9 million.

Clara Bryant Ford with a group of Henry Ford Hospital nurses in 1942. *(Detail From the Collections of The Henry Ford. ID:THF117576.)*

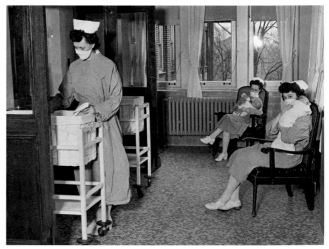

Above left: The American Legion Civil Defense Blood Bank truck donated by the Ford Motor Company in 1941. *(From the Collections of The Henry Ford. ID:THF117718.)*

Above right: The Henry Ford Hospital nursery in 1945. *(From the Collections of The Henry Ford. ID:THF117530.)*

It was a city pulsing with potential, and the hospital was one of the many bright spots. Research reached its pinnacle with physicians making significant medical advances within the halls of Henry Ford. However, the hospital's resolve would be tested as well.

Henry Ford Hospital had marked a quarter century with relatively little change in its core leadership, and with the continued financial support of the Ford family. But the next decade would be one of transition as the hospital lost virtually all of its connections to those visionaries who had founded it.

World War II Begins

The war had raged in Europe for two years, but the United States had done its best to offer support to Allied troops without getting engulfed itself. That changed when Japanese fighters attacked Pearl Harbor. The nation declared war against Japan, and Germany responded by declaring war on the United States. The US was at war on both the European and Asian fronts.

1940

Drs. Roy McClure, Frank Hartman, J. G. Schnedorf, and Victor Schelling exhibit "Phases of Anoxia" at the American Medical Association Meeting and are awarded a certificate of merit.

1940

Drs. Conrad Lam (pictured) and Edward Munnell redevelop the surgical glove originally designed by Dr. C. P. Bailey of Philadelphia. The new, six-finger glove, with a knife attached, is used for a technique in correcting mitral stenosis.

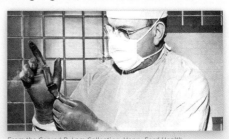

From the Conrad R. Lam Collection, Henry Ford Health System. ID=04-041. Credit: Detroit Free Press.

Panic ensued as Americans became concerned that opposing forces might be able to attack the US mainland. Henry Ford Hospital responded, crafting an elaborate civil defense plan to keep its staff and patients safe—and the facility functioning. Nurses on night duty carried flashlights and were in charge of pulling blackout curtains in case of an air raid. Physicians carried battery-operated blackout lanterns. Plans were made to move patients, if needed, to the hospital's second floor and the M-Unit. The hospital's side windows and skylights were bricked over, while the arched windows in the power house were painted black.[2]

The city mandated blackout periods, which put the staff into darkness. During these tests, observers flew over the city in military planes to ensure that the hospital was not visible. Special supplies such as fire extinguishers and gas masks were stored throughout the facility while mobile defense unit teams—each with a physician and nurse captain—were created. The hospital developed plans for dealing with a poison gas attack, including determining the location of de-gassing stations for men and women. Teams were formed to treat burns, shock, and fractures.[3]

Luckily, neither the hospital nor Detroit at large had to put these procedures in place, although they were practiced routinely through 1944. While these measures may seem extreme today, there was good reason for concern. The atmosphere was rife with rumor. More than 120,000 Japanese-Americans living on the West Coast were sent to internment camps in an unfounded attempt to prevent espionage.[4] On the East Coast, US military ships sank a German U-Boat just 70 miles off the coast of Massachusetts.[5]

The Department of Physical Therapy at Henry Ford Hospital, c. 1943. *(Detail From the Collections of The Henry Ford. ID:THF117548.)*

1941

The Japanese Imperial Navy attacks the US Naval Base at Pearl Harbor, and within days, US President Roosevelt declares war on Germany and Japan. After the attack on Pearl Harbor, Henry Ford and other auto company executives convert their factories to "Arsenals of Democracy," building rockets, planes, tanks, and military trucks on their production lines.

1941

Medical and surgical staff members of Henry Ford Hospital join the call to arms along with legions of Detroiters. Dr. Joseph A. Johnston, longtime head of pediatrics, edits a newsletter for staff members in the military. Photo: Dr. Johnston in his office, 1954.

Detail From the Conrad R. Lam Collection, Henry Ford Health System. ID=04-053.

1941

Henry Ford Hospital works with the American Legion to establish a blood bank for injured industrial workers and soldiers. Ford Motor Company supplies the vehicle that transports blood from donation points to the hospital.

That Detroit might come under attack was hardly a far-fetched notion. As the capital of industry, its war efforts were unmatched. Before Pearl Harbor, US manufacturers had ramped up production to assist Allied war efforts, and after the US joined the war, automobile manufacturers ceased production of cars for civilian use for four years. Automobile factories were quickly transformed to manufacture jeeps, tanks, and bombers. By 1944, Ford's Willow Run plant was building one bomber per hour.[6]

The patriotic sentiments engendered as the US officially entered the war swelled Detroit's population. By mid-1942, some 350,000 workers had moved to the city to join the war effort. Women took their places in factories, filling jobs vacated by men who had gone overseas to fight.[7]

Dr. Edward Quinn of the Division of Infectious Diseases, c. 1950. *(From the Conrad R. Lam Collection, Henry Ford Health System. ID=04-035.)*

Henry Ford Hospital Staff Goes to War

Henry Ford Hospital staff members felt the effects of World War II, as many joined the effort. By war's end, 182 physicians, 105 nurses, and 60 additional personnel had served in some capacity.[8]

While this depletion did not have the same effect as World War I, which rendered the hospital unable to function, it did make its mark. In an effort to keep in touch with those scattered from one end of the world to the other, Dr. Joseph A. Johnston, longtime head of pediatrics, created a newsletter that would be sent to Henry Ford staff serving in the military. Many Henry Ford Hospital leaders—including Dr. Frank Sladen, Dr. Roy McClure, and Dr. John Ormond—saw their children join the service. Two of Edsel Ford's sons, Henry II and Benson, also served.[9]

Dr. Edward Quinn: Infectious Diseases Pioneer

As a resident in Medicine at Henry Ford Hospital in 1942, Dr. Edward L. Quinn participated in the first clinical trials of penicillin in the US. He would become one of the nation's experts in infectious diseases and serve as consultant to the Food and Drug Administration and the pharmacologic industry on antibiotics.

Dr. Quinn joined the senior staff of Henry Ford Hospital in 1946, founding the Division of Infectious Diseases and the Infectious Diseases Research Laboratory in 1949. He established the division's fellowship program in 1955, one of the first in the country. He was a founding member of the Infectious Diseases Society of America and served as president of the Michigan Society of Infectious Diseases.

After nearly 40 years as chief, in 1983, Dr. Quinn became division head emeritus, working through the 1990s. "He was an amazing man," said Dr. Norman Markowitz, current staff member and former chief of the division. "For a clinical problem, you can read everything you can find, and when you don't know what to do, he would always have a way of telling you: 'Well, do this, and do this,' and have a procedure or a method or a pathway to either figure out what to do or to direct you. He was a wise man and knew how to proceed in the darkness."[1]

With some staff away and top leaders pressed into continuing medical training, residents took on larger roles. Dr. Edward L. Quinn was appointed chief resident in the Department of Medicine in 1943 while he and four colleagues assumed responsibility for more than 200 hospital patients.[10] That same year, the hospital brought in 27 interns and residents for an accelerated training program.[11]

The most profound effect was on the nurses and the School of Nursing and Hygiene. The war created a nationwide nurses' shortage. Although 41,397 women had been accepted into nursing schools around the country in 1941, that number was not enough. By 1942, the number had increased to 47,500. But with 10,000 nurses serving in World War II in April 1942, with a goal to double that within a few months, the need was great.[12]

Left to right: Henry Ford Hospital administrator Israel Peters, unidentified man, pathologist Dr. Frank Hartman, and surgeon Dr. Arthur McGraw at a Henry Ford Hospital School of Nursing graduation, c. 1940. *(Detail From the Collections of The Henry Ford. ID:THF117740.)*

1941

An elaborate plan for civil defense goes into effect and lasts until late 1944. By March 1942, more than 1,000 employees are trained in emergency details. Blackout curtains are installed at windows throughout the hospital.

1942

Contractors brick and smooth concrete over the huge windows and skylights in the surgical pavilion. Emergency circuits are placed in the operating room with backup power from emergency generators kept at the ready.

1942

A severe shortage of nurses occurs nationwide as trained nurses, including those from the School of Nursing and Hygiene, leave to serve overseas or in clinics for the tank factories. The US Cadet Nurse Corps is established at Henry Ford Hospital.

The US Cadet Nurse Corps from Henry Ford Hospital in 1943. *(Detail From the Collections of The Henry Ford. ID:THF117523.)*

In 1942 and 1943, Congress prepared several bills to offer funding for nurses' education, including the Bolton Act, which provided grants to institutions for training. Plans were to train 65,000 nurses in 1943.[13] The requirements were rigid, according to Lucile Petry, first director of the Public Health Service's Division of Nursing:

> *The schools are responsible, under the Bolton Act, for admitting more students and preparing them in shorter time. Production in the US Cadet Nurse Corps of the same quality of nurses as before should evolve from this acceleration. Educational standards will be maintained.*[14]

The Henry Ford Hospital School of Nursing and Hygiene was an enthusiastic participant, training 270 nurses in December 1943.[15]

1942

1942

Dr. D. Emerick Szilagyi leaves Henry Ford Hospital to take the physician position at Fordlandia, since Ford Motor Company is a large supplier of rubber to the US government during the war.

Dr. Edward L. Quinn begins his residency training at the hospital. After serving in the military, he joins the hospital staff in 1946. Dr. Quinn becomes one of the nation's experts in infectious diseases.

Successes on the Home Front

As the war raged on, physicians and researchers at Henry Ford Hospital continued research into infections and debilitating diseases, pushing medical science to new heights.

Henry Ford's surgeon-in-chief, Dr. McClure, served as a member of the National Research Council. The Council had been founded during World War I, bringing specialists in to assist the National Academy of Sciences in advising the government on scientific issues.[16]

During World War II, the Council launched a research project to study penicillin to combat infections. British researcher Alexander Fleming had discovered that Penicillium mold inhibited the growth of bacteria in 1928. Fleming's research was delayed several times—first by the inability to produce mold in sufficient quantities, and later by the war's impact on Britain.[17]

By 1941, research had moved to the United States, with major pharmaceutical companies investigating production while scientists studied penicillin efficacy. Under Dr. McClure's direction, Henry Ford Hospital became one of 10 facilities across the nation to participate in clinical trials. Dr. Conrad Lam and Dr. Edward Quinn oversaw a clinical trial that treated both surgical and medical patients.[18]

The resulting research proved the value of a new class of drugs: antibiotics. Their worth would prove both immediate and long-lasting. Throughout history, infection had been one of the leading causes of military deaths. In World War I, 18 percent of those who contracted bacterial pneumonia on the battlefield died. By World War II, that figure was less than 1 percent.[19]

Dr. Conrad R. Lam, c. 1940.
(From the Conrad R. Lam Collection, Henry Ford Health System. ID=04-037.)

1942

New hires to Henry Ford Hospital include Dr. Richmond Smith Jr., who founds the Division of Endocrinology in 1953; and Dr. Joseph L. Ponka, who later serves as chief of Surgical Division IV from 1958–1978.

Dr. Conrad Lam

Yale graduate Dr. Conrad Lam was hired as an intern at the hospital in 1932. He later served as a surgical resident and chief resident before joining the staff in 1938. Dr. Lam would go on to make significant contributions in research, including participating in the first penicillin clinical trials in the US and becoming the nation's first physician to administer purified heparin for the treatment of blood clots.[1]

Dr. Lam worked alongside his mentor, Dr. Roy McClure, on burn treatment advances. With Dr. Edward Munnell, he redeveloped a surgical technique for correcting mitral valve stenosis, creating a special six-finger glove in 1940.[2]

By 1950, Dr. Lam was again challenging himself in the area of cardiac surgery—a relatively new field at the time. He also helped pioneer the heart-lung machine, a tool that made open-heart surgery possible.[3]

After he retired from active surgery in 1975, Dr. Lam remained at the hospital as a consultant. In this phase of his career, he established the hospital's archives—later renamed in his honor. In 1980, he was named as one of the 10 pioneers of cardiac surgery.

At about the same time as the penicillin trials, the hospital established a Preventive Medicine Division under Dr. Louis Steiner. In addition to conducting physicals for Ford Motor executives, the division immunized businessmen who traveled overseas, including those going to Ford's rubber plantations in Brazil. This led to development of one of the country's first travel clinics, as Henry Ford Hospital became one of the first civilian facilities to administer a new yellow fever vaccine.[20]

Dr. McClure saw the long-lasting effects of his work on the Council and, in a newspaper interview, predicted a healthier post-war world because of the medical advances made by the coordinated efforts of the Council and the US Army and Navy Medical Corps.[21]

Medical Breakthroughs

Dr. McClure had a right to be optimistic about the future. Research continued aggressively during the war. Even physicians serving in the military continued to refine and explore. In the immediate post-war years, Henry Ford Hospital achieved a number of innovations.

Drs. McClure and Lam refined research into the use of tannic acid to treat burns. Noticing a pattern of liver necrosis in burn patients led to new methods of treatment.[22]

Dr. C. Paul Hodgkinson, a Ford physician who was stationed in Denver during the war, developed a technique for detecting breast cancer while overseeing care for women and children on the base as well as nurses stationed there. Dr. Hodgkinson's "scarf technique" placed a thin fabric between the doctor's hand and the woman's breast, making for a more accurate breast exam.[23] Once back at Ford Hospital, Dr. Hodgkinson, who later served as chief of the Department of Gynecology and Obstetrics for 24 years, continued to focus much of his research on early breast cancer detection.[24]

Opposite: A Henry Ford Hospital polio patient reading to his son in 1946. *(From the Collections of The Henry Ford. ID:THF117554.)*

Iris Dawson, R.N., in nursery, 1947. She participated in the penicillin trials, counting IV drips of the drug protocol for patients. *(From the Conrad R. Lam Collection, Henry Ford Health System. ID=04-047.)*

1943

Henry Ford Hospital participates in US government trials for use of the new antibiotic penicillin for the treatment of infection. Drs. Lam and Quinn supervise the work in both surgery and internal medicine.

1943

Detroit explodes in a race riot over jobs and available housing for all those who have come to work for the defense industry. The riots leave 34 people dead and hundreds wounded.

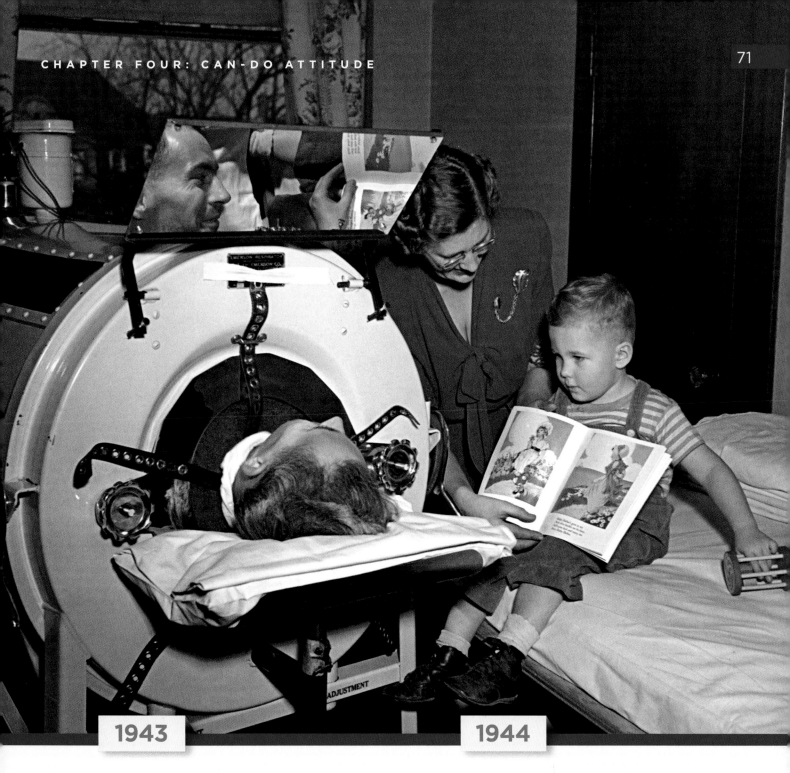

1943

1944

Dr. Louis Steiner establishes the Department of Preventive Medicine to provide physicals and vaccinations for executives traveling overseas for the war effort. This also becomes one of the first travel clinics in the US.

Since many male doctors are serving in the war, women medical interns are accepted for the first time in hospital history. Among the first at Ford Hospital are Drs. Magda E. Puppendahl, Department of Surgery; Louisa J. Piccone, Department of Obstetrics and Gynecology; Dr. Dorothy Finley, Department of Internal Medicine; and Drs. Edna I. Gordon and A. K. MacMillan, both of the Department of Neuropsychiatry.

Left: Dr. Frank Hartman, head of the Department of Pathology, c. 1945. *(From the Conrad R. Lam Collection, Henry Ford Health System. ID=04-040.)*

Right: A Henry Ford Hospital nurse using the liquid oxygen tent designed by Dr. Frank Hartman in 1948. *(From the Collections of The Henry Ford. ID:THF117533.)*

 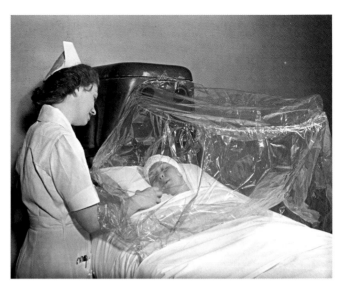

Inside the hospital's walls, Dr. Robert Ziegler became the first doctor to apply 12 leads in an electrocardiogram instead of the typical four. That was in 1944—years before the practice became routine. The next year, Dr. Ziegler developed a cardiology training program—one of the first in the United States—and began a program to study cardiac catherization.

Dr. Ziegler was far from alone in advancing cardiology. Around the world, tremendous developments in understanding the heart and its functions were occurred. Dr. Lam and Dr. Edward Munnell redeveloped a six-finger technique for mitral valve surgery, attaching a knife to a "sixth finger" in the middle of the palm.[25]

There were other advances to surgery during this time period. Dr. McClure, Dr. Frank Hartman, and physiologist Dr. Vivian G. Behrmann experimented with a photoelectric cell attached to a patient's ear during surgery. The cell would react to the color of the blood in

The Growth of Cardiovascular Services

During the 1940s, the medical field was rapidly gaining in its understanding of the heart and how it functioned—and Henry Ford Hospital was on the frontlines. In 1944, Dr. Robert F. Ziegler developed the now-common practice of multiple-lead electro-cardiograms, which the hospital was the first to put into place.[1]

Dr. Ziegler also established the cardiology residency training program in 1945, one of the first in the country, and in 1947 founded the Pediatric Cardiology Department. Meanwhile, Dr. Conrad Lam

was moving into the specialty from general surgery, and Dr. F. Mason Sones was a resident there. Dr. Sones would later be recognized as a pioneer in cardiac cinematography and leader of the Cleveland Clinic.[2]

By the 1950s, the hospital had begun conducting open-heart surgeries, and it was recognized internationally in 1955. In March of that year, the hospital hosted the Cardiovascular Surgery Symposium, where attendees heard renowned Dr. Denton Cooley lecture on treatment of aortic aneurysms.[3]

the ear, giving surgeons insight into the level of oxygen in the blood. By 1949, they, along with American inventor Charles Kettering, had introduced the oxyhemograph.[26]

"The possible applications of this instrument to physiology and clinical medicine are obviously numerous, but we have used it to date principally in the experimental and clinical study of anesthesia, congenital malformations of the heart, and cardiorespiratory insufficiencies," the physicians wrote in the *American Journal of Surgery* in 1949.[27]

Dr. Hartman is also credited with developing the liquid oxygen tent, which was patented in 1942. His patent filing included photos in which the tent was erected over a bed, "forming an air-tight enclose in which a patient may be placed. The apparatus conditions the air in the tent by removing the noxious gases of respiration given out by the patient, cooling the air and supplying oxygen to the air."[28]

The discoveries extended beyond medical devices to include new diseases. Dr. John Ormond, chief of urology, noticed similarities between two patients at the hospital. Both were men in the same age range and presented with back pain that could not be defined. Dr. Ormond identified retroperitoneal fibrosis, an inflammatory disorder in which abnormal tissue growth spreads from the cavity of the abdomen to the tubes that carry urine from the kidney to the bladder. This disorder has since come to be known as Ormond's Disease.[29] Dr. Ormond had joined the hospital as a surgical intern, founded the Department of Urology, and served as its chief until his retirement in 1952. Forever linked with the disorder, Dr. Ormond continued to write on the topic well into retirement.[30]

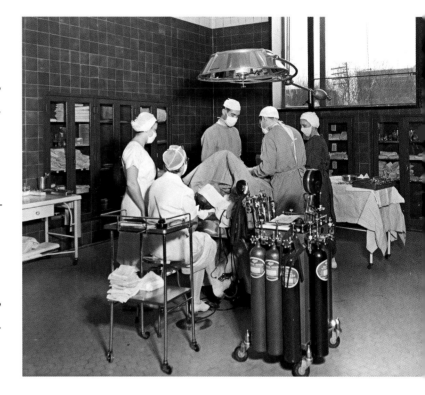

The surgical pavilion operating room, c. 1940.
(From the Collections of The Henry Ford. ID:THF117758.)

1944

1944

1945

Dr. Robert Ziegler begins the routine use of multiple chest electrocardiograms. Henry Ford Hospital is the first to do so.

The Henry Ford Hospital School of Nursing and Hygiene and Wayne State University begin an affiliation. Students expand their curriculum to include anatomy, physiology, microbiology, and chemistry.

Drs. Lam, Szilagyi, and Puppendahl research the use of tantalum gauze in the treatment of ventral hernias. Their research is published in the *Archives of Surgery* in 1948.

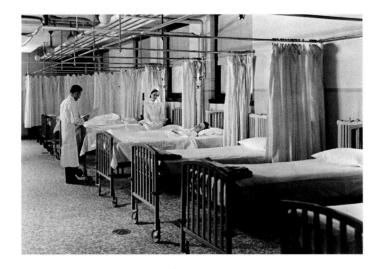

The Henry Ford Hospital recovery room, 1945.
(From the Collections of The Henry Ford. ID:THF117677.)

The hospital's dedication to research and advancing medical understanding had been a founding mission, and war would not abate that commitment. By the end of the 1940s, Henry Ford Hospital staff had published more than 1,000 medical articles in leading medical journals.[31]

With a focus on the innovative medical research occurring at the time, it could have been easy to lose sight of the main goal: improving outcomes for patients. That, however, was not the case. Dorothy (Dottie) Deremo was born at the hospital in 1946 with "immature lungs." Hospitalized numerous times during her first few years of life, Deremo says her earliest memory was "being in a yellow crib in the hospital, looking through the bars of the crib with an oxygen tent over me, and crying because my mother had to leave. Really, Henry Ford Hospital saved my life because that was just after the end of World War II, and penicillin had been discovered, and oxygen tents were used in the war, and those two things saved my life."[32]

Deremo would spend a lot more time at Henry Ford Hospital, joining the hospital's School of Nursing and Hygiene in 1966 and eventually rising to the position of chief nursing officer.

Growing Again

With the war's end, many of those drawn to Detroit for work stayed, while those who had gone overseas returned. In the 1950 census, Detroit ranked as the country's fifth most-populous city, with 1.84 million residents.[33]

1945

Henry Ford II becomes a member of the hospital's Board of Trustees.

From the Collections of The Henry Ford. ID:THF117769.

1945

Dr. Joseph P. Szokolay (pictured) in the employee health department, 1945.

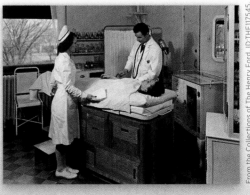

From the Collections of The Henry Ford. ID:THF117545.

The hospital's staff grew to 180 physicians, 70 residents, and 30 interns.[34] At the same time, enrollment at the hospital's School of Nursing and Hygiene topped 300. The growth put a squeeze on the facilities, with physicians sharing office space while private patient rooms became double occupancy.

Left: The Henry Ford Hospital Dental Laboratory, 1945. *(From the Collections of The Henry Ford. ID:THF117761.)*

Below: Dr. Magda Puppendahl, one of the first female doctors to enter Henry Ford Hospital, 1944. *(Detail From the Collections of The Henry Ford. ID:THF117529.)*

Specialties began emerging throughout medicine. Ford Hospital's Department of Medicine added divisions of Allergy, Pulmonary, Pediatric Cardiology, Rheumatology, and Infectious Diseases. New surgery specialties included Oral and Thoracic surgery.[35]

Dr. Joseph Ponka joined Henry Ford Hospital as an intern in 1942, launching a 50-year career that would be noted for excellence in teaching surgical techniques.[36] Dr. Sladen had convinced Dr. Richmond Smith Jr. to come as an intern in 1942. After military service and specialized studies, Dr. Smith returned to the hospital in 1949 in the Division of Metabolism, and in 1953, founded the Division of Endocrinology.[37]

The war years also opened up medical school positions for women, many of whom joined Henry Ford Hospital immediately after the war began. Dr. Magda E. Puppendahl had begun her career with a nursing degree before attending medical school at the University of Michigan.[38] After joining the hospital, she was a frequent research partner of Dr. Lam, co-authoring studies on burn treatments.[39] Dr. Dorothy Finley was also one of the hospital's first female surgeons.[40]

Dr. Louisa Piccone had first joined Henry Ford Hospital as a technologist in 1938. During the war, she pursued her medical degree at Wayne State University and returned to the hospital as an Obstetrics and Gynecology resident in 1948.[41] Dr. Edna Gordon and Dr. Edith Adams were among the first women in neuropsychiatry in 1946.[42] That same year, Dr. Elvina Anger became the hospital's first female senior medical intern.[43]

1945

As WWII ends, the large number of returning veterans requiring artificial limbs prompts the hospital to establish a Physical Medicine Division. Patients from around Michigan come for new limbs, physical therapy, and care of prosthetics.

1946

The Henry Ford Hospital orthopedic brace shop in 1946.

From the Collections of The Henry Ford. ID:THF117755.

Medical leaders Drs. McClure and Sladen—now past the age of 65—began to plan for the future of the hospital. The two presented a proposal to the Board of Trustees in 1946 to add two stories to the hospital—a possibility that had been accommodated when the foundation of the hospital was built decades earlier. The new floors would increase the hospital capacity to 800. A new clinical building—planned at 18 to 20 stories—would house outpatient clinics, physician offices, laboratories, and operating rooms.[44]

Drs. McClure and Sladen also proposed the hospital create a medical advisory board. The Board of Trustees took immediate action on that portion of the proposal and appointed Drs. McClure and Sladen, urologist Dr. Ormond, pathologist Dr. Hartman, cardiologist Dr. F. Janney Smith, gastroenterologist Dr. John Mateer, and obstetrician Dr. Jean Paul Pratt.[45]

Eleanor Clay Ford and Edsel Bryant Ford in 1943. (From the Collections of The Henry Ford. ID:THF117704.)

A Family in Transition

The decade between 1941 and 1951 marked a change between Henry Ford Hospital and the Ford family. In 1943, Edsel Ford died of stomach cancer. He had served on the hospital's Board of Trustees since it was founded in 1915, and, as Henry and Clara's only child, his loss was palpable. While the Fords grieved, the family also had practical matters to consider. Edsel had run the Ford Motor Company since 1919.

With Henry now 80, his return to daily oversight was impractical for the long term, and Edsel's two older sons were off at war. With no one left to run the company, Henry Ford II was released from military duty to return to Detroit and take the reins. Given Ford Motor's role in producing military equipment, ensuring a smooth operation was vital to the military effort.

1946

Dr. James T. Barron begins what would be a 25-year study of food pumps and other medical devices. The Barron Food Pump (pictured) helps reduce deaths in cases of ulcerative colitis. The American Medical Association and the International College of Surgeons document its impact.

From the Conrad R. Lam Collection, Henry Ford Health System. ID=05-043.

1946

The Edsel B. Ford Institute for Medical Research is established. Dr. Oliver H. Gaebler (pictured) becomes the head of the Department of Biochemistry, and Dr. John H. L. Watson is named head of the Physics Department.

From the Conrad R. Lam Collection, Henry Ford Health System. ID=03-031.

Henry II immediately began the process of transforming the Ford Motor Company by bringing in a new generation of leadership.[46] At the same time, the Ford family recommitted its ties to the hospital.

In 1945, Henry II joined the hospital's Board of Trustees, followed the next year by his brother Benson. Eleanor Clay Ford, Edsel's widow, remained on the board, joined by Anne McDonnell Ford, Henry II's wife, and Edith McNaughton Ford, Benson's wife.[47] Edsel and Eleanor Ford's two other children, Josephine and William Clay, would later become involved in the hospital as key benefactors. Josephine—known as Dody—would also later serve on the board.

From left, seated: Clara Bryant Ford holding Charlotte Ford, Henry Ford. Standing: Henry Ford II, Eleanor Clay Ford, unidentified girl, Anne McDonnell Ford, Josephine Clay Ford, and Edsel Ford, 1943. *(From the Collections of The Henry Ford. ID:THF117710.)*

While Edsel's death had put in place the next generation of Ford family leadership, the board would undergo transition again with Henry's death in 1947. His wife Clara was by his side when Dr. Mateer was summoned. Before the doctor arrived, Henry Ford—one of the greatest industrialists of the 20th century—died from a cerebral hemorrhage.[48] Little more than two weeks later, Benson Ford replaced his grandfather as president of the hospital's Board of Trustees.[49]

Within a week, Benson Ford and the board undertook steps to implement another aspect of Drs. McClure and Sladen's expansion proposal: establishing a separate research institute, the Edsel B. Ford Institute for Medical Research. The name, Dr. Sladen believed, was fitting:

No one knew the hospital and the staff better than he did or was more encouraging and inspiring to those eager to put the work of the institution on the highest levels of research, education, and medical care. The name itself gave assurance to the forward-looking staff of

1946

Benson Ford is elected to the Board of Trustees. He becomes the president in 1947 and serves the hospital board for 32 years.

1947

Polio afflicts thousands of Detroiters. Henry Ford Hospital installs negative pressure machines, or "iron lungs," that help polio patients breathe.

those days that the institute would grow in its way as differing from the activities of the clinical departments of the hospital proper, and, in due time, become indispensable as a basic source of new truths and inspiration to the hospital proper.[50]

Dr. Oliver Gaebler was named head of the Department of Chemistry while Dr. John H. L. Watson oversaw the Department of Physics. The institute was aggressive in its research, publishing 165 papers and 269 research projects in its first decade.[51]

The hospital would lose its last member of its Ford founders in 1950, when Clara died. Unlike her husband and son, who both died at their homes, Clara Ford died at the hospital to which she and her husband had devoted so much time and resources.

Benson Ford (left), Edith McNaughton Ford, and Dr. Roy D. McClure in 1947. *(From the Collections of The Henry Ford. ID:THF117560.)*

More Changes on the Horizon

The decade had seen great accomplishments in medical research and recruitment of key physicians. It also had seen the deaths of the Ford founders. And while the hospital's leaders continued to seek funding for expansion plans, they would also lose yet another vital connection to its earliest days.

In March 1951, Dr. McClure died in his sleep after a full day's work. Dr. McClure had served the hospital as its surgeon-in-chief since its founding. In the *Surgery* journal, Dr. McClure

1947

The 460-acre Clarkston estate of Colonel and Mrs. Sidney Waldon in Pine Knob becomes the hospital's first suburban purchase. Orthopedic, pediatric, psychiatric, and postoperative patients take advantage of the English-style manor and its beautiful surroundings (pictured, 1956).

From the Conrad R. Lam Collection, Henry Ford Health System. ID=04-044.

1948

Dr. Arthur B. McGraw and other members of the Division of General Surgery revamp their methods of handling acute appendicitis, resulting in zero mortality during a six-year span.

was remembered as "not only deeply interested in each individual patient, but he was world-conscious and gave of himself unstintingly that the field of medicine and surgery may be expanded to be of greater service to more people."[52]

With Dr. McClure's passing, only Dr. Sladen remained from the core leaders who had envisioned the hospital and seen it rise to prominence. A new leadership team would be tasked with pushing Henry Ford Hospital to even greater heights. But unlike its earliest days—when Ford recruited bright young physicians with potential—Henry Ford Hospital had earned enough cachet to recruit some doctors at the heights of their careers.

Clara Bryant Ford (far left in hat), Dr. Frank Hartman, unidentified nurse, Henry Ford, Dr. Roy D. McClure, and Elizabeth Moran, R.N., at the Henry Ford Hospital School of Nursing and Hygiene graduation in 1945. *(Detail From the Collections of The Henry Ford. ID:THF117730.)*

1948

Dr. John K. Ormond discovers retroperitoneal fibrosis, which becomes known as "Ormond's Disease." He describes two patients with diffuse fibrosis of the retroperitoneal tissues to establish the disease.

1949

Dr. Annetta R. Kelly, noted for her work in pharmacology, joins the hospital's Pathology staff. She is shown here in the laboratory with a 1952 Beckman D.U. spectrophotometer in 1986.

From the Conrad R. Lam Collection, Henry Ford Health System. ID=04-046.

Five

" *I regard it as an accidental stroke of good fortune that the beginning of my career as a surgeon coincided with the birth of a new branch of the surgical art: the surgery of the arterial system. Thus I had the rare opportunity of making and publishing observations that were original and useful, not because of their brilliance but because of the newness. The contribution for which I may perhaps take personal credit was a firm determination to describe my observations objectively and draw my conclusions honestly.*"

Dr. D. Emerick Szilagyi
VASCULAR SURGERY PIONEER[1]

INTERNATIONAL ACCLAIM

1952
1966

BY THE MIDDLE OF THE 20TH CENTURY, THE RECOGNITION OF SPECIALTIES ALLOWED physicians to become experts in various body systems. And with Henry Ford Hospital's commitment to research, physicians could explore the unknown, pushing into new techniques and developments.

Medicine in the 1950s was in step with what was occurring in the world. The Eisenhower Interstate System was created, which laid a path to the suburbs—a move that would become important to Detroit and to the hospital in the coming decades. The space race between Russia and the US produced a multitude of technological inventions. Television and computers were in their infancies. These were the first few steps in what would become a transformative marathon.

Meanwhile, at Henry Ford Hospital, a new lineup of leaders was ready to step into place in the effort to push the hospital to even greater heights.

Back of Henry Ford Hospital, preparing for construction of the Clinic building, January 1951. *(Detail From the Conrad R. Lam Collection, Henry Ford Health System. ID=05-045.)*

New Hands at the Helm

Since Henry Ford started the hospital in 1915, medical and business operations were largely separate and often competitive. The first administrator, Ernest Liebold, had come straight from Ford Motor's financial operations, though that did not prevent him from offering advice on the medical business. Drs. Roy McClure and Frank Sladen had long run the medical operations, though they often had an impact on financial decisions, especially when it came to expansions and funding medical growth. Hospital administrator Israel Peters had been involved in decisions, too, as a "lay" superintendent. Still, with Dr. McClure's death and Dr. Sladen's impending retirement, the hospital sought a professional hospital administrator. It found one who understood the careful balance of fiscal and medical needs.

Dr. Robin C. Buerki, who joined Henry Ford Hospital in 1951,[2] was considered one of the preeminent hospital administrators at the time. Dr. Buerki's resume included 19 years as the

Dr. Robin C. Buerki, c. 1955.
(From the Conrad R. Lam Collection, Henry Ford Health System. ID=05-003.)

head of Wisconsin General Hospital and Bradley Children's Hospital,[3] where he also served as Dean of the Medical School. He founded the American College of Healthcare Executives (ACHE)[4] in 1933.[5] In 1936, he served as president of the American Hospital Association[6] and followed that in 1938 as president of ACHE.[7] He was also one of the founders of the American Board of Medical Specialties and served as its president in 1947.[8]

Benson Ford traveled to Philadelphia, where Dr. Buerki was dean of the University of Pennsylvania Graduate School of Medicine, to offer him the job.[9] Dr. Buerki certainly had the administrative

1950

The Henry Ford Hospital School of Nursing and Hygiene celebrates 25 years of nurse training. The event draws the Ford family, Drs. Sladen and McClure, and Elizabeth Moran.

1950

The Henry Ford Hospital Alumni Association meets for the first time to help celebrate the hospital's 35th anniversary.

1950

The Korean War breaks out. Many house officers and staff leave for war, and several hospital staff members help set up base hospitals overseas.

credentials. But unlike most of his predecessors, he previously worked as a physician, receiving his certification from the American Board of Preventative Medicine.[10] Dr. Conrad Lam recalled his first introduction to Dr. Buerki—and to a new style of leadership at the hospital:

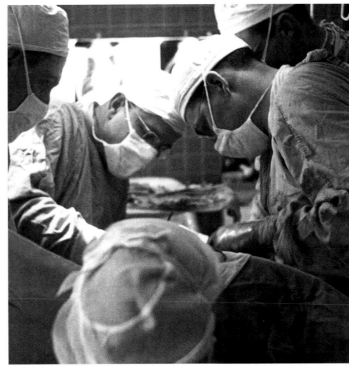

> When I returned to my office on A-4 after a month-long European trip, I heard a loud noise in what had been the office of Dr. Roy McClure, surgeon-in-chief. The secretary I shared with Larry Fallis, M.D., explained that the loud, commanding voice was coming from our new executive director, Dr. Robin Buerki, whose office was two doors away.
>
> I wondered how long it would be before I met Dr. Buerki. I did not have to wait long. That same day, a tall figure appeared at my door and said, "Hello. I'm Bob Buerki from down the hall. I heard you were back from Europe. How were things over there?" That was the beginning of a pleasant personal relationship.[11]

Dr. Conrad R. Lam in surgery, c. 1960. *(From the Conrad R. Lam Collection, Henry Ford Health System. ID=05-023.)*

Dr. Laurence Fallis, who joined the hospital in its early years as an intern and served Dr. McClure as second-in-command for many years, became surgeon-in-chief in 1952. Dr. John G. Mateer succeeded Dr. Sladen as physician-in-chief that same year,[12] while Dr. Sladen moved into a consulting role. Like Dr. Fallis, Dr. Mateer's resume at Henry Ford Hospital was lengthy, as he served as chief of the Division of Gastroenterology since 1920.[13]

1950

1950

Dr. Clarence Rupe (pictured) investigates the use of dialysis in the hypertension clinic.

In the hospital's 35th year, more than 600,000 people are registered as Henry Ford Hospital patients.

Dr. Jack Guyton of the Department of Ophthalmology, c. 1960. *(From the Conrad R. Lam Collection, Henry Ford Health System. ID=05-010.)*

Dr. Buerki also instituted an advisory group, which included Drs. Frank Hartman, Howard Doub, and Jean Paul Pratt, as well as Fallis and Mateer. It was modeled after the medical board formed seven years earlier to discuss issues related to the hospital's administration.

In the span of a few short years, Henry Ford Hospital had seen the transition of all its key leaders and several trustees. These new leaders would be charged with overseeing a massive expansion of the hospital—a plan their predecessors had put in place. They would also continue raising the hospital's reputation among the wider medical community. It was a far cry from Henry Ford's earliest days, when its closed system was met with skepticism by its peers.

Dr. Buerki in particular recognized the potential of learning from other leaders. In January 1955, he invited representatives from the Ochsner Clinic in New Orleans and the Cleveland Clinic in Ohio to share information and experiences. The group met again a few months later, expanding to include the Mayo Clinic in Rochester, Minnesota, and the Lovelace Clinic in Albuquerque, New Mexico. At the third meeting that year, the Lahey Clinic in Boston joined, and the Six Clinic Conference was born.[14] Since then, representatives from the same six institutions have met regularly to hear from top medical researchers and to learn from each other's experiences.

Dr. Jack Guyton: Mathematics and Medicine

Dr. Jack Guyton had been a "boy wonder" while a resident at Johns Hopkins University, pioneering new approaches in cataract surgery.[1] During World War II, he had been involved in research projects with gas casualties.[2]

By the time he was recruited to Henry Ford as chair of the Department of Ophthalmology in 1954, he could dictate his own terms, asking for—and receiving—a private bathroom in his office, the only one in the new Clinic Building.[3]

Dr. Guyton also had an interest in computers and created the Department of Biological Mathematics and Computer Sciences at the hospital in 1967. He was known to write programs for his own research, for departmental use, and for the computer systems staff.[4] He also served as a consultant for IBM.[5]

In addition, Dr. Guyton was known for an ability to concentrate on a task no matter how much chaos occurred around him[6]—and for his secret stash of Coca-Cola.[7]

Known as an avid recruiter of young medical interns, Dr. Guyton brought on board Cornelius McCole, whom he had mentored at Johns Hopkins[8] and who would later succeed him as department chair.

Medicine certainly ran in the Guyton family blood. His father Billy Guyton was an ophthalmologist/otolaryngologist and Dean of the University of Mississippi School of Medicine. His brother Arthur wrote the landmark *Textbook of Medical Physiology*.[9]

In assessing his impact on the field, Dr. A. Edward Maumenee wrote: "Dr. Guyton's career was very impressive, for it encompassed a rigorous dedication to truth and excellence, major contributions to medicine both at Johns Hopkins and Henry Ford, superb and successful care of his patients, and finally the inspiration of many young physicians."[10]

Expansion Plans

Drs. Buerki, Fallis, and Mateer inherited a construction project that had been years in the making. Drs. McClure and Sladen first proposed an expansion in 1946 as part of a massive restructuring that saw the advent of the Medical Advisory Board and the birth of a research practice that would honor Edsel Ford. However, the construction itself took much longer to begin.

With an initial price tag of $10 million, financing was complex. The Ford Foundation in New York was a logical first step, and, in 1948, the Foundation sent representatives to study the administration and the hospital's fiscal health.[15] It found a hospital that was sound. Given the Ford family's heavy investment through the years—and Henry and Clara Ford's willingness to balance the books at the end of each year—the hospital was operating in the black and had done so since 1940.[16]

In 1950, Benson Ford, along with Drs. Sladen and McClure, announced a multimillion dollar grant from the Ford Foundation to build the Clinic Building. The 17-story structure added new operating rooms, an expanded library, a pharmacy, and facilities for laboratory work and radiology.[17] The latter was badly needed, according to Dr. William Eyler, who was being recruited by Dr. Buerki and Dr. Doub, chief of radiology. "The hospital in general was considered a superior community hospital. The Department of

Dr. Frank Sladen (center) sharing the model of the proposed new Henry Ford Hospital campus with Eleanor Clay Ford; Henry Ford II; Marjorie Schultz, R.N.; Elizabeth S. Moran, R.N.; and Sally Brown, R.N., 1950. *(From the Collections of The Henry Ford. ID:THF117571.)*

1950

Dr. John Rebuck of the Department of Pathology reports the intracellular crystallization sequence of sickle cell hemoglobin for the first time.

1951

Dr. Laurence Fallis is appointed head of the Department of Surgery. He had been head of the Division of General Surgery since 1939 and is known for his work in hernia, colon, and abdominal surgery.

Construction of the Henry Ford Hospital Clinic Building, 1953. *(From the Conrad R. Lam Collection, Henry Ford Health System. ID=05-004.)*

Radiology's facility, however, was in very bad straits," Dr. Eyler said. "Very limited space, very limited equipment. … And why did I take the job under those circumstances? Well, steel was already up for the new building, and radiology was a fine department."[18]

Two years after he arrived, Dr. Eyler was appointed chief of the department. He noted:

I was given considerable freedom to do things the way I learned to do them where I had been trained to do things, which kept the department up at the cutting edge in technology. And we developed a staff over time, most of it inbred. People who trained here, stayed on with us. Overall, I would say that the ability to plan the programs and to determine the policies and practices of the department is what kept me here.[19]

Growing in Expertise

The 1950s were marked by the addition of numerous leaders who would spend many years at Henry Ford Hospital and make significant advances in their fields of study.

Dr. Raymond Mellinger began his association with the hospital in 1948, though his residency was quickly interrupted by military service. When he returned in 1953 in the Division of Endocrinology, Dr. Mellinger began a 36-year career that would be marked by his research into Cushing's syndrome,[20] a disorder caused by exposure to excessive amounts of the hormone cortisol.

1951

Dr. Robin C. Buerki is appointed executive director of Henry Ford Hospital. He helps to establish Henry Ford Hospital's reputation as a clinical, research, and education center through international symposia held at the campus.

1952

From the Conrad R. Lam Collection, Henry Ford Health System. ID=05-031.

Dr. Robert Knighton becomes the chair of Neurological Surgery. He helps establish the hospital's neurosurgery residency training program. He later is named chief of the conjoined neurology and neurosurgery department. Photo: Dr. Knighton, right, with his staff, 1974.

Dr. Robert Knighton came to head the Department of Neurological Surgery in 1952, while Dr. Boy Frame joined the General Internal Medicine staff in 1954, later founding the Bone and Mineral Division. Dr. Frame would become an internationally renowned bone and mineral specialist and be named chairman of the Department of Internal Medicine in 1985.[21] Dr. Harold M. Frost, chief of Orthopedic Surgery, began his research in 1958 and became regarded as one of the foremost experts on skeletal biology. Among the discoveries contained in his 500-plus published scientific papers and 16 books, Dr. Frost was the first to link bone density to hormone levels in women. His development of bone measurements is widely used by researchers to determine the effectiveness of new drugs.[22] Each year, the American Society for Bone and Mineral Research presents its Young Investigator Award, which is named after Dr. Frost.[23]

Henry Ford Hospital's group of bone and mineral disorders and genetics specialists were regarded as the field's research leaders. This group included Drs. Frost, Frame,

From left to right: Dr. William Eyler of the Department of Radiology, 1953. Dr. Raymond Mellinger of the Divison of Endocrinology, 1982. Dr. Harold Frost of the Department of Orthopedics, 1957. Dr. John Caldwell of the Hypertension Clinic, c. 1955. *(From the Conrad R. Lam Collection, Henry Ford Health System. ID=05-005, 05-006, 05-007, 05-041.)*

1953

1953

Henry Ford Hospital holds its first international symposium, "The Dynamics of Virus and Rickettsial Infections." Drs. Jonas Salk and Alfred B. Sabin are key speakers.

From the Conrad R. Lam Collection, Henry Ford Health System. ID=05-047.

The employee newsletter "Thermonitor" begins publication.

Left to right: Dr. George Mikhail, Dermatology, 1980. Dr. Melvin Block, Surgery, c. 1969.

Gene Jackson, A. Michael Parfitt, Henry Bone, Michael Kleerekoper, and Sudhaker D. Rao, along with nurse Evelyn R. Phillips.

Dr. John Caldwell joined the hospital in 1952, passionate in his fight against hypertension. He became physician-in-chief of the Section of Hypertension in 1955 and later started the first hypertension clinic with Nephrology.[24]

Dr. Clarence Livingood, dermatologist, was recruited in 1953 by Dr. Buerki, with an assist from Eleanor Clay Ford, who persuaded him to come to Detroit.[25] Dr. Livingood later recruited Dr. George Mikhail, a dermatologist who began the Mohs Surgery Clinic at the hospital in 1967—one of the few facilities at the time to offer the Mohs technique for removing skin cancer.[26]

Dr. Fred Whitehouse, who became interested in diabetes at the age of 12 when his 8-year-old brother was diagnosed with the disease, completed his residency at Ford Hospital

Dr. Clarence S. Livingood: Father of Dermatology

Although Dr. Frank Menagh had founded the Division of Dermatology in the hospital's earliest days, by his retirement it had grown into its own department. Dr. Clarence S. Livingood was recruited as its chair.

Dr. Livingood, who was already highly regarded in the dermatology field, established the department in 1953. During his military service as part of the Army Medical Corps, he co-wrote *The Manual of Dermatology*, which is still used today. "Diseases affecting the skin are of major importance to an army operating in the field because of the high morbidity and ineffectiveness that they can produce," he and co-author Donald M. Pillsbury wrote.[1]

In addition to his work at the hospital, Dr. Livingood was widely recognized as a pioneer in the field. He served as executive director of the American Board of Dermatology for more than 30 years and was a delegate to the Academy of the American Medical Association (AMA) from 1963 to 1988. He earned the AMA's

Distinguished Service Award in 1990.[2] The American Academy of Dermatology includes an annual lecture in his honor at its annual meeting.

Dr. Livingood spurred the development of sports medicine and served as team physician for the Detroit Tigers—and earned the World Series rings to prove it.[3] He worked with the Tigers for 30 years and hand-picked Dr. Michael Workings of Family Medicine to take his place.

"Dr. Livingood brought into sports the whole focus on taking care of not just the players but the whole corporation and the families of those players," said Dr. Workings.

In 1987, he and former Tigers manager Sparky Anderson founded Caring Athletes Team for Children's & Henry Ford Hospitals (CATCH), a charity to raise funds for pediatric patients.[4]

After Dr. Livingood's death in 1998, Rep. Carolyn Cheeks Kilpatrick (D-Michigan) paid tribute to his service on the floor of the United States Capitol.[5]

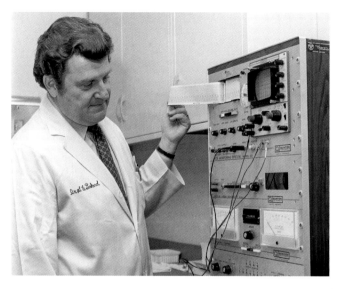

Left to right: Dr. Edward Krull, Dermatology, c. 1960. Dr. Sol Pickard, Cardiology, 1976. *(From the Conrad R. Lam Collection, Henry Ford Health System. ID=05-014, 05-017.)*

and trained in Boston with Dr. Elliott Joslin, "the father of diabetes care," before joining Henry Ford Hospital's staff in 1955. He became chief of the division of Metabolism in 1962 and subsequently Endocrinology and Metabolism until 1995. He would be one of the longtime physician-researchers at Ford Hospital, not retiring from clinical practice until 2014.[27]

For Dr. Melvin Block, a surgeon who joined the hospital in 1954 and later became the chair of the Department of Surgery, the choice to join Henry Ford Hospital was simple. "I wanted to be in a group practice involving all specialties, with a structured training program, a large volume of patients, and complete diversity of medical problems, from minor to major. At this institution, with the process of rapid growth encompassing a hospital and laboratories, library, research facilities … there was a great future."[28]

Looking back, Dr. Block discovered that the stimulating environment bred "strong bonds and clinical research and education and personal relationships, which extend to this

1953

Dr. Paul Dumke becomes the founding chair of the Department of Anesthesiology. He establishes the anesthesiology residency program at the hospital and is later deemed one of the most distinguished clinicians in the specialty.

1953

Dr. William Eyler joins the staff and two years later becomes chief of Radiology, succeeding Dr. Howard Doub. He becomes renowned in the specialty of Radiology, revered for his expertise in roentgen studies and analysis. Another longtime physician-researcher at Henry Ford, Dr. Eyler, remains part of the department in 2014.

1954

An expert on TB and lung diseases, Dr. E. Osborne (Os) Coates Jr. (pictured, right) joins the hospital to establish the Pulmonary division. He serves as chief until 1977, followed by Dr. Paul Kvale (pictured, left) who led the division until 1989.

From the Conrad R. Lam Collection, Henry Ford Health System. ID=05-051. Credit: Richard Hirneisen.

Above: Construction of two floors to Henry Ford Hospital, 1957. *(From the Conrad R. Lam Collection, Henry Ford Health System. ID=05-018.)*

Opposite: The first televised surgery at Henry Ford Hospital of the first graft of an abdominal aortic aneurysm, 1958. *(From the Conrad R. Lam Collection, Henry Ford Health System. ID=05-020.)*

day, probably, for those of us who are still alive. And this included all medical specialties. They were all represented at Henry Ford Hospital."[29]

The trailblazers of the 1950s were quickly followed by new leaders in the 1960s, including Dr. Edward Krull, who spearheaded the development of surgical therapies in dermatology. He was named chief of the department in 1976.[30] Other trailblazers included Dr. Sol Pickard, cardiovascular medicine; Dr. Howard Duncan, rheumatologist; and Dr. Paul Kvale, pulmonologist, who became head of the division of Pulmonary Medicine from 1977 to 1989 and conducted research into lung cancer.[31]

Building Again

Despite the massive investment in the Clinic Building, the hospital was bursting at the seams. Another expansion in March 1957 added two stories to the hospital. With an increase of 250 beds, patients enjoyed new rooms and modern maternity and newborn sections. The hospital's growth demanded additional parking spaces, too. In 1959, it added a new parking garage with room for 850 cars.[32] That addition sufficed for a few years, until construction began on an additional parking structure, which added 900 new spaces. That facility opened in 1968 and housed the hospital's main kitchen in the basement.

The changes to the physical structure of the hospital served to enhance the practice of innovative medicine that took place within its walls, as groundbreaking procedures began to occur with some frequency. Dr. D. Emerick Szilagyi was at the heart of three of them: one of the world's first grafts of an abdominal aortic aneurysm in 1952; establishment of a blood vessel bank in 1954; and one of the first televised surgeries in 1958.

1954

New arrivals to Henry Ford Hospital include Dr. Joseph P. Elliott, a surgical intern; and Dr. Jack Guyton, new head of Ophthalmology.

1954

Henry Ford Hospital hosts an international symposium on growth hormones, chaired by Dr. Richmond Smith.

1954

Dr. D. Emerick Szilagyi establishes the first homograft blood vessel bank in Michigan.

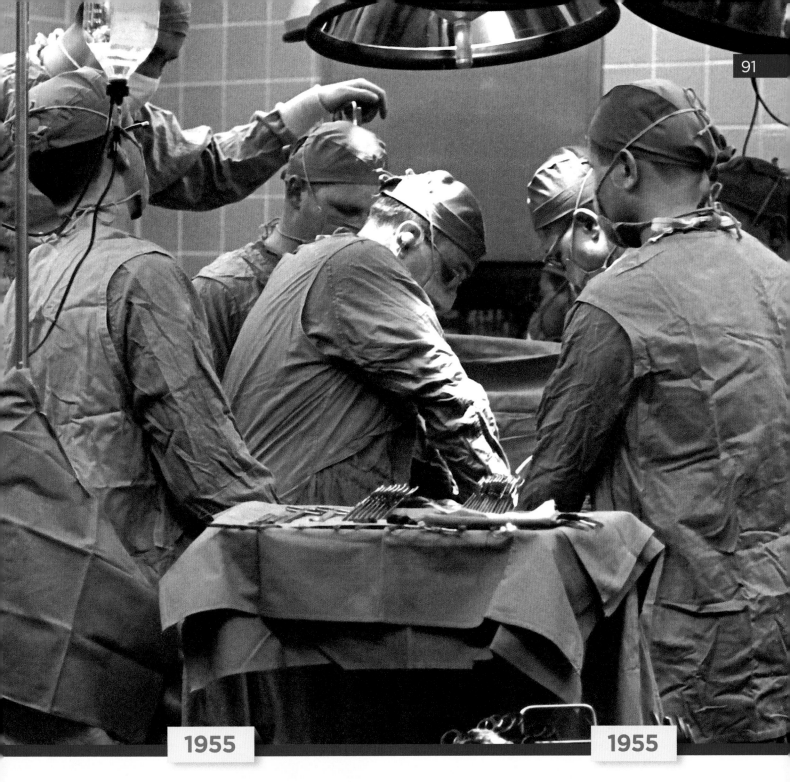

1955

1955

The Clinic Building opened with 131,000 square feet of new space, 14 specialty outpatient clinics, a 35,000-volume medical library, and 20 new operating rooms with special tile walls and television cameras to film procedures.

Dr. Joseph Beninson joins the Department of Dermatology. He studies pressure gradient dressings for the management of venous ulcers.

Dr. D. Emerick Szilagyi (seated, middle) and the Vascular Surgery staff, Drs. Joseph P. Elliott (seated, left) and Roger Smith (seated, right), Drs. W. Sherren, (standing, left) A. Gonzalez, S. Saksema, and J. Hageman, 1968. *(From the Conrad R. Lam Collection, Henry Ford Health System. ID=05-002.)*

Dr. D. Emerick Szilagyi: Vascular Surgery Pioneer

D. Emerick Szilagyi began his 50-year surgical career at Henry Ford Hospital in 1939. After his third year of residency, he was assigned by Dr. Roy McClure as the sole physician of Ford Motor Company's rubber plantation in Brazil, where he was called on to perform a wide variety of operations with only rudimentary support and his own talents. This experience proved formative for his future groundbreaking career; he returned to Detroit in 1945 as perhaps the best-prepared chief resident in the history of the institution.

As a staff surgeon and later chair of the Department of Surgery, Dr. Szilagyi developed an interest in vascular diseases and helped create the new specialty of vascular surgery. He was a daring surgical innovator and a superb clinical investigator. Among his many accomplishments:

- Performing the second-ever abdominal aortic aneurysm repair
- Developing the standard medical approach to the popliteal artery
- Initiating one of the first vascular training programs in the country
- Creating the world's largest vascular registry to study the natural history of vascular disorders and their treatment.

Many of the 250 research papers he wrote from this registry were seminal contributions to the literature and are still widely quoted today more than 50 years after their publication.

Dr. Szilagyi became an international leader in surgery and was recognized as one of Henry Ford Hospital's most famous physician ambassadors. He was a strong believer in the Henry Ford group practice model and an early champion of the satellite system, which he promoted wherever he went.

Even after retirement from clinical practice in 1984, he remained active as a founding editor of the *Journal of Vascular Surgery*, which has grown to become the preeminent journal for vascular surgery.

Primetime Pioneers

WWJ-TV had long been a pioneer in Detroit television. It was the first station to air a newscast and the first to televise the Tigers, Red Wings, Lions, and college football.[33] And when Dr. Szilagyi and Dr. Roger Smith performed surgery, removing a section of the aorta and replacing it with an artificial graft, the television station provided live commentary. Dr. Henry Bahnson of Johns Hopkins Hospital, Dr. Marion S. DeWeese of the University of Michigan, and Dr. Eugene Osius of Harper Hospital helped viewers understand what they were seeing.[34]

During the 1950s, Dr. Lam performed open heart surgery using total heart-lung bypass. Following the surgery, Dr. Lam saw cardiology patient referrals all the way from South America.[35]

"In every field I can think of, there was at least one person who was a world authority or close to it," radiologist Dr. Eyler said. "And that was a form of excellence which I appreciated. I felt I was practicing with experts."[36]

Dr. Eyler also appreciated Dr. Buerki's style, which provided a quick answer when requesting some sort of capital outlay. "You prepared yourself to meet with him," Dr. Eyler said. "You presented your case and you got an immediate decision. And usually going in well-prepared, the answer was, 'Yes, go ahead.'"[37]

But with 40 years as a hospital administrator behind him, Dr. Buerki was ready for retirement. In 1964, the hospital's Board of Trustees took his recommendation of Dr. James (Ted) Howell as his successor. Dr. Howell joined the hospital in 1944 as an intern and had worked as

Dr. Richmond Smith, seated at the head of the table with house officers, 1968. *(From the Conrad R. Lam Collection, Henry Ford Health System. ID=05-021.)*

Dr. John Rebuck develops the "human-skin window" procedure, a test to monitor a patient's ability to fight infection. The doctor would examine white blood cells in a man-made window in the skin of the forearm. Students could then study the inflammatory process and better understand the immune system's role in such diseases as ulcerative colitis, diabetes mellitus, allergies, and organ transplant rejection.

Henry Ford Hospital holds a symposium, "Cardiovascular: Surgery Studies in Physiology, Diagnosis and Techniques." The proceedings are edited by Dr. Conrad R. Lam and published by the W. B. Saunders Company.

From the Conrad R. Lam Collection, Henry Ford Health System. ID=07-026.

Dr. Buerki's administrative assistant since 1955. Dr. Howell became the hospital's fifth administrator in its 50-year history.[38] He would have new medical leaders at his side in 1966, when Dr. Szilagyi would be named surgeon-in-chief and Dr. Richmond Smith Jr. physician-in-chief.

A New World

Medicine and Henry Ford Hospital leadership were not the only things changing. How the cost of services was covered also underwent a revolution. Medical insurance was growing, and more were using it to pay for their health needs. Community Health Association (CHA),

Dr. Richmond Smith: Endocrinology Leader

As with many of Henry Ford Hospital's leaders, Dr. Richmond Smith (pictured, 1979) spent the vast majority of his career in one location. While at Henry Ford Hospital, Dr. Smith served in a variety of capacities.

In 1942, he arrived at the hospital as an intern. By 1953, he was charged with founding the Division of Endocrinology and served as its first chief.[1] During Dr. Smith's tenure there, the division grew to include thyroid specialist Dr. Martin Miller and Dr. Raymond Mellinger, an Endocrinology Fellow who later became an expert in Cushing's syndrome. Dr. Mellinger succeeded Dr. Smith as division chief in 1966, when Dr. Smith moved to the role of chair of the Department of Internal Medicine.[2]

Dr. Smith played an instrumental role in obtaining the $100 million grant from the Ford Foundation. He retired in 1979 and moved to Maine to explore carpentry. Unable to leave medicine altogether, Dr. Smith served as a consultant to two local hospitals there.

"Richmond Smith as Chairman of Medicine was a scholar and a gentleman, and I appreciated his support on a number of occasions," said Dr. William Eyler, chair of the Department of Radiology. "He was devoted to the proper care of patients and to some modest scientific efforts being conducted at the same time. Just, in my view, a very ideal person for the position."[3]

1955

From the Conrad R. Lam Collection, Henry Ford Health System. ID=05-049.

Dr. Robert C. Horn Jr., becomes chair of Pathology, succeeding Dr. Hartman, who retires after 33 years of service.

1955

The first meeting of the Six Clinic Conference occurs at Henry Ford Hospital to discuss medical issues in closed practice hospitals. Ford Hospital, Ochsner Medical Center, Lahey Hospital and Medical Center, Lovelace Health System, Cleveland Clinic, and Mayo Clinic would continue to meet for decades.

which later evolved to be the Health Alliance Plan (HAP), was formed in 1958 by Walter Reuther and the United Auto Workers (UAW) to provide a health plan for UAW employees.[39]

Henry Ford Hospital formed an insurance department in 1957 to process claims of patients who used insurance to pay for their medical care. By 1962, the collections department had become computerized. That was just in time for the complexity that came with the creation of the country's new health insurance programs: Medicaid and Medicare. Medicare was designed to provide health care for those over 65, while Medicaid covered children without parental support and the disabled. When the programs launched in 1966, about 19 million people enrolled.[40]

Population was shifting, too. In the mid-1960s the African-American population accounted for 30 percent of Detroit's 1.6 million residents. The number of African Americans had increased by 50 percent over the previous decade and was coupled with a significant decrease in the white population.[41]

Despite the numbers, though, African Americans were just beginning to integrate many of the positions at the hospital. Wilma Gandy, hired as a ward clerk in 1955, was one of the first African Americans to be employed at the hospital.

"There were no blacks in any supervisory capacity," Gandy said. "There was a black nurse. Other than that, I didn't know of anybody else with a title or within the kitchen. They started hiring us as clerks, and nurse's aides at the hospital, orderlies."[42]

The hospital had taken its first steps in diversifying its staff, a commitment that would become deeply ingrained through the years. However, making such a massive societal change was not without turbulence. As the 1960s moved into its latter years, Detroit would feel this evolution. And while the hospital felt the unrest, too, it used this opportunity to remake itself to better serve its patients.

1956

Dr. Conrad Lam performs the first successful open-heart surgery at Henry Ford Hospital using a heart-lung machine.

1958

WWJ-TV in Detroit broadcasts a live telecast of a surgical procedure involving the resection of an aorta, which was replaced with an artificial graft. A distinguished group of doctors narrates the procedure while Drs. D. Emerick Szilagyi and Roger F. Smith conduct the surgery. The event is sponsored by the Wayne County Medical Society and the Michigan State Medical Society, along with the 12th Annual Michigan Clinical Institute.

1959

Proposed rendering of the Henry Ford Hospital parking structure. Designed by Albert Kahn Associates, the structure features hyperbolic parabolic concrete panels and wins the excellent design award in 1960 from the Detroit Chapter of the American Institute of Architects.

From the Conrad R. Lam Collection, Henry Ford Health System. ID=05-019.

Six

We are part of Detroit. We have our roots here. We've grown here."

Dr. Richard Smith
DEPARTMENT OF OBSTETRICS AND GYNECOLOGY
AND FORMER CHAIR OF THE HENRY FORD MEDICAL GROUP BOARD OF GOVERNORS[1]

A CITY IN TRANSITION

1960
1970

THE UNITED STATES WAS IN TRANSITION AS THE LANDMARK CIVIL RIGHTS ACT of 1964 was enacted. Passing the bill was contentious enough in Congress. But once the bill became law, it set in motion a tremendous social change—one that would not necessarily come easily, even in northern cities like Detroit.

While southern cities were in consistent upheaval as African Americans fought to see the benefits that the Civil Rights Act promised, northern cities had their own issues with discrimination. Dr. Martin Luther King Jr. had come to Detroit in 1963, urging better pay for workers.

But in the heat of the summer of 1967, peaceful protests turned violent. A four-day riot filled the city with violence, looting, and more than 1,600 fires. The injured poured into the emergency rooms of neighborhood hospitals, especially at Henry Ford Hospital, which was near the most serious rioting.

From the top of the hospital's Clinic Building, west view of the Detroit riots, July 1967. *(Detail From the Conrad R. Lam Collection, Henry Ford Health System. ID=06-002.)*

Eventually, the fires ceased and the injured healed. But the scars on Detroit's psyche would be long-lasting. The events shook the city and reshaped how Henry Ford Hospital approached its work and its community.

Freedom March

Detroit roiled throughout much of the 1960s. In 1963, Dr. Martin Luther King Jr. came to the city to lead the Walk to Freedom—two months before the famous March on Washington. It was here that 125,000 participants—the largest civil rights demonstration at the time—heard King deliver a version of his "I Have a Dream" speech.[2]

The purpose of the Detroit walk was twofold: to address the segregation and brutality occurring in the Deep South, and to focus on the plight of African Americans in northern cities. In the North, discrimination was evident, and the walk focused on the bias that blacks faced in housing, hiring, pay, and education.[3] The date of the event—June 23, 1963—marked the 20th anniversary of the 1943 Detroit Riots, in which 34 people were killed.

Walter E. Douglas Sr., who has served continuously on various Boards of Trustees for the institution since 1978 and was made an honorary trustee in 2010, had just moved to Detroit to help establish the Internal Revenue Service data center. "When we got here in 1966, we moved into Green Acres, which is a northern suburb inside the city, just below Eight Mile Road," he said. "Two or three days later, we got some nasty letters from our neighbors asking us why we sneaked into the community in the middle of the dark and why we had all these strange foods. These were things I wasn't really prepared for."[4]

Douglas also noticed that promising African-American students would attend university and come home only to find a job at the post office. White-collar positions were not, he believed, open to them. Meanwhile, Henry Ford Hospital had not fully diversified its staff.

1960s

1960s

Nursing starts to become specialized into areas of critical care, medical-surgical care, and other fields. Photo: Head Nurse Carolyn Hutchens in the coronary care unit, 1967.

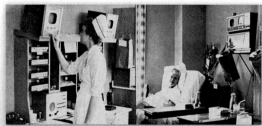

From the Conrad R. Lam Collection, Henry Ford Health System. ID=06-027.

Dr. Gerald M. Breneman of the Division of Cardiology helps establish the first coronary care unit (CCU) at Henry Ford Hospital. After CCUs were established in the US, mortality rates of heart disease patients drop from 30 to 18 percent. "It is the specialized nurses that make the unit so vital," he says.[1]

The hospital made efforts to hire African Americans and Hispanics, but typically in lower-level jobs.

"In the African-American community in particular, there were not the kind of expectations of seeing a doctor of color, any color, in any hospitals, and there was always that kind of tension that occurred," said former Detroit Mayor Dennis Archer, who, in 1959, was the first African American to work in Henry Ford Hospital's medical records department.[5]

The hospital's wards were typically segregated, too. From the Henry Ford Hospital's formation until the 1960s, all non-whites were hospitalized in the M-Unit, except for children. The segregated culture within the hospital may have prevented Dr. Alfred Blalock from accepting a staff appointment to Henry Ford Hospital in the 1930s, fearing that his assistant Vivien Thomas—an African American—would not be treated well.[6]

"I felt we got good service on the wards in the front of the hospital because I worked there most of the time," said Wilma Gandy, a Henry Ford Hospital ward clerk at the time. "But I cried if I had to relieve on the M-Unit. There was no air-conditioning and there were two bedrooms with two patients in each one. The rest was a ward with curtains in between. I just couldn't see how they could, on the one side, be doing so well. And these people over here, what they had to endure bothered me."[7]

The roots of dissension in the city—and the hospital—ran deep. "I could sense, because of our treatment, there was a lot of hostility that had been built up in the city among blacks about how they were treated," Douglas said. "And I don't consider 1967 to be as much a riot

Walter E. Douglas Sr., 2009. *(From Henry Ford Health System. ID:74506_Douglas, Walt.)*

Walter E. Douglas Sr.: Committed to the Community

With an MBA from North Carolina Central University, Walter E. Douglas Sr. joined the Internal Revenue Service, which brought him to Detroit in 1966. Detroit's 1967 riots spurred Douglas to volunteer to help the city's people. He became vice president in 1972 and president in 1978 of the non-profit New Detroit, which aimed to address racial and employment issues. When he heard about the formation of the health insurer Health Alliance Plan (HAP), he urged the leaders to include someone from a minority group on the board.

"At the time, most hospitals in metropolitan Detroit had no diversity at all," Douglas said. "They were mostly made up of white men and white women. No Hispanics, no African Americans, no Arabs, or anyone from the Middle East."[1]

He was appointed to HAP's board in 1978, serving as chair from 1985 to 1999, and also served on the boards of Henry Ford Hospital and the health system. He completed a minority training program offered by the Ford Motor Company in 1985 and subsequently became an owner of the Avis Ford auto dealership in 1986 and majority owner in 1992. He became an honorary trustee at Henry Ford Health System in 2010.

Reflecting on his continuous service since 1978, he commented:

I saw the hospital being an important institution in the city. I saw the need for quality health care being important to the citizens, not only in the city but in this metropolitan community. And I believe that a hospital in Detroit— just like hospitals in Baltimore, where you have Johns Hopkins, and other hospitals around—could be a world-class entity, and I wanted to be a part of it.[2]

1961

1961

Henry Ford Hospital establishes a Division of Emergency Medicine with Dr. Robert Kandel as chief. Photo: The hospital's emergency entrance, 1961.

Ernest R. Breech steps down from an executive position at Ford Motor Company and becomes a member of the hospital's Board of Trustees. In the late 1960s he was among the first to suggest the concept of medical satellites in the suburbs.

From the Conrad R. Lam Collection, Henry Ford Health System. ID=06-023.

as a rebellion. I think that as [the character] Howard Beale said in the movie *Network*, 'I'm sick and tired of this. I'm not going to take it anymore.' I think there was some of that, and the reaction people had to what was going on in 1967. And that certainly was kind of what I felt among people when I first moved here."[8]

A City on Fire

It started simply. Police raided an after-hours establishment—known as a blind pig—at 12th and Clairmount, within a mile of Henry Ford Hospital. As the officers arrested 82 patrons, a crowd gathered, taunting officers. A bottle smashed through the window of a police car, putting in motion days of turmoil that would become one of the most violent riots in the nation's history.

Fires burned throughout the city—with 1,600 blazes counted. Stores were looted and burned.[9] Dorothy (Dottie) Deremo, then a student at Henry Ford Hospital School of Nursing, was among those who went to the hospital's top floor to watch the fires burn. "There were windows all the way around that allowed us to see the entire city, and it looked like it had been bombed," she said. "There was smoke and fires everywhere. I was distraught to see the city that I loved in flames."[10]

Opposite: Tank outside Henry Ford Hospital's parking garage during the riots, 1967. *(From the Conrad R. Lam Collection, Henry Ford Health System. ID=06-001.)*

Below: Dorothy (Dottie) Deremo, R.N., 1989. *(From the Conrad R. Lam Collection, Henry Ford Health System. ID=06-021. Credit: Richard Hirneisen.)*

A Diverse Community Emerges

From its founding, Henry Ford Hospital has served all who came through its doors. As medicine changed to include women and all races, the hospital was well-suited to adapt. Students and physicians from around the world have always come to Henry Ford Hospital to learn from pioneers such as Drs. Conrad Lam and D. Emerick Szilagyi in the earlier years and Dr. Mani Menon and Dr. William O'Neill more recently.

Dr. Kent Wu came to the United States from China in 1958, practicing as an orthopedic surgeon from 1971 to 1999. His specialties were bone cancer and foot surgery. He holds patents on a number of instruments. Other international physicians included Dr. Mohammed R. Ansari from India, Drs. Riad Farah and Farouk N. Obeid from Syria, Dr. Ghaus Malik from Pakistan, and Dr. Enrique Enriquez from Mexico.

African-American house officers at the hospital in the 1970s paved the way for senior staff. Drs. Ray H. Littleton, T. Jann Caison-Sorey, and Richard Smith were among the first group of African-American physicians at the hospital.

Still, the hospital had a ways to go in improving perceptions in the African-American community. "There's always a perception of Henry Ford Hospital back then, that it was a hospital for the affluent whites that didn't want to take care of African Americans," said Randy Walker, Henry Ford Health System's former chief diversity officer. "Over the years, Henry Ford has done a really good job working on that perception. You look at the number of organizations that Henry Ford supports, the number of employees that are involved ... It wasn't just a PR piece. Henry Ford practices what it preaches."[1]

Inside the hospital, staff members feared that the fires would spread. Firefighters were pelted with bricks and rocks if they tried to put out the flames. Television reports carried interviews with those who made threats and urged those inside nearby buildings to leave.

When the riots broke out, Gandy was at home. Her husband urged her to stay there. She refused and headed to the hospital. "I stayed all day and that night because I didn't want to hear my husband say I couldn't go back. There was so much talk on the radio about it, and some were getting riled up the wrong way, and so there was some fear the next day."[11]

Lee Gooden, c. 1970.
(From the Conrad R. Lam Collection, Henry Ford Health System. ID=06-003.)

Lee Gooden was working his shift as midnight supervisor: "Those who were at work at the time, they asked them to stay on. I was here I think about two or three nights before I could go home. Those who were out couldn't come in, and those who were here couldn't go."[12]

For those outside of the hospital, getting into the area was a challenge. Security personnel were sent to retrieve any emergency workers who could not get there on their own. Nurses carpooled, and volunteers showed up. "You have to screen volunteers," said Joan Daniels, former nursing supervisor, "and know what their capabilities are, so it was a pretty intense situation for a few days. There was a motel over on West Grand Boulevard and the Lodge Freeway, and somebody was killed there from an exchange of gunfire. So it was pretty intense, pretty frightening."[13]

Dr. Evelyn Fisher, who would become a renowned infectious disease specialist, drove to the hospital to work. She had just started her residency. "At the doctors' parking garage, there were eight policemen standing in a row holding guns at the opening to the garage, and

Lee Gooden: Problem Solver

Lee Gooden was on his way from Alabama to Seattle when he stopped in Detroit to visit an aunt. After about a week in the city, he decided to look for a job. If he found one, he would stay. If not, he would move on to Seattle. Though jobs were not easy to come by in 1953, he happened in to Henry Ford Hospital to fill out an application. When the receptionist noticed his retail experience, she sent him to the general store to learn more. Within a few minutes, he was on the job and worked 10 hours that day.

He worked in the general store for three years before moving over to payroll as a timekeeper. Promoted to payroll clerk, he was asked to move to medical records as a midnight supervisor and was promoted again, back to payroll. Eventually, he made his way into human resources, where he retired as a senior associate.

Though it may not be reflected in his various job titles, Gooden was often called upon by his peers to assist with problems. "If there was any problem where the employee felt that they were being neglected or underpaid, they would come to me, and I would go to the supervisor or their manager, and we would try to resolve it," he said. "And that's where mostly my knowledge of counseling came in, because I guess the word got around that I was kind of good in that. And the supervisors and the employees were always knocking on my door."[1]

Additionally, in the effort to ensure that the racial tensions felt in the city did not permeate the hospital, Gooden and others formed the Fordsmen, a small group of employees that hosted after-work events for Henry Ford Hospital staffers of all races.

I thought they must be having some kind of special drill … It wasn't until I got in to the hospital that I found out the riots had started during the night. I was there for three days," said Dr. Fisher.

Within a day, Governor George Romney had declared a state of emergency and sent in 7,300 National Guard and 400 state police to quell the rioters.[14] The Guard took up positions at Henry Ford Hospital and Herman Kiefer Hospital—putting both medical facilities at risk as snipers took aim. Lights were shut off at night to keep the hospital shrouded in darkness for fear of potential attacks.[15]

Even in the darkness, though, the hospital staff was busy. The emergency room treated gunshot wounds, stabbings, and serious lacerations. The ER treated 656 cases related to the riot during a four-day period—including 400 serious traumas.[16] With police officers and National Guardsmen stationed in the hospital's garage, the dietary department had the extra task of feeding the troops each day. It was a time that tested all of the hospital's infrastructure, proving that while the world burned around them, the hospital staff could—and would—keep the focus on treating patients. Deremo recalled:

A Henry Ford Hospital nurse using an early computer at a nurses station, 1968. *(From the Conrad R. Lam Collection, Henry Ford Health System. ID=05-048.)*

> *There was all this insanity outside the campus, including in the nurses' residence. We had to crawl along the floor by outside windows because snipers were shooting into the building, and we worked 18 hours and then we had six hours of rest for that whole week because we had to take care of patients that were still in the hospital. But inside the hospital was an island of sanity, really. We were white, brown, all different skin colors, races, ethnic origins, religions. … I saw the best of Detroit inside the hospital while the worst was going on outside.*[17]

1961

Doctors come from around the globe to attend the Henry Ford International Symposium, "The Etiology of Myocardial Infarction." Drs. Thomas N. James and John W. Keyes edit the proceedings for publication.

1962

Henry Ford Hospital hosts an oral cancer symposium with the Michigan Department of Health, the Michigan State Dental Association, and the Detroit District Dental Society. Dr. Michael Brennan (pictured, c. 1980s), physician-in-chief of oncology, presents the final lecture.

From the Conrad R. Lam Collection, Henry Ford Health System. ID=06-020.

A New Conversation

The riots shook the city to its core. Racial tensions that had long simmered were out in the open. The response to this horrific event—which killed 44 people—set Detroit on a path to a new conversation.

"There were a lot of dialogue sessions where blacks and whites sat down—in our view, sometimes for the first time—to talk about the kind of things that had separated us for years," Walt Douglas said.[18]

The nonprofit organization New Detroit was born out of the riots at the request of the governor and the mayor, Jerome Cavanagh. Under the direction of business executive Joseph Hudson Jr., New Detroit began by gathering a diverse committee to listen to and understand the perspective of others.[19]

The riots had captured the attention of leaders and average citizens alike. "It showed me the level of anger and despair that existed in the city and the racial tension," Deremo said. "It was at that time when I made a personal commitment to not only heal bodies but to try to be a part of the solution to heal that schism that existed among the races within our community."[20] After graduating from the School of Nursing, Deremo joined the nursing staff at the hospital, eventually serving as its chief nursing officer.

Impact on the Hospital

While the riots had revealed divisions between the city and some of its constituents, the shared experience helped to nurture a feeling of camaraderie within the hospital. That was largely due to the work of the Fordsmen, a group of 10 or so employees who hosted dances and social gatherings.

1963

More than 25,000 people come to hear Rev. Martin Luther King Jr. speak at Cobo Hall and join a march for freedom in Detroit afterward.

1965

Pharmacists at Henry Ford Hospital, 1965. Left to right: Robert Reoch, Donald F. Lovelace, Charles P. Morrison, and Janice A. O'Reilly.

From the Conrad R. Lam Collection, Henry Ford Health System. ID=06-026.

1965

Henry Ford Hospital celebrates its 50th anniversary with a special meeting of the Henry Ford Hospital Medical Association for a two-day reunion. The Board of Trustees names its auditorium for Dr. Buerki, the medical library for Dr. Sladen, and the operating suites for Dr. McClure.

"After work, there was nothing to do, no association," said Lee Gooden, one of the early—and longstanding—Fordsmen. "You could socialize here at work, but there was no association after work among the blacks and whites. And so we got together and formed a group and promoted dances and brought people together. We booked some of the best musicians, and, most of the time, the dances were well-attended. It would only cost a dollar and 25 cents for the tickets to come in, and that would give you a pop and two glasses of ice. That, again, brought people together. That softened the racial divide that we had here at the time."[21]

The Fordsmen grew to include charitable works, including raising funds for those who had been affected by floods or fires. Eventually, the social dances stopped, and the Fordsmen became known as the Old-Timers, who still gathered for an annual picnic.[22]

Despite the Fordsmen's efforts, the racial tension had birthed damaging reverberations, especially since the riots had gained national attention. "It was a disaster for the training programs because the spouses of potential house officers said, 'No way. It's not going to be Detroit,'" said Dr. Bruce Steinhauer, a renowned physician who was an internist at the hospital during the riots. "That picture on the cover of *Time* magazine with the flames was nationally published, and people just decided against Detroit. So we plowed on, largely, thank goodness, because we got some very high-quality foreign medical graduates who, in those years, kind of dominated the program."[23]

The Fordsmen's Club, 1961. First row left to right: Felton Petty, Ernest Slaton, Charles Robinson, and Fletcher Jefferson. Back row left to right: Virgil Waters, Lee Gooden, and George Smith. (Robert Haskett not shown.) *(From the Conrad R. Lam Collection, Henry Ford Health System. ID=06-004.)*

1966

Dr. Richmond W. Smith Jr., founder of the Division of Endocrinology, is appointed by the Board of Trustees as chair of Internal Medicine.

1966

Dr. Laurence Fallis retires after heading the Department of Surgery for 14 years. Dr. D. Emerick Szilagyi is appointed chair of the department.

1966

Dr. Clarence S. Livingood becomes the team physician of the Detroit Tigers Baseball Club. He holds the position until 1997 and initiates use of sports medicine at Henry Ford Hospital.

The Long, Slow Process of Integration

Healing after the riots was not an easy task. Integration was slow. As a ward clerk, Gandy and others began the process slowly, urging some African-American patients to refuse to go to the M-Unit. "One night, a white woman came in, and we had a full house," Gandy said. "She wanted to go into the room with a black patient, but the husband didn't want her to go in. He finally agreed, and so from then on, if there was a full house, a white patient could share a room with a black patient."[24]

Wilma Gandy, 1972.
(From the Conrad R. Lam Collection, Henry Ford Health System. ID=07-031.)

Detroit's landscape was changing. The creation of the interstate highway system a decade before led to the development of suburban housing and business. The riots had served to open the floodgates, with whites in particular moving out of the city's core. Businesses followed their customers, and houses in the city were abandoned, but Henry Ford Hospital stayed. "We made our firm commitment by Henry Ford to stay here when everyone else left," said Dr. Richard Smith, longtime obstetrician and leader. "If you look around our neighborhood, there were many hospitals that are now gone. But we remained ... because this is our community."[25]

Staying was, in reality, a simple decision. Henry Ford Hospital was a Detroit institution—one that had earned the kind of reputation that would draw patients who knew they would receive outstanding care. Dr. John Popovich, the hospital's current president and CEO, commented:

Wilma Gandy: Ward Clerk to Advocate

During her 44 years at Henry Ford Hospital, Wilma Gandy had a front row seat to many changes. In some instances, she had a hand in moving them along a bit faster.

Gandy joined the hospital in 1955 as a ward clerk. "I loved the contact with the patients," she said. "Everything that I could do for the patient, I did. My mother and father taught me to love my neighbor, but at Henry Ford, I learned to be compassionate."[1]

When Gandy saw disparities among where patients were housed based on skin color, she began to work to integrate the hospital. Blacks typically were sent to the M-Unit, unless it was at capacity. Then, they were treated in other parts of the hospital. There, Gandy and others would encourage the African-American patients to stay in the newer part of the hospital, rather than transferring to the M-Unit as beds opened up. "We had to pick the black patients and tell them, 'You can refuse to go back. Doctors have patients all over this hospital.' Through three clerks, I would say, we integrated the place."[2]

Gandy also was instrumental in founding the Henry Ford Hospital Employee Credit Union in 1972. She had seen the model work through her church and was the first employee to pay the $5 to join. She later became its vice president. "Anything I get carried away with, I will push it down everybody's throat. But I really made a commitment, I made a vow that I would do everything I could to support Ford Hospital and give them a good image at all times."[3]

The faculty here, as well as the Board and administrative staff, were really Detroiters. Real Detroiters have grit. They look at achievement much more than, perhaps, background. There are many other hospitals that were moving out at that time. You can see them continuing to be part of the landscape in health care in southeastern Michigan. But there was much more attention by all of the people here to continue to do the work on this campus and in this city. I think there was this commitment to the importance of what a central city hospital means to a population in general. And the commitment of the Ford family to the city absolutely couldn't be changed. They were committed to this city, and they were committed to the ups and downs of this city.[26]

Internal Changes

The hospital had to make changes in business strategy after the riots. In 1968, the Board of Trustees and Benson Ford asked for the resignation of Dr. James (Ted) Howell, the hospital's administrator. Howell had lost the confidence of many medical leaders since replacing Dr. Robin Buerki in 1964. Dr. Buerki returned temporarily while the institution sought Dr. Howell's permanent replacement.

It would take several years to find the right person to fill the position. The new administrator would be charged with helping the hospital better integrate its staff while responding to a significant population change in Detroit and the suburbs.

1967

Riots break out in the city of Detroit within a mile of Henry Ford Hospital.

1968

The first allogeneic kidney transplant is performed by Drs. D. Emerick Szilagyi, Joseph Elliott, and Roger Smith.

1968

From the Conrad R. Lam Collection, Henry Ford Health System. ID=06-005.

Surgeon Dr. Joseph Ponka (pictured, second from right, c. 1968) teaches residents at the hospital.

CHAPTER

Seven

"*There's no question that since the riots, the city changed dramatically.
Downtown was a vibrant, exciting place, and, after the riots, much of the economic
lifeblood of the city moved out. One of the things that's remarkable has been that, in
spite of that, the hospital was able to thrive and grow, and, not only maintain and
enhance its reputation as an academic health care center, but to grow as a facility
that provided care for the local residents. So even back then in the Seventies, it was
clear that this organization had figured out how to thrive in an environment when
it was easy and even when it became more difficult.*"

Dr. Robert Chapman
DIRECTOR, JOSEPHINE FORD CANCER INSTITUTE
AND DIVISION HEAD OF HEMATOLOGY/ONCOLOGY[1]

most polarized metropolitan area in the country in terms of the city and the suburbs. And, of course, we were in the city where many of the doctors, and many of the hospitals, had already bailed out. ... And that posed some very significant problems.[4]

The challenges in Detroit were unique to Nelson, whose previous turnaround experience took place in a much different culture in Minnesota. Like many, Nelson found Detroit deeply divided and overly reliant on automobile manufacturing. He was intrigued, however, by the institution's employed physician group.

"Henry Ford was this hospital that had the large, multi-specialty group practice," Nelson said. "The clinic is an integral part of the organization. Vastly different. That was one of the main reasons I went to Henry Ford. I wanted to see how that kind of an organizational structure, with the physicians as an integral part, how that was different, how it was better, how it worked, and what it was all about."[5]

"How Do We Survive?"

Once in place, Nelson began addressing the significant challenges of the hospital, including staff frustrations and patient concerns. He also looked a little longer term. "One of our challenges was, 'How do we survive? How do we grow? How do we interface with what we have demographically?'" Nelson said. "And, at that time, with most health care, the hospital is the center of the health care industry. My thinking was that somehow we had to penetrate the suburbs because that's where the strength was of the metropolitan area. But we couldn't go out and build hospitals there because of the certificate-of-need regulations."[6]

The 1974 Health Planning and Resources Development Act required medical facilities to propose and obtain approval from a state agency before beginning any major capital

---

1972

Henry Ford Hospital appoints Mary Morris, R.N., as its first African-American director of nursing and Theresa Jones, R.N, as the first African-American director of the School of Nursing.

1972

Henry Ford Hospital records its millionth patient, a 16-month-old baby with a heart condition, under the care of Dr. Roger M. Folger, chief of the pediatric cardiology division.

projects such as a building expansion.[7] If Henry Ford Hospital wanted to place significant facilities into the suburbs, it would have to prove they were needed—a challenge, as many hospitals had already established operations there.

The hospital would have to find a new way to expand into the suburbs without going the standard route of simply building a new facility. Nelson brought in C. Thomas Smith, who joined the hospital in 1971 as vice president and executive director of hospitals and clinics, and others such as Patrick Hays as administrator for operations. "[Nelson] taught me that if you enter an organization that needs to be changed, you do it with class and a certain amount of subtlety," Hays said.[8]

Though Nelson's approach might have been subtle, his moves were not. He found the hospital almost totally dysfunctional, as he described it:

C. Thomas Smith, Henry Ford Hospital vice president, c. 1977. *(From the Conrad R. Lam Collection, Henry Ford Health System. ID=07-021.)*

> *Anywhere you turned, you could find a problem, including the need of repair of the building. The one that attracted the most publicity was that my predecessor had attempted to install an automated, computerized financial system for the hospital and the clinic without adequately testing the system, without adequately running parallel for any period of time, and it blew up and didn't work. And they couldn't generate any bill that made sense. When I walked in that place, they had 250 people sitting at card table chairs in the corridors in the basement and everyplace else, correcting by hand the bills that the computer was kicking out. I didn't understand why or how they were meeting the payroll and other expenses if they couldn't generate a bill that could be reimbursed.[9]*

Because of the cost-reimbursement formula that insurance companies—as well as Medicare and Medicaid—operated under at the time, doctors submitted costs and were paid. At the end of each year, the books were settled as reconciliation determined whether

1972

Henry Ford Hospital's Troy facility opens with financial services, later adding dialysis and psychiatric services.

1972

Michigan's first computed tomographic scanner opens in the Department of Radiology.

1972

Dr. Mary Logan starts the first Henry Ford Hospital Pediatric Multidisciplinary Care Clinic with Dr. E. Dennis Lyne of pediatric orthosurgery.

the costs were accurate or too high. In the latter case, the hospital would reimburse the insurers. Because of the mess with billing, financial auditors would not certify the hospital's books for a period of three years—from 1968 to 1971.[10]

"The financial statements didn't mean anything," Nelson said. "As nearly as we could figure out, we owed those third-party payers something like five to six months' revenue, which meant we were technically bankrupt."[11]

Solving the computer issues was no small task. No off-the-shelf solution would work because of the hospital's unique arrangement with its physicians. Nelson sought the advice of experts who recommended slugging it out one phase at a time. "You start with your receivables, and you get those going right. And then you've got to move to the rest of it," Nelson said.[12]

The NCR 315 Computer at Henry Ford Hospital, 1962. *(From the Conrad R. Lam Collection, Henry Ford Health System. ID=07-012.)*

The hospital purchased a former bank building in the Troy suburb to overcome another issue: the computer's mainframe in the basement. "Every time there was a heavy rain, the sewers would back up, and the computer would be under a foot of water," Nelson said. "The location in Troy was bigger than we needed, but it was immediately available. We moved the whole operation out there to isolate the problem and to get all these people out of the corridor in the basement and give them adequate work space and resources. It took us a while—I'd say two to three years— to get it fully straightened out."[13]

1972

Dr. Evelyn Fisher volunteers as director of the outreach Pallister-Lodge Methadone Maintenance Clinic, one of the first of its kind at the time.

1972

Drs. Stanley Dienst, John Caldwell, Joseph Cerny, and Fred Whitehouse represent Henry Ford Hospital at the 11th annual Kidney Disease Symposium, held at Detroit's Mercy College.

1972

Henry Ford Hospital develops a single symbol logo (pictured) to establish visual identity, which was considered important as operations expanded to metropolitan Detroit.

From the Conrad R. Lam Collection, Henry Ford Health System. ID=08-042.

The Troy Medical Center, 1973. *(From the Conrad R. Lam Collection, Henry Ford Health System. ID=07-019.)*

The improvements started small, said Steve Velick, former CEO of the hospital who was a manager of billing at the time:

> *We really worked with IT back then to put some checks and balances in order for us to get a more accurate billing. If there was an operating room charge before, we would send a bill out, a flag would go out and we'd say, "There should be an anesthesia charge, a physician billing charge, there should be supplies," things like that. As simple as you think that is, that was a significant improvement to billing.*[14]

1972

The hospital selects Dr. Nathan Levin as its first head of the Division of Nephrology. Dr. Levin helps to expand dialysis services and make kidney transplantation possible.

1972

The hospital honors Dr. Jonathan Parsons of the Edsel B. Ford Research Institute for his pioneering work with kidney stones. Dr. Parsons developed methods of X-ray diffraction in the analysis of biological and medical compounds and substances.

1972

The hospital purchases 78 acres of land in West Bloomfield Township to develop a health care satellite facility.

Staffing Challenges

The computer challenges—and the related payment issues they brought—were not Nelson's primary concern. It was the nursing shortage. The hospital's nursing staff had dwindled to 110 nurses for the 1,000-bed hospital. "That kept me awake a lot of nights because I'd never heard of such a thing," Nelson said. "And that was something that had developed over a several-year period."[15]

The nursing shortage also was a bit of a head-scratcher as the hospital's School of Nursing continued to thrive, graduating dozens each class. Nelson was asked to present diplomas at graduation: "I'm sitting on the stage there with a couple of faculty members, the director of the school, and I turn to the faculty member next to me, and I think there were 70 students in the class, and I said, 'How many of these students will be staying with us?' She said 'Seven.' I knew we had a problem because normally a school like that would keep two-thirds. And where I'd been before, the schools of that same nature, we'd done that."[16]

Recruiting at the national level was equally challenging, especially since the riots were still in everyone's memory. Nelson recalled:

We said, "If we're going to solve this problem, we've got to do it from the inside out." We redesigned the whole organization

Henry Ford Hospital School of Nursing Graduation, 1972. *(From the Conrad R. Lam Collection, Henry Ford Health System. ID=07-006.)*

1972

Henry Ford Hospital hosts a four-day international symposium on metabolic bone disease led by Dr. Boy Frame (pictured, 1984).

1973

Henry Ford Hospital announces a $100 million grant from the Ford Foundation for projects in medical education and research, community health care, and facilities improvement.

1973

The Pelham Community Health Station (pictured, 1974), a hospital outreach facility, opens in Pelham Middle School to serve local residents.

Left to right: Mary Morris, R.N., director of nursing at Henry Ford Hospital, c. 1972. Theresa Jones, R.N., director of the Henry Ford Hospital School of Nursing, 1975. *(From the Conrad R. Lam Collection, Henry Ford Health System. ID=07-005, 07-004.)*

of the nursing depart-ment. We created four subsets of this large hospital; 1,000 beds is more than anybody should try to manage, whether it's nursing or whatever it is. So we broke the hospital into four units with a director of nursing for each one. And the message to the management team was "This is not a nursing department problem. It's a management problem. And everybody in this organization has to help solve it." So we paid a lot of

Nursing Integrates and Reorganizes

In the 1960s, African-American nurses were still uncommon at Henry Ford Hospital. But by 1972, two key leadership positions in the nursing department were held by women of color: Theresa Jones, director of the School of Nursing and Mary Morris, director of nursing for the hospital.

Jones was still a new hire at the hospital in 1967 when she began working at the School of Nursing. At the time, the field of nursing was changing, and the accreditation board was seeking more applicants with bachelor's degrees. With a Master's degree, Jones was one of two nurses at the hospital to have received that level of education.[1]

Integrating the nursing staff was a complicated undertaking. "It was lonely," Jones said. "You didn't see yourself at all, and when you'd see a black resident, you'd go: 'Oh, thank God! There's somebody else here besides me.'"[2]

At the time, there was a large fence that surrounded the hospital, and Jones urged administrator Stan Nelson to remove it:

I don't think anybody liked the fence, and they needed to expand the parking lot, so the fence had to go. The community was telling people, "You're sitting in

the middle of a predominantly African-American neighborhood, and we have no contact with them. We don't have anything." So we had a lot of meetings where hospital leadership consulted with individuals from the community about what things they could do to improve the relationship. They made an honest effort to try and integrate the community and Henry Ford Hospital.[3]

During her tenure at the School of Nursing, Jones offered opportunities to everyone, including male students and those who were openly gay. She later was appointed by President Jimmy Carter to the Nurse Training Advisory Commission. "When I started getting a lot of publicity for the hospital as well as for the School of Nursing, you could kind of see a change occurring."[4]

Jones retired from Henry Ford Hospital in 1986 and planned to complete a PhD. While she was preparing her doctoral defense, her husband died in 1990. She then made the decision to take over the family's automotive dealership, Northwestern Dodge. This was another industry which, at the time, was underrepresented by minorities—particularly women.[5]

attention to the students in the unit with activities, and recognition, and then faculty improvement. Next year, we kept about two-thirds of the class.[17]

The new leadership positions allowed the hospital to address another damaging oversight: the lack of women of color in key roles. Mary Morris became the hospital's first African-American director of nursing and Theresa Jones became the School of Nursing's first African-American director. Both positions were filled in 1972.[18] Jones worked tirelessly to recruit nurses to the hospital.

The changes clearly worked. By 1974, the hospital had 450 nurses.

Aerial view of the West Bloomfield Medical Center site, 1972. *(From the Conrad R. Lam Collection, Henry Ford Health System. ID=07-025.)*

To the Suburbs

With those two immediate crises solved, Nelson and his leadership team could turn their attention to the hospital's longer-term challenge: serving the customers who had moved out to the suburbs. The Troy facility included a dialysis clinic and outpatient psychiatric services—the hospital's first attempt to dip its toes outside of the city center. By 1975, two additional 78,000-square foot facilities would open in Dearborn and West Bloomfield.[19]

The move to suburban medical clinics would prove again Nelson's "unerring knack for identifying where the field ought to be heading and then getting there ahead of anyone else," said C. Thomas Smith.[20] Nelson did not see the move as visionary, but obvious:

1973

Richard Krolicki (pictured, c. 1975), who would become vice president for Corporate Facilities, works with hospital

chief Stan Nelson on locating the land for proposed satellites. His father, August Krolicki, was hired by Henry Ford and had also been head of facilities at the hospital.

From the Conrad R. Lam Collection, Henry Ford Health System. ID=09-029. Credit: Richard Hirneisen, Royal Oak, MI.

1973

Virgil Waters (right) is appointed as the first patient advocate in Emergency Medicine. Dr. Richard Nowak (left) was chief of Emergency Medicine from 1988 to 1992.

From the Conrad R. Lam Collection, Henry Ford Health System. ID=07-035.

If we are confined to the city, and confined to running the hospital, the future looks a little bleak. We figured we had to get into the suburbs somehow. The idea of moving to the suburbs with ambulatory care was one of the strategies that we identified and started looking at very seriously. There really were two schools of thought involved. One was what I called the sender excellence theory. That is the traditional kind of thinking in the medical centers that says, "if you build excellence, people will come." The other school of thought was, "unless we can bring our health services to where the people are, they're getting what they need in the suburbs, and they will continue to get it within the suburbs."[21]

Opposite: Benson Ford at the Fairlane Medical Center groundbreaking, February 21, 1974. *(Detail From the Conrad R. Lam Collection, Henry Ford Health System. ID=06-007.)*

While the expansion may have been obvious to Nelson, there were significant discussions and disagreements among leadership. "We felt that we actually had to do it but not at the exclusion of developing the excellence," Nelson said. "So we sort of developed a duality of strategy. We'd go into the suburbs with ambulatory care, which was legal and permissible, much to the consternation of the hospitals and doctors out there. Plus we'd build the excellence on the main campus. That is basically what we pursued."[22]

Dr. Bruce Steinhauer, an internist at the hospital, suggested that the new ambulatory centers had to be open around the clock, which meant adding emergency rooms at some of the centers. He recalled:

That made a tremendous difference to the comfort level, because what we didn't want is people using these facilities during the day but getting sick at night and saying, "Well, now I have to find my way to the local hospital." If we were going to have a system, we had to have 24-hour coverage. It was expensive keeping them open around the clock, but it was one of the important differences we had.[23]

1973

State Sen. Coleman A. Young is elected the first African-American mayor of Detroit and retains this position for five consecutive terms.

1973

Dr. Robert Horn, chief of Pathology at Ford Hospital, serves as president of the American College of Pathology.

Above: The Ernest and Thelma Breech Pavilion at the Fairlane Medical Center, Dearborn, 1981. *(Detail From the Conrad R. Lam Collection, Henry Ford Health System. ID=06-014.)*

Above right: West Bloomfield Center, c. 1975. *(From the Conrad R. Lam Collection, Henry Ford Health System. ID=06-008.)*

The move was so innovative that when the hospital sought an architect with expertise in building ambulatory clinics, it could not find one. "When it was finally designed, and opened, it looked a lot to me like a hospital without any beds," Nelson said. "Instead of beds, we had physician offices."[24]

The Dearborn facility "took off like a rocket," Nelson said. "We were growing 15–18 percent a year." West Bloomfield was another story. Henry Ford Hospital arrived well before the population boom, but it was clear the future was there in terms of growth because of the geographic barrier of the US-Canada border to the north. "Northwest was going to be the direction that, over time, over decades, the city would expand," said Nelson. "I can remember driving past the cornfields to get to the ambulatory care center out on West Maple, wondering what in the world we were doing out there. And we got some flack in the sense that it was two or three years before we could break even out there."[25]

1974

Dr. Donald Ditmars serves as president of the Michigan Academy of Plastic Surgeons. Dr. Ditmars is later appointed chief of the Division of Plastic and Reconstructive Surgery at Ford Hospital in 1981.

1974

Dr. Sidney Goldstein, a specialist in the prevention of sudden cardiac death and a pioneer in clinical trials, is appointed chief of the Division of Cardiovascular Medicine.

Within just a few short years of arriving in Detroit, Nelson had revolutionized the hospital's structure and set it on a course that it could follow for many years.

Not Abandoning Detroit

Despite the expansion to the north and west, Henry Ford Hospital remained committed to the city as well. Community outreach became more important than ever. Theresa Jones, the School of Nursing director, took initiative to visit people in the suburbs to encourage people to come downtown to the hospital.

The hospital joined with the City Health Department and the Michigan State Department of Social Services to create the Community Health and Social Services Center (CHASS). CHASS would provide free health services to those living in primarily Spanish-speaking neighborhoods. A staff of bilingual physicians and social workers would be devoted to the patients. Henry Ford physicians such as Drs. Evelyn Fisher, Mary Logan, Ramon Del Busto, and Harry O. Davidson routinely devoted their time to the clinic.[26]

Commitment to the Community

In the 1950s, Ford Hospital doctors had started volunteering time at the St. Francis Cabrini Clinic in downtown Detroit. Henry Ford Hospital reinforced its commitment to the city of Detroit by providing care for the underserved communities with the opening of the Community Health and Social Services Center (CHASS) in 1971.

CHASS initially served primarily non-English speaking, low-income families.[1] The City Health Department and the Michigan State Department of Social Services were vital partners.

CHASS' physician services were contracted through Henry Ford and allowed the physician staff to consult with the Henry Ford Medical Group as needed.

By 2012, CHASS had built a new $17 million facility to expand its services to include more primary care and wellness services. Henry Ford Health System contributed $3 million to the new facility. The clinic would serve 28,000 patients, compared to 11,000 served at its previous location. The facility also offered a time to reflect on CHASS' success.[2]

"Over the years, CHASS has successfully overcome the three main barriers to care in the community we serve—access, language, and transportation—and today, CHASS is a model of quality health care delivery to urban populations," J. Ricardo Guzman, CHASS CEO, said.[3]

The hospital's commitment to serving anyone who needed medical assistance extended well beyond CHASS and the Cabrini Clinic, which continue today.

"I think, in many instances, Henry Ford took a proactive approach in terms of addressing the community's health." said Dr. Kimberlydawn Wisdom, currently the health system's senior vice president of community health and equity as well as chief wellness officer. "It was open, as an organization, to looking beyond its four walls and saying, 'Let's see how we can move upstream as an organization.'"[4]

Moving "upstream" also harkened back to the hospital's foundation, when auto magnate Henry Ford felt that the facility should benefit the community. "It was just so great to feel very much aligned with the spirit of Henry Ford himself," Dr. Wisdom said. "The health system, over time, continued that commitment at some level."[5]

Dr. Mary Logan with pediatric patient, 1973. *(From the Conrad R. Lam Collection, Henry Ford Health System. ID=07-040. Credit: Richard Hirneisen Photography.)*

While CHASS was a unique model, it was hardly the hospital's first commitment to the city's poor patients. The Cabrini Clinic, which had been developed in the 1950s, continued with the assistance of Henry Ford physicians who volunteered their time.

A Much-Needed Financial Boost

The hospital may have appeared to have it all, but what it lacked was significant. It had relied on the Ford family for support for decades but was without an endowment, which could provide vital financial stability for the long term.

As far back as the late 1960s, physicians began to explore ways to secure an endowment. One idea was to approach the Ford Foundation, which had provided a significant grant in 1950. Though the Foundation had been created by Edsel Ford in 1936, it did not typically support health care institutions.

Cristina Ford, Henry II's wife, was a patient of Dr. Richmond Smith, who had been one of the physicians working on the endowment. Dr. Smith and Stan Nelson took Cristina Ford on a visit to the Mayo Clinic and St. Mary's Hospital in Minnesota to show the level of excellence that they expected for Henry Ford Hospital.

Dr. Smith told Dr. Oscar Carretero, who had come to the hospital to open the Hypertension Research Laboratory in 1968, about his plans for a $50 million grant. "I thought, 'Well, he's gone crazy,'" said Dr. Carretero. "Fifty million dollars? I had just spent a year preparing a grant for $250,000 from the National Institutes of Health, and I worked day and night

1974

Dr. Robert Knighton serves as president of the American Neurological Society of America. He was chief of neurosurgery at Ford Hospital from 1953 to 1971 and of the combined department of neurology and neurosurgery from 1971 to 1978.

1975

Dr. Paul Stein founds the Cardiovascular Research Laboratory at Henry Ford Hospital.

1975

The second Henry Ford Hospital International Symposium on Cardiovascular Surgery, organized by Drs. Julio C. Davila, Ellet H. Drake, and Wolf Duvernoy, draws more than 450 physicians from the US and 12 foreign countries.

generating data, writing, and so on, and he talks about $50 million? Well, I was right. He didn't get $50 million. He got $100 million."[27]

Henry Ford II played a significant role in landing the grant. He had worked with the Foundation since 1943 and helped it grow to one of the largest philanthropic organizations in the world. He had overseen a diversification in the Foundation's assets as it divested itself of Ford Motor Company stock.[28]

With his knowledge of the Ford Foundation dynamics, Henry Ford II recommended to Nelson and Dr. Smith that the hospital propose a $200 million grant. Nelson remembered:

To my credit, I didn't fall out of my chair. I just swallowed and asked, "Could we put in brick and mortar?" The Ford Foundation did not give to brick and mortar. And to that Mr. Ford said, "Well, they don't give to health care either, so we would be breaking that rule. Let's break the other rule, too." I told him, "If I can put in brick and mortar, I can get the grant up to $200 million." And he said, "If you can get it up to $200 million, I think I can get you $100 million." I thought that sounded pretty good.[29]

Since the Foundation did not typically award grants to health care facilities, it engaged the Boston Consulting Group to assess the hospital. The report raised flags about the hospital's recruitment of staff and physicians, its lack of fundraising programs,

Dr. Oscar A. Carretero in the Henry Ford Hospital Hypertension Research Laboratory, 1978. *(From the Conrad R. Lam Collection, Henry Ford Health System. ID=07-014.)*

1975

From the Conrad R. Lam Collection, Henry Ford Health System. ID=07-038.

Dr. H. Mathilda Horst (pictured) becomes the first woman surgeon trained in vascular surgery at Henry Ford Hospital under Dr. D. Emerick Szilagyi.

1975

From the Conrad R. Lam Collection, Henry Ford Health System. ID=07-036.

West Bloomfield Medical Center opens with Dr. Charles Wolf (pictured) as medical director. Wolf-Peterson-Weiss Syndrome is named after him and his Ford Hospital colleagues Drs. James Peterson and Lester Weiss. They reported in 1967 on the chromosome abnormality that causes dwarfism.

and the rising number of uncollectable and charity care cases. The hospital was able to rebut the report by pointing out several programs which had already been put in place.[30]

By Christmas, Henry II had requested an immediate meeting with Nelson. "He got the grant," Nelson said. "There were some strings attached. But the [requirements] were not difficult to meet." It was an unparalleled contribution at that point in time. Nelson added, "It's ironic. In this day and age, $100 million doesn't sound like maybe all that much, but it was an unprecedented gift. And he [Henry II] instinctively saw that the institution needed something to move it to the next level."[31]

Let the Games Begin

The hospital staff had been through a few challenging decades. While the Fordsmen had provided a much-needed social outlet during the immediate post-riot days, team building continued to be vital, so in 1977, the hospital launched its first Olympiad.[1]

The goal was to raise money for toys and medical equipment in the pediatrics unit. It would do so through a series of "chariot" races in the hospital's student housing parking lot.

The event had its own mascot—Ollie Olympiad—and its own Olympic "torch" lighting, using a bedpan designed by the facilities staff. To compete, employees wore togas, and departments' teams raced hand-constructed chariots.

As the Olympiad grew in subsequent years, added events included foot races and administrative tricycle races. Cardiac surgeon Dr. Conrad Lam directed the accompanying band. In 1979, the Olympiad had more than 3,000 in-person spectators who paid $5 admission.[2] The event made TV news that year.

Through the years, the event grew to include other hospital affiliates and new pre-race activities, such as a bake-off and toga party held at nearby pizza joint, Dino's. The Olympiads were a beloved annual event through 1991.

"Everybody came to the Olympiads," said Randy Walker, who started at the hospital in 1978 as a dishwasher and recently retired as chief diversity officer. "You had thousands of people. And it really created camaraderie around Henry Ford. And people knew about the Olympiads. It was just a big party."[3]

Employee Deborah Babcock at the Olympiad games, 1978.
(From the Conrad R. Lam Collection,
Henry Ford Health System. ID=07-022.)

From the Conrad R. Lam Collection. Henry Ford Health System. ID=06-011. Credit: David Welsh, Romulus, Michigan.

R.W.Smith Jr. M.D.   McGeorge Bundy   Benson Ford   Stanley R. Nelson

In 1973, Benson Ford, the hospital's Board of Trustees chair and McGeorge Bundy, the Ford Foundation president, announced the grant. The gift would be given in two parts: $25 million up front and a $75 million annuity, which would pay out in equal parts over the next decade. The hospital put the $25 million into construction of the education and research building. "We at Ford Hospital believe in Detroit and are committed to its growth," Benson Ford said at the grant announcement. "We mean to contribute our full share to the revitalization of the city."[32]

The grant required the hospital to create a development office to seek other support, strengthen medical education, upgrade facilities, and increase its outreach programs.[33]

The Henry Ford Hospital press conference announcing the Ford Foundation grant with Dr. Richmond Smith Jr. (left), chief of medicine; McGeorge Bundy, Ford Foundation president; Benson Ford, Henry Ford Hospital board chief; and Stanley R. Nelson, executive director, Henry Ford Hospital; 1973.

1975

1975

From the Conrad R. Lam Collection. Henry Ford Health System. ID=07-039.

Dr. Frank Cox becomes the first director of medical education at Henry Ford Hospital.

The Virginia Park/Henry Ford Hospital Non-Profit Housing Corporation is founded. The program is a joint venture of Henry Ford Hospital and Virginia Park Citizens District Council and the City of Detroit to provide housing for people with low and moderate incomes.

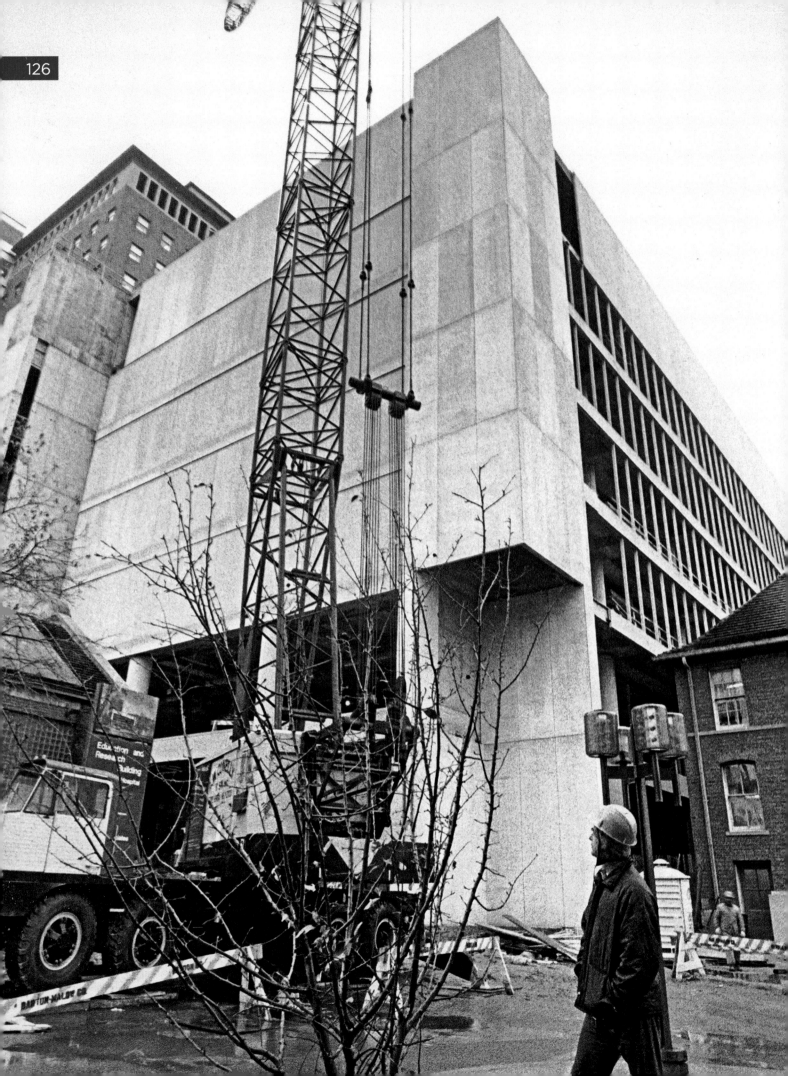

Opposite: Construction of the Benson Ford Education and Research Center Building, c. 1975. *(Detail From the Conrad R. Lam Collection, Henry Ford Health System. ID=07-016.)*

From left: President Gerald R. Ford at the opening of the Benson Ford Education and Research Center with Benson Ford and Carlton M. Higbie Jr., 1977. *(From the Conrad R. Lam Collection, Henry Ford Health System. ID=07-020.)*

The education and research building construction began almost immediately, and the facility opened in 1977. "The building was the first thing built with that part of the endowment," Dr. Carretero said. "Then they created the [research grant] endowment, and that has allowed a lot of different people to work in research at the hospital."[34]

The Ford Foundation had made a timely investment in Henry Ford Hospital, one that would position it to take advantage of the broad medical advances happening at the time—and to drive numerous innovations.

1976

Dr. Brock E. Brush serves as president of the Michigan State Medical Society. A distinguished surgeon and chief of General Surgery at the hospital, Dr. Brush served as president of multiple societies and was a founder of the Michigan Cancer Foundation.

1979–1980

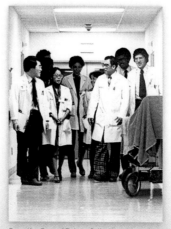

From the Conrad R. Lam Collection, Henry Ford Health System. ID=07-013.

By the end of the 1970s, the culture of hospital staff becomes more diverse. Photo: Doctors on rounds at Henry Ford Hospital, c. 1980.

Eight

" *In a traditional academic institution, each researcher has to go out and find the money to do his project. We organized a big hypertension program, and everybody didn't have to be equally productive in it. They had different responsibilities, and as a result of that, to some extent, we outdid some of the traditional academic organizations in accomplishments. By being able to not have to follow the traditional thing that everybody had to get tenure and had to get grants by themselves, we got grants together, and it was an extremely productive model.*"

Dr. Bruce Steinhauer
INTERNIST, FORMER SENIOR VICE PRESIDENT FOR MEDICAL AFFAIRS
AND CHAIR OF THE BOARD OF GOVERNORS[1]

Integrating Clinical Care, Education, and Research

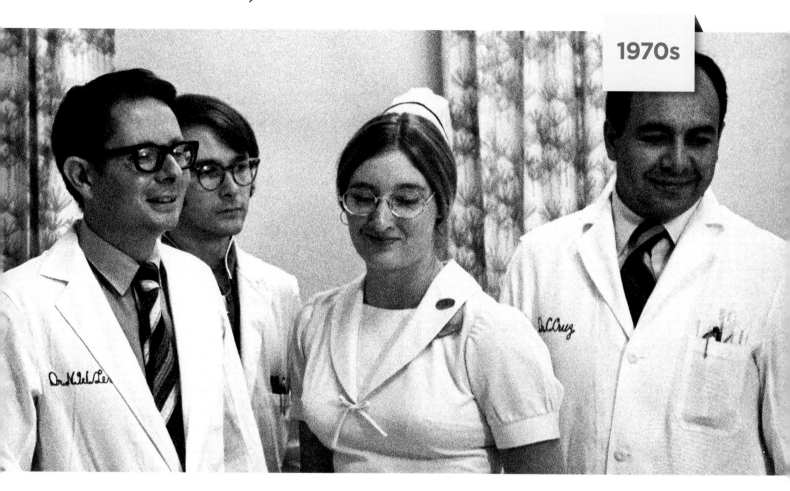

1970s

W ITH THE FORD FOUNDATION $100 MILLION GRANT SECURED, THE hospital could focus its efforts on building the world-class facility that it believed the money could deliver. While the ideal might seem obvious, research had previously been conducted somewhat independently of the hospital. With the birth of the Benson Ford Education and Research Center in 1977, the hospital now had a way of integrating scientific and clinical research.

The hospital continued to aggressively develop the next generation of medical leaders. It did so with the devotion of its staff, which generously shared its knowledge. Access to world-renowned experts made recruitment easier. A world of possibilities was open, but difficult choices lay ahead. It was apparent that the hospital could better steward the resources of the grant money by focusing on a few specific areas of research.

Dr. Nathan Levin, chief of Nephrology (center) on patient rounds with (from left) Joan Spilis, R.N.; Judy Moses, R.N.; Patricia Rykaczewski, dietitian; Dr. Jose Galvez; Dr. James Williams; unidentified nurse; and Dr. Cosme Cruz, 1972. *(Detail From the Conrad R. Lam Collection, Henry Ford Health System. ID=08-026.)*

"It was always difficult to identify where we should focus research," said Dr. Melvin Block, the former chairman of surgery at Henry Ford Hospital. "Was it going to be cancer? Transplantation? What was it going to be? What we did in surgery was to identify our objective to do our research, and it involved transplantation. … That later developed to liver transplantation, cardiac transplantation, and so forth, the full scope there. But that was all being developed during that period of time, which was exciting. Everything was a challenge, but really exciting everywhere."[2]

Pioneering Surgeries

While it may have been somewhat overshadowed by both the expansion plans and the outreach, another prong of hospital executive Stan Nelson's plan was to build Henry Ford Hospital into a nationally recognized center of excellence. This would be accomplished largely by continuing the tradition of research and pioneering medical procedures that had been a part of Henry Ford Hospital since its establishment.

During this time period, vascular surgery continued to expand. Drs. D. Emerick Szilagyi, Joseph Elliott, and Roger Smith had pioneered the first allogeneic kidney transplant—meaning the kidney was transplanted between relatives—in 1968. Dr. Roger Smith recalled the procedure:

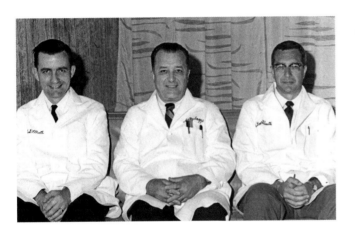

From Left: Drs. Joseph P. Elliott, D. Emerick Szilagyi, and Roger F. Smith, 1968. *(From the Conrad R. Lam Collection, Henry Ford Health System. ID=05-008.)*

We had two teams. There were two operating rooms next to each other. I was working to remove the kidney, and in the meantime, Szilagyi and Elliott had prepared the artery to receive the kidney. After I had finished, I took it next door and they made the vascular connections.

1970s

One of the nation's oldest free clinics, Cabrini Clinic in the Corktown neighborhood of Detroit, offers primary medical care, prescription assistance, mental health counseling, and health education to people of minimal means. Dr. J. Martin Miller, Dr. Martin Zonca, Dr. David Leach, and other doctors at Henry Ford Hospital volunteer there for patient care.

1970s

From the Conrad R. Lam Collection, Henry Ford Health System. ID=08-045.

Dr. J. David Carey becomes the director of the Ophthalmology residency training program in 1976 and serves in this position for 25 years. The program becomes one of the largest in the US. From left, standing: Drs. Gilbert O'Gawa, J. David Carey, Cornelius McCole. Seated: Drs. Jack Guyton and Philip Hessburg, c. 1974.

Then the urology chief, [A. Waite] Bohne, did the ureteral implant into the bladder, and that was very successful. That kidney worked for a short time, but it started to reject. Ultimately, the patient was re-transplanted successfully, this time with a cadaver transplant, and she went on and got a college education. … It was all very satisfactory, the way it worked out.[3]

Dr. Joseph Elliott, along with Drs. Edwin Guise and John Hageman, surgically reattached the arm of a 7-year-old girl—a complicated and rarely successful surgery at the time—who had been injured in a snow blower accident. With 18 months of therapy, the young girl regained significant use of the arm.[4]

"With the national reputation of the staff at Henry Ford Hospital, we attracted unusual cases, and we were in a large population group. There was not a lot of other competition, so a lot of special cases would gravitate to us," Dr. Roger Smith said.[5]

Above: Dr. A. Waite Bohne of the Department of Urology, c. 1970. *(From the Conrad R. Lam Collection, Henry Ford Health System. ID=08-002.)*

Left: Dr. Edwin R. Guise of the Department of Orthopedics with transplant patient Marcia Grimm in a Detroit television interview, 1972. *(From the Conrad R. Lam Collection, Henry Ford Health System. ID=08-003.)*

1970s

J. Edward Lundy suggests the Ford Land Development Company make a gift of 21 acres along Hubbard Drive near the Southfield Freeway to Henry Ford Hospital. This land is the site of the future Fairlane Medical Center.

From the Conrad R. Lam Collection, Henry Ford Health System. ID=08-052.

1970s

Dr. Lester Weiss (pictured) becomes chair of Pediatrics in 1974 and later also chief of Medical Genetics in 1980. He pioneered research in birth defects and the concept of satellite genetics clinics. His innovative telemedicine technology was featured by *Time* magazine in 1996.

It was certainly a time of significant advances. But even smaller forward movements would prove tremendously beneficial for patients. Dr. Donald Ditmars, division head emeritus of Plastic and Reconstructive Surgery, remarked:

It was not all major surgery. Some of it was minor surgery, such as what we now do in the clinics. I came along at the time when ambulatory surgery was first developed, which really made a big difference in how we did things. We used to admit people to the hospital after ganglion excisions on the wrist and carpal tunnel surgery. Now it's not only done as an outpatient in the ambulatory surgery unit, but it's also being done in the clinics. And that has been a real progress over a period of time. … We were at the forefront of that progress.[6]

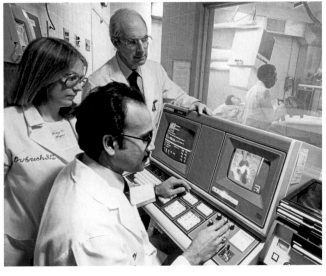

These groundbreaking surgeries, among other areas of medical expertise, provided young doctors with a rare opportunity to witness legends in the field in action. Dr. Robert Chapman, current director of the Josephine Ford Cancer Institute and then a resident in Internal Medicine in 1976, commented on his experience with two of his mentors:

When I came, some of the physician leaders were national icons at that time. The chairman of the Department of

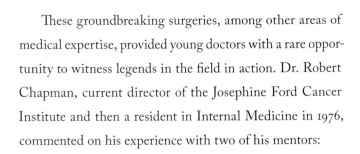

1970

1970

The Genetics Laboratory opens with early research studies by Drs. Charles (Gene) Jackson, Boy Frame, and Lester Weiss on the Amish communities in the Midwest. Pictured, from left: Drs. Lester Weiss and Gene Jackson, c. 1990.

Drs. Charles (Gene) Jackson, Melvin Block, and J. Martin Miller are among the first in the country to use calcitonin testing for the early detection of medullary thyroid cancers. The research is published in the *Annals of Internal Medicine* in 1973.

Diagnostic Radiology was Dr. William Eyler, who was one of the most prominent diagnostic radiologists in the country. Everyone knew that if you wanted an elegant interpretation of a chest X-ray, you sat down with Dr. Eyler, and he would point out things that the average person would never appreciate. There was Fred Whitehouse, who at the time was the head of Metabolism, certainly one of the most prominent diabetologists in the country. You couldn't help but spend time with him and just learn, even by osmosis. One of the things I've always felt about both Drs. Eyler and Whitehouse is that if one imagined what was meant by the phrase, 'a gentleman and a scholar,' these two were the absolute epitome of what that meant in the best possible sense.[7]

Henry Ford Hospital's group practice model was a catalyst to innovation, bringing together physicians and scientists from every field of medicine. Dr. Daniel Reddy, who joined the hospital in the 1970s and later became chief of Vascular Surgery, added:

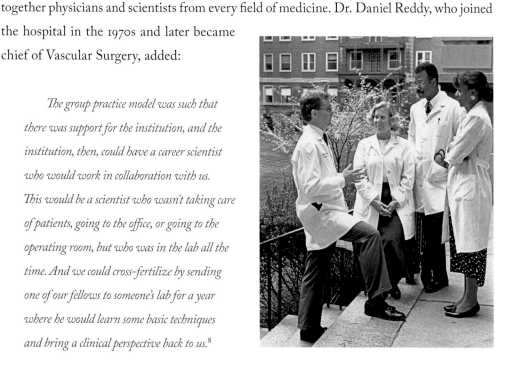

> *The group practice model was such that there was support for the institution, and the institution, then, could have a career scientist who would work in collaboration with us. This would be a scientist who wasn't taking care of patients, going to the office, or going to the operating room, but who was in the lab all the time. And we could cross-fertilize by sending one of our fellows to someone's lab for a year where he would learn some basic techniques and bring a clinical perspective back to us.[8]*

Above, from left: Dr. Fred Whitehouse, diabetes nurse Davida Kruger, and patient, 1989. *(From the Conrad R. Lam Collection, Henry Ford Health System. ID=08-016.)*

Left: Drs. Daniel Reddy, Vascular Surgery; Dorothy Kahkonen, Endocrinology; Raymond Littleton, Urology; and T. Jann Caison-Sorey, Primary Care, c. 1990. *(From the Conrad R. Lam Collection, Henry Ford Health System. ID=08-013.)*

1970

1970s

Dr. Enrique Enriquez, from Mexico City, comes to Henry Ford Hospital for a surgery residency from 1970 to 1973, followed by a vascular surgery fellowship from 1973 to 1974. He joins the staff of Emergency Medicine in 1974 and remains there until his retirement in 2013.

Dr. Sudha R. Kini (pictured, 1989) joins the pathology staff as director of the Cytopathology Laboratory. From Bombay, India, Dr. Kini came to Detroit earlier for her residency. Dr. Kini helps to establish fine needle aspiration as the preferred method to determine thyroid cancer. This pivotal study is published in *JAMA* with Dr. Kini and endocrinologist Dr. J. Martin Miller as the lead authors.

Above left: Dr. A. Michael Parfitt, 1977. Above right: Dr. Michael B. Kleerekoper (left) on patient rounds, c. 1990. *(From the Conrad R. Lam Collection, Henry Ford Health System. ID=08-051, 08-034.)*

A Time of Growth

The 1970s brought a renewed focus on recruiting new staff. Drs. Michael Parfitt and Michael Kleerekoper joined Dr. Boy Frame in the developing specialty of Bone and Mineral Disorders. This group, working with Dr. Harold Frost in bone research and Dr. Charles (Gene) Jackson in genetics research, came to be known internationally for osteoporosis research and treatment.[9] Others who would join at this time and become leaders in their specialty fields included Drs. Kenneth Greenawald, Pathology; Sudha Kini, Cytopathology Laboratory; Joseph Cerny, chief of Urology who helped to expand medical education; and Riad Farah and Ray Littleton, both in urology.

Dr. Ghaus Malik, a neurosurgery resident in the 1970s, worked with two renowned cerebrovascular neurosurgeons at Ford Hospital, Dr. Robert Knighton and Dr. James Ausman. Dr. Malik now has among the largest case experiences with cerebral aneurysms and

1970s

1970s

Dr. Kenneth A. Greenawald joins the Pathology staff in 1970, becoming department chair in 1977. Under his leadership, the Pathology laboratories across the health system began to be integrated in the 1990s. He is named medical director of the Henry Ford Health System's Integrated System Laboratories in 1996. Photo: c. 1990.

From the Conrad R. Lam Collection, Henry Ford Health System. ID=08-032.

Dr. Louis D. Saravolatz joins the Internal Medicine residency program, followed by a fellowship in Infectious Diseases. He serves as head of Infectious Diseases from 1982 to 1996. Photo: c. 1980.

From the Conrad R. Lam Collection, Henry Ford Health System. ID=08-036.

Left: Dr. Raymond Littleton, Department of Urology, performs a percutaneous nephroscope extraction to remove renal stones, 1983. Right: Dr. Ghaus Malik, Neurosurgery, c. 1980. *(From the Conrad R. Lam Collection, Henry Ford Health System. ID=08-008, 08-010.)*

arteriovenous malformations in the US. He became vice chair of neurosurgery at Ford Hospital and later simultaneously held the position of chief of neurosurgery at William Beaumont Hospital. Dr. Reddy, a future chief of the Division of Vascular Surgery, joined the residency program to work with Dr. Szylagyi, and rose to become one of the nation's recognized experts in aortic aneurysm surgery.

Ford Foundation Grant Provides for the Long Term

Administrator Stan Nelson, Chief of Medicine Dr. Richmond Smith, and Henry Ford II were able to secure a $100 million award from the Ford Foundation ($25 million for construction on the hospital campus and a $75 million endowment). While the number itself was impressive, the return on the investment was even more significant.

Five years after the grant was initially awarded—to be paid in installments over a decade—Institutional Strategy Associates of Boston provided an evaluation of the grant's results. The consultants—hired by the foundation to initially assess the hospital's fitness to receive such a grant—reported that 1 million patients had visited the hospital in 1977. That made Henry Ford Hospital the most-visited hospital in the country.[1]

The report also praised the hospital's commitment to the city, its undergraduate medical education program, and recruitment of new physicians: "In our view, Henry Ford Hospital is now, in the heath care mainstream of the 1970s,

fully contemporary on all fronts, and well-positioned to play a dynamic leadership role in American medical practice, with great future promise."[2]

Long term, the $75 million endowment produced significant income for research and other hospital needs. As of 2013, the endowment has produced more than $600 million in proceeds, with $350 million spent on the hospital. Of that $350 million, 68 percent has gone to research initiatives. Over the past decade about 64 percent of researchers receiving internal funding from the hospital also received outside grants from organizations such as the National Institutes of Health (NIH).[3]

Since the late 1980s, the endowment has supported research activities annually, ranging from $5 million in 1989 to $11 million in 2013. This research support by the endowment has directly contributed to growth in research grant funds received by the NIH and other sources, which reached $60 million in 2013.[4]

In 1971, Dr. Richard Nichols was named chair of the Department of Otolaryngology. He was one of the youngest chairs at Henry Ford Hopsital at the time. He would later be the first doctor at the hospital to implant a cochlear device in the attempt to give hearing to deaf patients.[10]

In 1979, Dr. Farouck Obeid joined the Division of Trauma and Emergency Surgery and Critical Care Medicine at Henry Ford Hospital. The Syrian native came to the United States to complete his surgical residency and a fellowship in vascular surgery. He was a devoted teacher, holding professorships at University of Michigan Medical School, Case Western University, and Michigan State University.[11] In addition, Dr. Obeid became the director of the Trauma Services and Minimally Invasive Surgery Center at Hurley Medical Center in Flint, Michigan.[12]

A Chance to Learn

While the hospital had first aligned with the University of Michigan in 1937, in 1969 a formal affiliation agreement would bring third- and fourth-year medical students to the facility to learn. The mix of a diverse population base in Detroit, along with the hospital's recognized leaders in their fields and groundbreaking medicine combined to deliver an excellent education.

"I went to medical school in a small town, and the clinical material wasn't that great. I wanted to be challenged more," said Dr. William A. Conway, who came to the hospital in 1973 as a resident. Dr. Conway joined the staff in the Division of Pulmonary Medicine in 1977. "A classmate of mine was in a residency here at Ford. He said, 'This is really unusual. You will see things that are only written about in textbooks.'"

Dr. Oscar Careterro: Hypertension Research Pioneer

In medical school in Argentina, Oscar Carretero was taught by Dr. Juan Fasciolo, who was part of a group of renowned Argentine physiologists pioneering work in hypertension research. That Argentine group identified a pressor substance which became known as angiotensin. Like his mentor, Dr. Carretero wanted to focus his career on hypertension research.

He came to Henry Ford Hospital in the 1960s after research work in Mendoza, Argentina; Basel, Switzerland; and the Cleveland Clinic in Ohio. The connection was a fellow Argentine who worked at Ford Hospital. Medicine Chair Dr. Richmond Smith Jr. and Metabolism Division Head Dr. Fred Whitehouse offered Dr. Carretero the opportunity to create a research program from scratch and have full freedom to pursue his ideas.

Today the Vascular and Hypertension Research Laboratory at Henry Ford Hospital

The young resident not only saw interesting cases, but he also had a front seat to significant changes in health care. He later served as the hospital's chief medical officer, chief quality officer, and as the CEO of Henry Ford Medical Group.

Many of the hospital's key future leaders started as a medical student or resident. This included Dr. Kimberlydawn Wisdom, currently senior vice president of Community Health and Equity, and the health system's chief wellness officer.

"There were a lot of physicians that were very interested in young medical students and just helping them understand the field of medicine," Dr. Wisdom said. "There were physicians who were trained during the war so they had to be trained very quickly, and they would share their experiences a lot. There was a lot of time to talk, to share experiences when you went on rounds, in between rounding with patients, eating lunch, evening meetings. There were a lot of opportunities to hear from senior leaders across the system and it really began to socialize you very much into the profession of medicine."

Dr. Wisdom recalled one summer between her first and second year of medical school, which she spent at the hospital:

Dr. Kimberlydawn Wisdom, c. 1980. *(From the Conrad R. Lam Collection, Henry Ford Health System. ID=08-048.)*

> *I had a tremendous opportunity to round with some of the best physicians, probably, in the country in terms of addressing the multidisciplinary needs of children that were affected by neurologic conditions and brain tumors, very intractable seizures. … While I learned about bedside manner, I learned a lot about how to talk to families and share very unpleasant diagnoses.*[13]

The skills acquired in the summer helped her make the shift to emergency medicine. "In the emergency department, you have to gain a skill of really getting to know people very quickly and earning their trust," Dr. Wisdom said. "That's what I was able to learn from

is world-renowned. Dr. Carretero is one of a few scientists ever to be awarded five Program Project research grants from the National Institutes of Health. He has brought in more than 75 million dollars in external funding, published over 390 manuscripts, trained more than 100 postdoctoral fellows, collaborated with hundreds of scientists, served as president of scientific organizations, and received major awards.

Dr. Carretero has greatly contributed to understanding the role of vasoactive hormones in the regulation of blood pressure and kidney function, as well as the pathogenesis of hypertension and target organ damage. He has pioneered the field of kinin research, showing that kinins act to regulate organ blood flow and kidney function as well as participate in both the acute antihypertensive effect and the chronic cardiovascular protective effect of angiotensin-converting enzyme and endopeptidase inhibitors.

Dr. Richmond Smith told Dr. Carretero "the sky's the limit" and Dr. Carretero is still following that advice as he continues his lifelong work in hypertension research and education.

1976

Dr. Thomas Fox, a staff physician since 1964 and division head of general surgery in 1968, founds the Division of Colon and Rectal Surgery. He remained in that position until he retired in 1995. He established the fellowship program in colon and rectal surgery in 1976 and served as program director until 1995.

1976

The Computed Tomography Scanning Center, featuring the first full-body scanner in Michigan, opens at Henry Ford Hospital.

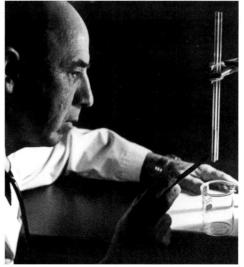

people like Dr. Hugh Walker and Dr. Gene Jackson, that you've got to develop that rapport with people very, very quickly, and especially when you're dealing with profoundly ill patients whose diagnoses were very challenging."[14]

Some of the hardest lessons were learned in the toughest times. Dr. William O'Neill, current medical director at the hospital's Center for Structural Heart Disease, was a fourth-year medical student on a rotation in cardiology at Ford Hospital when a 45-year-old patient was talking to him one minute. "Then all of a sudden, his eyeballs roll up and he drops over and he's done, a cardiac arrest. People tried to do CPR. I'd never seen anybody die before. It really struck me how catastrophic heart attacks were."

Educating these young physicians brought light moments, too. Dr. John Popovich spent his third year of medical school at Henry Ford Hospital as part of the relationship with the University of Michigan Medical School. He was invited to a party at one of the apartments—Georgetta—that housed residents. "I went down the steps into Georgetta and there's a man sitting there with a keg and he's pumping the keg and he said, 'Hey would you like a beer?' I said, 'Oh, absolutely.'" The keg operator and Dr. Popovich exchanged pleasantries

Opposite: Dr. Michael Tomlanovich (left) and Dr. Hyde Richardson (center) of Emergency Medicine, c. 1978. *(Detail From the Conrad R. Lam Collection, Henry Ford Health System. ID=08-017. Credit: Richard Hirneisen, Royal Oak, Michigan.)*

Above left: Dr. Loeto Mazhani and Dr. Hugh Walker (right) of the Department of Pediatrics, c. 1983. Dr. Walker established the pediatric neurology program at Ford Hospital.

Above: Dr. Charles (Gene) Jackson of Clinical Genetics, 1977.

1976

Dr. Cornelius (Con) McCole serves as acting chief of the Ophthalmology Department from 1976 to 1978 and as chief until 1992. He brought the department to a new level of excellence. He insisted on the highest standards in patient care and education. His genuine interest in people from a variety of walks of life made him beloved by many. His friend and former Ford auto executive J. Edward Lundy established an endowed chair in Dr. McCole's name.

1977

Dr. John Sigler (left), Dr. Jeanne Riddle, and Dr. Gilbert Bluhm, 1977, receive the Hektoen medal for their research in platelets and gout.

for a few minutes before Dr. Popovich asked the man's name. "He said, 'I'm Stan Nelson. I'm the president of the hospital.' Stan was a person who was genuine and he took the time to know a lot of people at the hospital. As a medical student and as a resident, your separation from administration is pretty significant. But you could always tell he was tremendously respectful and positive."[15] Beyond the fun, there was a heritage of education and investigation, as Dr. Popovich pointed out:

Education—which sometimes in academic institutions like medical school plays a lesser role than research—was a major focus of the academic enterprise here. All those individuals were people who wanted to train and mentor the next generation. They weren't necessarily sitting in a laboratory hoping not to be interrupted by an intern or resident. … I had the opportunity to walk into Fred Whitehouse's office and ask a question about diabetes. He wasn't bothered by it, but felt that it was the reason he was there, from an academic standpoint. … It was just a collaborative environment.[16]

Dr. David Leach, a pediatric endocrinologist who became the hospital's second director of medical education, joined the faculty in 1975. "One of the things I was interested in was teaching medical students, so I was looking after the 36 medical students from the University of Michigan as they rotated through the various departments."[17] Dr. Leach, who maintained his position as a pediatric endocrinologist, added, "To teach, you have to practice what you're teaching and demonstrate how you practice. You can't just go in a classroom and speak in the abstract."

From Left: Dr. Michael Eichenhorn, Dr. Joaquin Arciniegas, and Dr. John Popovich, chief residents, Internal Medicine, 1977–1978. *(From the Conrad R. Lam Collection, Henry Ford Health System. ID=08-047.)*

1977

The hospital's Division of Cardiovascular Medicine receives a grant from the Lilly Research Laboratories to study a new drug that stabilizes irregular heart rhythms in patients with coronary heart disease.

1977

The National Institutes of Health awards Dr. Oscar Carretero, director of the Hypertension and Vascular Research Laboratory, two grants to study the role of isorenin and pressor factors in hypertension.

1977

The hospital's switchboard and mailroom are overloaded when superstar Detroit Tigers pitcher Mark "The Bird" Fidrych is admitted for knee surgery. The hospital responds with the first press conference in its history, led by Development Officer William Wildern.

Research Takes Focus

The hospital was not waiting for the Ford Foundation grant to be delivered—or for the Benson Ford Eduation and Research Center building to be ready. Research was well underway on a number of fronts. In 1970, the hospital set up a state-of-the-art genetics laboratory. Dr. Charles (Gene) Jackson, who would later go on to be a noted researcher in genetics, including multiple endocrine neoplasia and muscular dystrophy, joined the team. He also would become head of the Third Medical Division and chief of the Clinical Genetics Division.[18] Dr. Boy Frame, an expert in bone and mineral diseases, and Dr. Lester Weiss in pediatrics, were also instrumental in creating the genetics lab. "You have to do research in medicine to advance knowledge," said Dr. Oscar Carretero, hired as director of the Hypertension Research Laboratory. "Research is a frustrating activity, but it's a fun activity. When you get things done and you show something new, it becomes very, very exciting."

When Dr. Carretero arrived in 1968, he was one of the first physicians hired in the medical group as a bench scientist. Previously, most bench research had been conducted as part of the Edsel B. Ford Institute. "When I started, the Henry Ford Hospital was known as an outstanding health care and educational organization with some clinical research," Carretero said. "There was very little basic research. In that regard, we were behind Mayo Clinic or the Cleveland Clinic. Now, I think that, thanks to the Ford Foundation grant and other grant funds, we have a large group that does research in multiple areas."

When the Benson Ford Education and Research Center opened in 1977, it provided a prime opportunity for scientists to come together under one roof—and remain connected to the hospital at large. The hospital also benefited from the National Institutes of Health (NIH)-funded Sleep Research Center, among the first of its kind in the United States, established by Dr. Thomas Roth. He recruited Drs. Frank Zorick and Mark Kaffeman.

Dr. David Leach of the Department of Internal Medicine, c. 1980. *(From the Conrad R. Lam Collection, Henry Ford Health System. ID=08-020.)*

1977

The hospital's recreation association organizes the first Henry Ford Hospital Olympiad on the grounds of the main campus. Joseph Madej, Debbie Babcock, Bob Scavone, Chuck Ruzicska, and Tom Ross help create the event.

1977

The Henry Ford Hospital apartments for students and house officers, designed by Albert Kahn Associates, open after two years of construction. The building is funded by a grant from the Kresge Foundation.

1977

Dr. Louise Liang of the Department of Pediatrics at Fairlane Center is appointed a White House fellow to assist the president and vice president with health care legislation.

From the Conrad R. Lam Collection, Henry Ford Health System. ID=Liang-Louise-L.

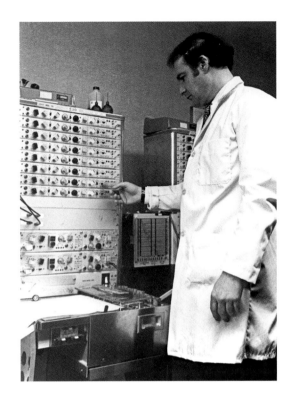

Dr. Thomas Roth of the Sleep Disorders Research Center, the first of its kind in the US, in 1978. Photo: c. 1980. *(From the Conrad R. Lam Collection, Henry Ford Health System. ID=08-022.)*

"We built a six-room laboratory, which was pretty big in those days," said Dr. Roth. "I had a tremendous amount of support from the institution in terms of doing this. They were very enthusiastic, and they saw this as the future. Henry Ford Hospital was visionary enough to undertake that."

Referrals came quickly, primarily from patients with sleep apnea, which causes sufferers to temporarily stop breathing during sleep. "One of the people who was highly motivated to recruit me and collaborate with me was Dr. Bill Conway from pulmonary medicine," said Dr. Roth. "The treatment for sleep apnea in those days was tracheotomy. A Ford ear, nose, and throat (ENT) surgeon named Shiro Fujita developed a new surgery for sleep apnea (uvulopalatopharyngoplasty), which was the mainstay of treatment until continuous positive air pressure was discovered. We also very quickly developed a strong relationship with the Department of ENT."

Current ENT chief Dr. Kathleen Yaremchuk, who joined the staff in 1984, recalled, "It was a really exciting time. Dr. Fujita recognized that some patients responded wonderfully to the new treatment whereas there was another group he called 'non-responders.' He spent the rest of his career trying to decide what produced the non-responders."

As the state's first ENT surgeon to become a certified sleep specialist, Dr. Yaremchuk noted, "In the last 10 years we were finally able to separate patients and predict which patients would do well or not with surgery. I worked with Dr. Fujita, and there was this great debt that I needed to carry on the tradition."

By 1979, Henry Ford Hospital's research programs had grown from 23 laboratories to 145 professionals in 31 laboratories with 160 projects and more than $6 million in grant funds.

1977

Actors Laurence Olivier and Tommy Lee Jones work with staff members at the Clara Ford Nurses Home for two weeks during the filming of the movie *The Betsy*.

1977

Wanda Szymanski, R.N., (pictured, left) in the neonatal intensive care unit, 1977. A longtime nurse at Henry Ford Hospital, Szymanski later became part of the team to develop the Bariatric Surgery Center.

Advances in Medicine

The 1970s were a time of significant growth in medical treatments and cancer breakthroughs throughout the world. At Henry Ford Hospital, Drs. Gene Jackson, Melvin Block, and J. Martin Miller were among the first in the country to test for the early detection of a specific familial thyroid cancer using the hormone calcitonin. For cancer patients in the 1970s, there was still significant progress to be made in treatment, as oncologist Dr. Robert Chapman remembered:

> *The mindset of those who treated cancer was, 'Okay, you have cancer. It's a terrible, deadly disease, so whatever side effects or toxicity you might have to put up with in terms of trying to treat it is worth it, because the disease is so bad.' At that time, there really wasn't a lot of emphasis on care designed to minimize the side effects of the patient who suffered either from the disease or the treatments. Both were brutal, and it was later, really in the early and mid-eighties, that people even began to think, 'Well, we should really focus on trying to dampen the side effects of the chemotherapy, the radiation, and the cancer itself.' That new emphasis changed the landscape of what cancer treatment was all about.*[19]

Dr. Shiro Fujita of the Department of Otolaryngology, c. 1984. *(From the Conrad R. Lam Collection, Henry Ford Health System. ID=08-023.)*

Cancer advances since the 1970s are proof that the Henry Ford Hospital model—merging laboratory and clinical research—paid off. As Dr. Chapman said:

> *I've always felt that clinical trials were absolutely essential to the practice of oncology, and the way I thought about it is that the state-of-the-art is fine for now, but it's not really acceptable for anybody. Nobody wants cancer care 10 years from now to be identical to what it is now. It's certainly much better in many areas than it was 10 years ago. We can't make it*

1978

Dr. Thomas Roth begins researching normal and pathological sleep processes and newly established sleep disorders.

1978

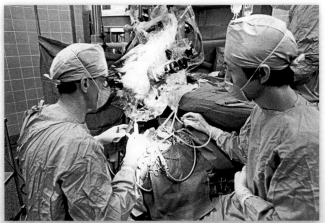

From the Conrad R. Lam Collection, Henry Ford Health System. ID=08-011.

Dr. James Ausman serves as chief of neurosurgery from 1978 to 1991. He became known as one of the premier neurovascular surgeons. Photo: Dr. Ausman (left) in surgery, c. 1979.

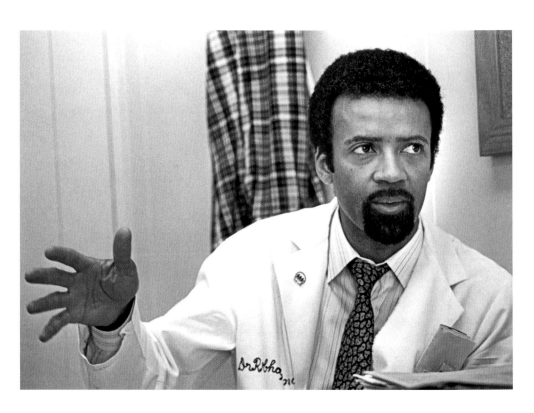

Right: Dr. Robert Chapman, c. 1986. *(From the Conrad R. Lam Collection, Henry Ford Health System. ID=08-049.)*

Bottom: Henry Ford II (right) with Edsel Ford II at the dedication of the Edsel B. Ford Center located at the Henry Ford West Bloomfield Medical Center, 1983. *(From the Conrad R. Lam Collection, Henry Ford Health System. ID=08-030.)*

better unless we come up with innovative new approaches, compare them to what we're doing already, and then make improvements, let that become the new standard, and then evaluate them against additional new ideas. This has led to many developments of greater understanding in molecular biology and molecular genetics, which we apply very directly to how we treat cancer. … All of this comes back to research, some of it in the lab, some of it at bedside, and most importantly, correlating what we've learned in the lab to how it will impact patients at the bedside.[20]

Henry Ford II: Behind the Scenes Supporter

When Benson Ford died, his brother Henry II succeeded him as chair of the Board of Trustees of Henry Ford Hospital in 1978. Henry II initially had been appointed to the Board when his father died, though he largely left the hospital business to his brother's care. Henry II had concerns of his own: the family's automotive business.

After his father Edsel's death in 1943, Henry Ford II was brought back from military service to assist with the running of Ford Motor Company. When his grandfather Henry retired in 1945, the title of Ford Motor Company chair was passed to Henry II.

With the motor company, Henry II's legacy was one of "managing it from the brink of disaster to the top rank of industrial power," as the *Los Angeles Times* reported at his death.[1] While the hospital's situation was not quite as dire, Henry Ford II's work on gaining the Ford Foundation a $100 million grant also helped position it as a top institution.

Progress in Understanding

Cancer treatment was not the only area seeing significant progress at the hospital. The 1970s brought tremendous advances in issues related to kidneys. In 1973, Dr. Stanley Dienst pioneered the first kidney transplant to a diabetic patient in Michigan. Just a year prior, the hospital had created the Division of Nephrology under the leadership of Dr. Nathan Levin.[21] Dr. Francis Dumler interned, served a residency, and then completed a fellowship in nephrology before joining the staff. He would serve as physician-in-charge of the Fairlane dialysis center. His research made possible significant strides in the understanding of diabetes' impact on kidney disease.

Cardiology was also seeing significant developments. In 1975—the 20th anniversary of its famed international cardiology symposium—the hospital again opened its doors to cardiologists from around the world. "The division at the time was small, made up of eight or 10 cardiologists who were doing a lot of different things and, in my estimation, doing them very well," said Dr. Sidney Goldstein, an Associate Professor at the University of Rochester who was appointed Division Head of Cardiology at Ford Hospital in 1974.

Dr. Stanley G. Dienst of Transplant Surgery, 1982. *(From the Conrad R. Lam Collection, Henry Ford Health System. ID=08-025. Credit: Joe Crachiola.)*

Dr. Goldstein had a prime view of the potential when research, education, and medicine were combined. "When I came, I thought it would be to develop some specialty interest within the division, and develop some areas of expertise that could be a focus for future clinical research and the cardiac catheterization laboratory, the [electrocardiograph] laboratory of the intensive care units," he said. "I saw those as areas where focused research, particularly clinical research, could provide a good environment for teaching and expand our expertise within the institution and in the community."

1978

Dr. Joseph Ponka becomes director at the West Bloomfield Center. He remains in this post until 1985.

1978

Dr. Robert S. Brown heads up the newly formed Division of Trauma and Emergency Surgery.

1978

Dr. Ellis J. Van Slyck becomes head of the Division of Hematology from 1978 to 1987. He codirected the weekly Hematology-Hematopathology conference for 10 years.

From left: Drs. Hani Sabbah and Paul Stein in the cardiovascular research laboratory, 1980. *(From the Conrad R. Lam Collection, Henry Ford Health System. ID=07-037.)*

Dr. Goldstein was later involved in planning the landmark beta-blocker heart attack trial, which studied the use of beta-blockers in the treatment of patients with acute myocardial infarction. "That study is probably the most important clinical research and had the most profound effect on cardiac mortality in the last half century," Dr. Goldstein said. "It decreased the mortality rate of patients with acute myocardial infarction by about 35 percent, which over the years has also become the quality standard for the treatment of acute myocardial infarction. Henry Ford Hospital provided the platform for me to develop and direct that research project."[22]

1979

Several Detroit companies, including General Motors, donate a former Howard Johnson's Motor Lodge to the hospital, which uses the building to house its School of Nursing and the Sleep Research Center.

1979

Negotiations between Henry Ford Hospital, Metro Health Plan, and business and labor leaders form the federally licensed Health Alliance Plan.

1979

The School of Nursing affiliates with University of Michigan Dearborn for first-year courses in biological and behavioral sciences.

1979

Dr. Joseph Beninson and Joseph Madej, the hospital's film director, win the Golden Eagle Award from the Council on International Non-Theatrical Events (CINE) for the film *Pressure Gradient Prophylaxis of Thrombosis.*

Dr. Sidney Goldstein (left) of the Division of Cardiology in consultation, c. 1980. *(From the Conrad R. Lam Collection, Henry Ford Health System. ID=08-027.)*

Eleanor Clay Ford and Benson Ford: Decades of Support

With 53 years as an active member of the hospital's Board of Trustees, Eleanor Clay Ford—Edsel's widow—remained an important connection to the hospital's founding family. She joined the hospital board just a few years after her marriage to Edsel, juggling motherhood of her four children with her charitable works. At her death in 1976, she had seen the Ford family's commitment to the hospital transition to her children.

"I cannot emphasize enough that if it had not been for Mrs. Eleanor Ford, there would just not be a Henry Ford Hospital as we know it today," Dr. Clarence Livingood, the hospital's chair of the Department of Dermatology from 1953–1976, once said.[1] The Eleanor Clay Ford Pavilion at Henry Ford Hospital was named in her honor.

While other members of Edsel and Eleanor's family supported the hospital, second son Benson became chairman of the Board of Trustees in 1947 and held the position until his death in 1978. He oversaw significant growth, including the addition of the clinic building and, upon securing the Ford Foundation grant, the Education and Research Building, which was named in his honor. Like his father, Benson Ford died relatively young—at age 59—after several years of ill health.[2]

Benson's wife, Edith, was also involved in the hospital's board, serving for 36 years and continuing to financially support the hospital until her death in 1980.[3]

Benson was at the helm when the West Bloomfield land was purchased with the vision to build a hospital there one day. "He'd be very proud and honored to be part of the growth and development of a fantastic world-class hospital in the suburbs and the neighborhoods," Benson Ford Jr. said of his father. "I believe that Henry Ford Hospital is part of the glue that's holding the city together now, too."[4]

New Leaders Take Hold

The 1970s had seen a significant shift in the world—and at Henry Ford. Medicine showed new promise and research led to important discoveries. The hospital had taken the first steps towards its future with the birth of the satellite system, all while remaining committed to the city of Detroit through its community services.

As the decade came to a close, several changes would be needed on the Board of Trustees. First, Eleanor Clay Ford died in 1976. She had served on the hospital's Board for 53 years. Son Benson Ford—chair of the Board of Trustees—died in 1978, followed by the death of his wife Edith McNaughton Ford in 1980. She had served on the Board since 1943.

Though the Ford family lost Eleanor, Benson, and Edith within a short span, other members of the family continued their commitment to the hospital. Benson was succeeded by his brother Henry II, who served as Board chair from 1978–1983. And Edsel Ford's remaining children, Josephine and William Clay, continued on the Board until the early 1980s.

Hospital leadership was changing, too. Dr. Thomas Killip (of the Killip classification scheme) joined as chief of the Department of Medicine, succeeding Dr. Richmond Smith in 1979, while Dr. Melvin Block succeeded Dr. D. Emerick Szilagyi as chair of the Department of Surgery in 1975. He was followed by Dr. Roger Smith in 1979.

Together, these new leaders would be vital in helping Henry Ford Hospital grow and respond to a rapidly changing business environment.

Opposite: (From left, seated) Benson Ford, Edith McNaughton Ford, Stanley R. Nelson. (Back row) Lynn McNaughton Ford (Alandt) and Henry Ford Health Service Award recipients, c. 1970. *(From the Conrad R. Lam Collection, Henry Ford Health System. ID=08-029.)*

1979

1980

Henry Ford Hospital's cardiology staff, led by Dr. Fareed Khaja, pioneers use of coronary angioplasty, the balloon procedure that revolutionizes heart patient care.

Dr. C. Paul Hodgkinson (center) is honored by his former staff, including Dr. Dorothy Porter (far left), Dr. Richard Smith (left), and Dr. Brent Davidson (fourth from right).

From the Conrad R. Lam Collection, Henry Ford Health System. ID=03-039.

Dr. Hodgkinson began his career at Henry Ford Hospital in 1937 and served as chief of Obstetrics and Gynecology from 1958 to 1973. He was renowned for his research in breast cancer detection and urinary incontinence. Photo c. 1980s.

CHAPTER

Nine

"*Acquisitions or partnerships, joint ventures, those are the ways of the private sector. That's the way you grow, that's the way you handle competition. And I thought those were astute ways for Henry Ford to expand its tentacles in all of the markets without having to do all of the construction that it would take in order for that to happen. It was consistent with a strategic plan that says, 'We believe our model is the best and we want to work with other organizations and seed our model into those organizations as well. Acquire them, if necessary, and become the dominant health system in metropolitan Detroit.' And that's what Henry Ford has done.*"

Walter Douglas Sr.
LONGTIME BOARD OF TRUSTEES MEMBER[1]

The Business of Health Care

Aerial view of the Maplegrove
Treatment Center, c. 1980.
*(Detail From the Conrad R.
Lam Collection, Henry Ford
Health System. ID=09-039.)*

I N THE 1980S, THE BUSINESS WORLD WAS CHANGING. COMPUTERS AND OTHER TECH-
nological advances were beginning to make an impact. Many businesses found that
survival would come through dominating a market, which would come by acquiring
competitors as well as expanding into new territories.

The hospital world—and Henry Ford Hospital in particular—would find itself in a
similar position. It was the era of major hospital mergers for nonprofits and for-profits alike.
The mergers coincided with dramatic shifts in the way hospitals and physicians were paid,
both through insurers and government programs.

Detroit was changing, too. Japanese automakers had come to the United States to build
plants—but not in Michigan. Chrysler struggled, posting a $1.1 billion loss in 1979. The fol-
lowing year, the federal government guaranteed loans totaling $1.5 billion to keep
Chrysler solvent.[2]

From the Conrad R. Lam Collection, Henry Ford Health System. ID=09-027.

From the Conrad R. Lam Collection, Henry Ford Health System. ID=09-001.

Henry Ford Hospital would meet these shifting business demands head on, serving diverse populations in the urban core and growing suburbs. By the end of the decade the hospital would look dramatically different.

Above: The Eleanor Clay Ford Pavilion at Henry Ford Hospital, 1982.

Above right: Detroit Mayor Coleman Young (center) at the dedication ceremony of the Eleanor Clay Ford Pavilion with (from left) Doug Peters, hospital executive; Erma Henderson, city council member; Henry Ford II; Cynthia Ford; and Kathleen DuRoss Ford, 1982.

Responding to Community Needs

As 1980 dawned, the hospital began work on a five-story addition, the Eleanor Clay Ford Pavilion. When it was opened in 1982, the addition brought new operating rooms, a modern emergency facility, intensive care units, and a new radiology facility.[3] In all, the hospital had added 210,000 additional square feet of space to serve growing demand.

The early part of the decade also brought the development of the William Clay Ford Center for Athletic Medicine, named in Ford's honor for his significant contribution. The focus on the field of sports medicine was groundbreaking at the time. The center offered orthopedics, physical therapy, and athletic fitness programs to help injured athletes heal and provided educational oppor-

1980s   1980

From the Conrad R. Lam Collection, Henry Ford Health System. ID=09-038.

Henry Ford Hospital opens more satellite medical centers and expands existing centers. Photo: Thelma Breech and her sons, Robert and William Breech, at the dedication of the Ernest and Thelma Breech Pavilion at the Fairlane Medical Center in Dearborn, 1981.

Dr. Joseph Ponka completes the textbook *Hernias of the Abdominal Wall*.

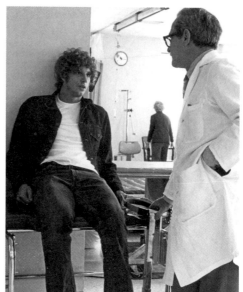

tunities for medical professionals to prevent injuries. As team physician for the Detroit Tigers, Dr. Clarence Livingood worked closely with the orthopedic specialists in the care of the athletes. The Department of Orthopedics and the Center for Athletic Medicine specialists also served as team physicians throughout the years for the Detroit Tigers, Lions, Red Wings, Pistons, and Shock.

During this time, the hospital also continued its move into the suburbs. It opened new satellite centers in Sterling Heights, Plymouth-Canton, and Royal Oak. The hospital's largest venture occurred during the early part of the decade. William Clay Ford and his wife, Martha Firestone Ford, were responsible for the hospital's recognition of the need to treat alcohol and chemical dependency. Their commitment resulted in the establishment of the Maplegrove Center, an inpatient and outpatient substance abuse treatment facility in West Bloomfield.

When Maplegrove opened in 1981, former First Lady Betty Ford—a longtime advocate for those dealing with addictions—came to the dedication ceremony. She also spoke before

Above left: Gail Warden (left) and Bill Ford Jr. at the William Clay Ford Center for Athletic Medicine, 1996. (From Henry Ford Health System. ID:101494_819.)

Above: Dr. Clarence S. Livingood with Detroit Tigers baseball player Mark Fidrych at Henry Ford Hospital, 1977. (From the Conrad R. Lam Collection, Henry Ford Health System. ID=09-002.)

1980

Henry Ford Hospital's archives are established by Sladen Library director Nardina Mein and Dr. Conrad Lam. The archives are later named in honor of Dr. Lam.

1980

Dr. Charles Barone joins the Henry Ford Hospital staff. He later becomes chair of the Department of Pediatrics. Photo: Dr. Barone, 1994.

William Clay Ford, Sr. and Martha Firestone Ford at the Maplegrove Treatment Center, c. 1980s. *(From the Conrad R. Lam Collection, Henry Ford Health System. ID=09-010.)*

the Economic Club of Detroit, advocating for treatment of alcoholism and pointing to Maplegrove as an innovative solution.[4]

Addiction challenges presented learning curves for all involved, including Maplegrove's Board of Trustees. "I had to learn about chemical dependency, about alcoholism," said Jane Muer, founding Maplegrove Board of Trustees chair. "All of our trustees on that board had to learn about what this was. It's a different type of medicine than being a heart surgeon, a neurologist. It is very difficult being a doctor in psychiatry and a doctor that is involved with behavioral health."[5] Dr. Michael F. Boyle III, an internist at Bi-County Hospital, became medical director of the Maplegrove Center in 1984. He also served with Dr. Livingood as team physician for the Tigers. A specialist in Addiction Medicine, Dr. Boyle became a beloved physician at Maplegrove, where he worked until his death in 2011.

Dr. C. Edward Coffey, who became chief of Psychiatry in 1996 and later CEO of Henry Ford Behavioral Health Services, called substance abuse "one of the most prevalent mental illnesses." He cited the organization's "long history of a commitment to understanding

1981

The William Clay Ford Center for Athletic Medicine (CAM) is established by the Department of Orthopedics. CAM is housed in the old education building on Ford Hospital's campus until the new athletic and fitness center opens nearby.

1981

Robert and Marjorie Herndon donate 500 acres of land to Henry Ford Hospital, including the Rush Lake Hills Golf Club. The proceeds from events held at the course assist in funding cancer research and patient needs.

substance abuse, to understanding addiction and to its treatment, and that commitment has been nowhere better manifest than in the creation of Maplegrove Center. ... The Ford family has been very instrumental in this facility, which today continues to save lives by the thousands every year."[6]

Benson Ford Jr., son of the longtime Board of Trustees chairman Benson Ford, was—by his own admission—one of those lives saved. "Once I walked through the doors of Maplegrove, I gave up my resistance to fighting drug use and alcoholism. I just listened to them, listened to their messages, listened to their lectures, and took it one day at a time."[7]

Addiction services quickly expanded with the addition of a Youth Treatment Center in 1985 and programs at the hospital's campus, in Dearborn, and in Troy. Thomas Groth was named director of operations for the substance abuse program at Henry Ford Hospital, and worked closely with Maplegrove. In 1988, Groth, who later became interim chief of Henry Ford Hospital, worked with Sis Wenger to train community volunteers who then presented education programs throughout the city.[8] The community education program was later recognized by President Ronald Reagan.

Dr. Michael Boyle. *(From the Conrad R. Lam Collection, Henry Ford Health System. ID=09-046.)*

Expansion of Services

The 1980s were a time ripe for health care expansion. Under President Reagan, the diagnosis-related group (DRG) payment system for health care began. These fiscal changes for the health industry in the 1980s produced consolidation of hospitals and development of the corporate-led health system. The hospital's board reorganized in 1983, incorporating Henry Ford Health Care Corporation to oversee the hospital and its two subsidiaries: Henry Ford Fairlane Health Services, which would explore new business opportunities, and Greenfield Health System Corporation, which primarily offered dialysis.

1981

From the Conrad R. Lam Collection, Henry Ford Health System. ID=09-008.

Sis Wenger (left, with Tom Groth) establishes Maplegrove Community Education, staffed by volunteers from the Junior League of Birmingham. This program later wins a US Presidential award.

1981

Former First Lady Betty Ford speaks at the dedication of Maplegrove Center in West Bloomfield, which specializes in the treatment of substance abuse.

From the Conrad R. Lam Collection, Henry Ford Health System. ID=09-006.

The board reorganization had a practical purpose, in addition to better serving growing needs. Henry Ford II had just retired from Ford Motor Company when he was recruited to the Henry Ford Hospital Board of Trustees after his brother Benson's death. Robert J. Vlasic, who served on the Henry Ford Hospital Board at the time, remembered persuading Henry Ford II to come aboard. "He said, 'I'm not taking on any more responsibilities,' " said Vlasic. "And we kept pestering him and said, 'Look, we'll do it any way you want to do it.' He said, 'If you set up the organization so that I only had one person reporting to me and we only had two meetings a year and one of those in Palm Beach, I'd consider it.' And that was the birth of the system."[9] Henry II served as chairman of the Henry Ford Health Care Corporation (HFHCC) while Vlasic was the only one reporting to him as chairman of the hospital's Board of Trustees.

Robert J. Vlasic, Henry Ford Hospital Board Trustee, 1981. *(From the Conrad R. Lam Collection, Henry Ford Health System. ID=09-013.)*

Over the course of the next few years, HFHCC expanded its business via affiliations and partnerships. In 1986, the hospital affiliated with Kingswood Hospital, a psychiatric inpatient facility that had been founded 20 years prior. Cottage Hospital in Grosse Pointe and its two related nursing homes also affiliated with HFHCC in 1986. And in 1988, the corporation signed a 20-year agreement with the city of Wyandotte to operate the hospital there.[10]

Wyandotte was a community hospital in every sense of the word. "These are people taking care of their neighbors," said William Alvin, who became Wyandotte Hospital's CEO in 1991. "These nurses who worked at Wyandotte Hospital, they weren't just taking care of people that they didn't know. It's a key asset to that community. The people who work there are primarily the people who live in that community. And Wyandotte Hospital particularly was made up of a core of very loyal, very capable employees and doctors, and that was the core of it and the intrinsic link with the community itself."[11]

1981

Dr. K. M. A. Welch arrives at Henry Ford Hospital as the founding chairman of the Department of Neurology. Dr. Welch becomes an internally renowned neurologist, establishing both an NIH-funded Stroke Center and NIH-funded Headache Center at Ford Hospital.

1982

Dr. Mary Cantrell (pictured, 1977) is appointed chair of the Department of Anesthesiology at Henry Ford Hospital, making her the first woman to chair any medical department at the hospital.

From the Conrad R. Lam Collection, Henry Ford Health System. ID=06-024.

Caring for the Patient Wherever Needed

Good medical care does not end when patients leave the hospital or physician's office. Ensuring that they have the care they need for the next stage is vital. Henry Ford Health System's Community Care Services (CCS) provides services that range from annual eye exams to end-of-life care.

Before CCS began, hospital case managers would work with patients after their hospital stay to determine where the patient could find services. But just as the hospital saw potential in ambulatory services when no one else did, adding another level of care made sense. "This was no different than owning an ambulatory system and building the continuum of care," said John Polanski, president and CEO of CCS since 1990.[1]

CCS grew out of Greenfield Health Corporation, which offered outpatient services such as dialysis, and Fairlane Health Services, which focused on new business development. Polanski had recommended the hospital start a home health products arm in 1982. The hospital also provided hospice care. Eventually it made sense to merge all of the entities into CCS.

By 2014, CCS had expanded to serve virtually any health need outside of a hospital or doctor's office. Whether a patient needed a private-duty nurse, home health care, pharmacy services, or medical supplies, CCS had a program that was available to help. Home health care also saw growth in the use of technology, including: Home Care, which offered a medication dispensing service; Lifeline, an emergency response system; and Telehealth, a remote monitoring system for chronic conditions. Regarding the future of CCS, Polanski stated:

The Henry Ford Health System is well-positioned, as we continue to integrate and bring the pieces forward, for how I believe health care is going to be delivered in the future. Whether it's what we're doing with home health care or telemedicine or pharmacy or home dialysis or even Henry Ford OptimEyes or hospice, these programs will all play a very significant role in how health care is delivered in the future. I think, ultimately, the government is looking at quality. I think we've built very high-quality programs. And I think they're looking at cost. There's no doubt that hospitals or inpatient facilities are incredibly expensive and that we need to learn, as an organization, how to transition patients who are on that continuum of care. We have to continue looking for ways that we can provide the very best quality but also at the very best price. In the long term, I see this division only growing and expanding because those service offerings that we've started with are going to get more complicated, more important.[2]

Community Care Services includes:

• Henry Ford Health Products, a medical supply retailer with 10 retail sites.

• Fairlane Home Infusion, which provides education and supplies for in-home intravenous care.

• Ambulatory Pharmacy Services, operating 23 retail pharmacies.

• Greenfield Health Systems, dialysis services in two states.

• Henry Ford Extended Care, a private-duty service.

• Henry Ford Home Health Care, a Medicare-certified home health care agency.

• Henry Ford Continuing Care Corporation, operating two long-term care facilities.

• Henry Ford Hospice

• Henry Ford Center for Senior Independence.

• Occupational Medicine, providing five on-site contracted industrial medical clinics and three clinics located at Henry Ford Satellites.

• Henry Ford OptimEyes, including 20 optical sites.

Above: The Kingswood Psychiatric Hospital, c. 1986. *(From the Conrad R. Lam Collection, Henry Ford Health System. ID=06-025.)*

Above right: Christine Cole Johnson, Ph.D., c. 1995. *(From the Conrad R. Lam Collection, Henry Ford Health System. ID=09-018.)*

Henry Ford Hospital continued its emphasis on satellite centers, too. As the suburbs grew, it became clear that large parcels of land would be harder to purchase. Just as it had done in the 1970s when it launched its first two clinics, the health system strategically began purchasing large parcels of land in areas in which it planned to grow.

Without the growth—and diversification of business interests—that occurred during this period, Henry Ford Hospital would look very different today. "I think the satellites also helped us acquire the suburban hospitals," said Dr. Vinod Sahney, former senior vice president of the health system.[13]

The diversification served the research interest, too. "Because it's this system, you have populations and communities that you can study," Dr. Christine Cole Johnson said. Later the chair of the Department of Public Health Sciences, Dr. Johnson joined the health system in 1985 as an epidemiologist. "A health system more representative of the general population is more of a real-world setting to do research."[14]

1982

Henry Ford Hospital establishes the Home Health Care program.

1982

Stanley Nelson serves as chairman of the American Hospital Association Board.

1982

From the Conrad R. Lam Collection, Henry Ford Health System. ID=09-040.

Dr. Joseph Shore, who joined the Edsel B. Ford Institute for Medical Research in 1966, becomes Director of Research for Henry Ford Hospital. He also served as chief of Biochemical Research and received two US patents for his work.

Changing Payment System

In 1983, in the midst of the rapidly changing health care environment, the federal government—typically one of the largest lines of business for a hospital—made some of the most dramatic changes to Medicare and Medicaid since the program's inception. The new DRG

Cottage Hospital: A Long History, Poised for the Future

The influenza epidemic of 1917 first brought Cottage Hospital to Grosse Pointe, Michigan.[1] As the village grew into a town, it became a popular location for some of Detroit's wealthiest families, including the Fords.

While it did not officially affiliate with the Ford family's other medical facility— Henry Ford Hospital—until 1986, Cottage Hospital remained close to the Ford family's interest. Soon after the acquisition, John Polanski, president and CEO of Community Care Services since 1990, witnessed a conversation between Henry Ford II, chairman of the Board of Trustees for Henry Ford Health Care Corporation, and Stan Nelson, hospital executive:

The conversation revolved around Mr. Ford asking Stan, "How are you going to run the place now that you have two hospitals?" And for the first time in my life, I saw Stan short on words. I could see that he really wasn't giving Mr. Ford the kind of answers Mr. Ford wanted, and I recall being deathly afraid that they were going to ask me, and I'll tell you, I did not have the answer. And after what seemed to be a half hour—it was probably 10 minutes—Mr. Ford put his hands on his knees and looked at Stan, and he said, "Stan, you're going to run Cottage Hospital like I run my truck division. You're going to make sure you have good leadership there, and then you're going to leave them alone. You're not going to bring them into these everyday meetings that large corporations have. You're not going to expose them to the bureaucracy that is inherent in a large organization. Make sure you have leadership, give them the vision, and let them go."[2]

In 1998, Cottage Hospital was acquired as part of the Bon Secours Hospital, forming Bon Secours Cottage Health Services. Henry Ford Health System (HFHS) owned 30 percent of the joint venture. In 2007, Cottage become owned solely by HFHS.[3]

By 2010, Cottage Hospital had been converted into a multi-specialty outpatient center. Henry Ford Medical Group added more than a dozen outpatient specialties and boosted the number of physicians. It also added a senior center and expanded women's health services and athletic medicine.

"There is a great need for a contemporary ambulatory surgery center in that market," Bob Riney, HFHS' chief operating officer said. "Ambulatory care can be difficult to do successfully for some hospitals. At Henry Ford, it is a strength for us."[4]

payment system offered predetermined payments based on the diagnosis regardless of the actual cost of treatment. Steve Velick, president of Greenfield Health Systems at the time and later CEO of Henry Ford Hospital, said:

It was revolutionary. We knew we had to focus on the business aspect of how we ran things and create accountability. I think it was philosophically, "How do we run this like a business? How do we hold people accountable? How do we still, as part of that, deliver high-quality care?" So it was really broadening the responsibility and creating alignment in not just top leadership but throughout a business unit, an organization.[15]

From left: Sandy Herring, Steve Velick, and Sandra Dorsey, at the Henry Ford Quality Expo, 1990. *(From the Conrad R. Lam Collection, Henry Ford Health System. ID=09-024.)*

It was not just the government payments that were changing. Around the same time, health maintenance organizations (HMOs) had become one of the largest types of insurance. Henry Ford Hospital executive Stan Nelson immediately saw the potential in tying together the HMO movement with the hospital's emphasis on ambulatory care services in the suburbs. "There would be synergy between the health plan and the clinic-service plan," Nelson said. "If you get a new program going, it's going to open up new options that you could never anticipate without the new program."[16]

The United Auto Workers (UAW), with the support of Ford Motor Company, was seeking an alternative plan to the union-managed HMO which had been established in the

1980s

1980s

Drs. Michael Tomlanovich, Richard Nowak, and Gerard Martin—each of whom serves as chief of Emergency Medicine at separate times across the decades—begin research studies to improve emergency care of cardiac arrest.

From the Conrad R. Lam Collection, Henry Ford Health System. ID=09-041.

Volunteers always play a crucial role in helping at Henry Ford Hospital and other facilities. Photo: Georgetta Woodson, hospital volunteer, and Dan O'Donnell at the Henry Ford Hospital information desk, 1985.

With the addition of the health care products business, the health system offered various services to patients recovering at home. This employee works on fabrication for a wheelchair, HealthCore, Southfield, 1997. *(From Henry Ford Health System. ID:101494_732.)*

late 1950s. In 1979, the UAW's Metropolitan Hospital and Health Centers, and Metro Health Plan, Inc., partnered with Henry Ford Hospital to create the Health Alliance Plan (HAP).[17] By 1986, HAP became part of the health system.

"A lot of hospitals tried and failed, mostly because they didn't understand the business," Nelson said. "They didn't understand it was a different business. You couldn't assign an assistant administrator from the hospital to run an HMO. You had to hire somebody who understood HMOs and insurance, and health concerns. I think it served a very good purpose for the organization. And it's very synergistic with the ambulatory care people."[18] It was not an easy integration, however. Douglas Peters, who joined Henry Ford Hospital in 1977 and later served as its president, noted:

1980s

Dr. John Popovich in the Division of Pulmonary Medicine and his colleagues work to establish critical care units at Ford Hospital. The first such units are set up in the M-Unit building. By 1989, construction begins to add a sixth floor onto the Eleanor Clay Ford Pavilion to house 36 intensive care beds.

1982

The Eleanor Clay Ford Pavilion is dedicated. Eleanor Clay Ford served on the Ford Hospital's Board of Trustees from 1919 to 1973. The five-story building houses a new emergency center, operating rooms, radiology, and intensive care units.

1982

From the Conrad R. Lam Collection, Henry Ford Health System. ID=10-005.

Betsy Brieder, R.N., "capping" Cynthia Criger, R.N., at her graduation from the Henry Ford Hospital School of Nursing. Ford Hospital nurse graduates wore a white cap with black band, whereas the nursing students wore a plain white cap. All nursing schools in the US designed their own caps to distinguish their graduates.

The Health Alliance Plan
building in Detroit, c. 1990.
*(From the Conrad R. Lam
Collection, Henry Ford Health
System. ID=09-025.)*

*The whole concept of an HMO is to promote health
and keep people out of doctors' offices and hospitals.
And the intent of the hospital portion of our organization
was to treat, care for, rehabilitate, etcetera. So there was
a natural tension, but over time, I think, it became
obvious that having the Health Alliance Plan was a
significant factor in our relationships with Blue Cross
Blue Shield of Michigan and other insurers. They knew
we had that capacity and we could promote it and
market it and gain enrollment and take care of a
population that would not necessarily be any longer with
Blue Cross. So it created, initially, some internal challenges and tensions. Externally, those
tensions were by design, and we welcomed them.[19]*

In-Home Care

The coming changes to reimbursements—particularly the Medicare payments—drew John
Polanski's attention. Polanski, who had started at the hospital as a respiratory therapist and
later became director of that program, thought that the reimbursement changes would drive
a need for home health care products. He considered leaving the hospital to start his own
home health venture when Stan Nelson urged him to stay and start the new business for the
health system. "We started with very specific focus on the home health care products and
services," said Polanski, longtime CEO of the health system's Community Care Services
business unit. "Along the way, we developed many products and services that, I think, create great value. We're currently organized as 11 unique businesses, a very diverse portfolio,

1983

The Henry Ford Health Care Corporation is formed as the parent
organization of the hospital and
two subsidiaries: Fairlane Health
Services, for the development of
new business, and Greenfield Health
Systems Corporation, for varied
services, including kidney dialysis.
Henry Ford II is chair of the Corporation Board and Robert Vlasic serves
as chair of the Board of the hospital.

1984

The Lakeside Medical
Center groundbreak-
ing for a new facility.
Photo, from left: Mike
Proach, Mike Slubowski,
Michigan's Lieuten-
ant Governor Martha
Griffiths, Dr. Jan
Radke, and Dr. Bruce
Steinhauer, 1984.

that all contribute significantly to Henry Ford Health System, both financially and in terms of creating great service for our patients and our customers."[20]

Henry Ford Hospital's first venture into home health actually started a few decades earlier with the nurses. Elizabeth Moran, director of the School of Nursing, had hired Genevieve Dunworth in 1950 to work in the hospital and teach in the nursing school. In 1953, Dunworth began coordinating care for the hospital's patients who needed home care. It was one of the

James Walworth, c. 1980.

From the Conrad R. Lam Collection, Henry Ford Health System. ID=09-042.

Health Alliance Plan (HAP) Rounds Out Health Offerings

Whereas the auto magnate Henry Ford founded a hospital for his auto workers and the community, the United Auto Workers (UAW) President Walter Reuther can be considered the founder of the first health maintenance organization plan in Detroit.

Health Alliance Plan's (HAP) origins date to 1956 when Walter Reuther sought an alternative to traditional health insurance for union members. The UAW purchased Metropolitan Hospital in 1958, formed a salaried physician group practice, and created the Community Health Association (CHA) as a health plan that revolutionized the way health care is delivered in Michigan.

Opened in 1960, the CHA had many features today's consumers would recognize: an office visit copayment; a monthly premium; and preventive care coverage that encouraged members to schedule regular physical exams. President Roosevelt's daughter, Anna Roosevelt, was one of CHA's first employees. She referred to CHA as "The New Deal in Health Care." In 1972, CHA was renamed Metro Health Plan Inc.

During the 1970s, Ford Motor Company wanted all of its employees to have the same type of health plan. The auto company utilized the medical expertise of Henry Ford Hospital physicians. Ford Motor commissioned California's Kaiser Permanente to study the Detroit market. The Kaiser study indicated that an integrated health care delivery system with a health plan could inspire community support and offer a viable alternative to traditional health care coverage.

Negotiations between Henry Ford Hospital, Metropolitan Hospital and Health Centers, and Metro Health Plan forged a new partnership in 1979—the Health Alliance Plan.

"Prevention, regular doctor visits, and health education were part and parcel of the health plan. That was a much broader approach than just taking care of people when they were sick, and that was the pivotal difference between HMOs and traditional health care coverage," said William Alvin, a former President of HAP. "There was also a focus on efficient use of care—delivered at the right time, in the right setting."

As Henry Ford satellites opened, HAP brought new patients there, and as HAP expanded its membership, Henry Ford doctors were there in the communities to care for them. "There was tremendous synergy, mutual growth, and benefit between HAP and Henry Ford at that time," said Alvin.

In 1986, HAP joined the Henry Ford Health System. "Our experience was witnessed by hospital systems across the country as a successful integrated model that could be brought into their communities," said James Walworth, the founding president of HAP. "Among the elements was that a hospital-based medical group could get into the marketplace through a health plan. Around Michigan, in particular, some healthcare plans are associated with a health system and hospitals."

earliest services of its kind, drawing coordinators from around the country to see how Henry Ford Hospital provided for its patients in this way. Dunworth retired in 1980, creating the need—and the opportunity—for a more formal home health nursing program.

Greg Solecki, who had been in the Human Resources Department since 1976, was tapped to head home health care, which launched in 1982. Though Henry Ford Home Health Care began with just 10 employees, including nurses and business staff, mere word that the hospital had entered the arena caused concern among others at the Michigan Home Health Association meetings, as Solecki recalled:

Home Health Care executive Greg Solecki (center), Wyandotte Hospital CEO James Sexton (right), and others at the opening of the Wyandotte Hospital's Henry Ford at Home site, 2008. *(From the Conrad R. Lam Collection, Henry Ford Health System. ID=09-026.)*

People would actually come up and say, "Well, we know who you are. You're the one who's going to be taking our business away from us." And I had no idea how competitive this whole home health thing was. There were a lot of freestanding, mom-and-pop providers out there that had been doing this all along, and this was at the advent of hospitals and, later, systems owning their own home health outfits. And you know, they were right. They began to see their market share dwindle as hospitals and systems preferred to refer patients to their own providers who were aligned with their mission and with their policies and practices and protocols. Of course, we always honored patients' choice, but there's definitely an advantage to being a part of the system. We were very fortunate that we were at the front end of something that subsequently turned out to be very big.[21]

1983

Dr. Michael Somand (left, with administrator Tom Groth) becomes the medical director at the Fairlane Medical Center.

1983

The Edsel B. Ford Center is dedicated at the West Bloomfield Medical Center. Henry Ford II and his son, Edsel B. Ford, along with Jane Muer, Robert Vlasic, Dr. Joseph Ponka, and Rabbi Richard C. Hertz of Temple Beth El, dedicate the center.

1984

Dr. Roger Smith proposes The Heart and Vascular Institute to the Henry Ford Health Care Corporation Board of Trustees, which approves the concept the same year. The Institute consists of cardiac surgery, vascular surgery, cardiology, and hypertension research.

In 1984, Henry Ford Home Health Care, led by Solecki, became a part of the overall home health products and services business unit led by Polanski. As business evolved, the large group of health products and services became known as Community Care Services, with Polanski as CEO and Solecki as vice president of Henry Ford at Home. This robust division included Henry Ford Extended Care, a private-duty nursing and supplemental staffing agency; Henry Ford Home Infusion, in which pharmacists and nurses assisted patients with IV therapies; and Henry Ford Health Products, which provided medical supplies for patients.[22]

John Polanski outside Perry ComfortCare, Inc., 1985. (From the Conrad R. Lam Collection, Henry Ford Health System. ID=09-011.)

1986

Kingswood Hospital, a psychiatric hospital in Ferndale, becomes affiliated with the health system.

1986

The health system affiliates with Cottage Hospital in Grosse Pointe and its nursing homes.

1988

The health system becomes affiliated with Wyandotte Hospital in the Downriver area.

1988

Gail Warden is recruited to be CEO of the health corporation.

A New Leader

The changes that led Henry Ford from a hospital to a health system had taken visionary leadership. Now it was time for another round of changes.

Henry Ford II died in late September 1987 following a three-week bout with pneumonia. That same year, Stan Nelson began to recruit his successor. At the top of the list: Gail Warden, from the Group Health Cooperative of Puget Sound in Seattle. "They were looking for somebody who had a background in prepaid health care and HMOs as well as running an academic medical center," Warden said. "It looked like a perfect job for me because they do all the things that I enjoy and had experience in."[23] Bill Alvin, former CEO at Henry Ford Wyandotte Hospital and a former HAP president, remarked on Warden's election to the CEO position:

It was a perfect match. Gail continued the evolution of Henry Ford becoming known nationally and respected nationally.

Henry Ford Medical Group

The closed staffing model Henry Ford selected for his hospital in 1915 spurred recruitment of physicians from top training institutions around the country during the following decades. These physicians saw the benefit of practicing in an institution unencumbered by the financial concerns of running a practice. Collaboration rather than competition was the result. These early principles of collaboration and teamwork enabled the group to excel in the areas of clinical care, education, and research.

As the health system began to develop in the 1980s, the physician group of Henry

Stanley Nelson started that. Gail Warden continued it. Gail Warden came from a system, the Group Health Cooperative in Puget Sound, which was an employed physician group plus a health plan, so he conceptually spent much of his career in what Henry Ford Health System was in the process of becoming. He had an idea in his head from his experience how this system should evolve to its next level. … Somebody once told me that almost in any conversation or meeting, the most prepared person in the room was Gail Warden because he just had such a breadth of experience, and he was very conscientious and hardworking.[24]

Opposite: From left: Gail Warden and Stanley Nelson at Henry Ford Hospital, 1988. *(From the Conrad R. Lam Collection, Henry Ford Health System. ID=09-030.)*

In his time at Henry Ford, Nelson made his mark, taking one hospital to a system with several hospitals, 25 outpatient centers, nursing homes, and home health services.[25] "He was an extraordinary guy, one of the best executives I've ever had the privilege of working with," Bob Vlasic said. "He was an extraordinary executive and very thoughtful."[26]

Nelson had created a path for the health system to grow. It was now up to Warden to take some of Nelson's ideas, in particular ambulatory care centers and Health Alliance Plan, add in his own, and lead the health system to the next level.

One of the first orders of business would be a reorganization that would again position Henry Ford for the future. Henry Ford Health Care Corporation and Greenfield Health Systems merged, creating the Henry Ford Health System, effective December 31, 1989.

Ford Hospital and the growing medical centers officially established the Henry Ford Medical Group, governed by the elected Board of Governors. Former Chair of the Board of Governors Dr. Richard Smith, said, "We set our policies for the group, the behavior of the group, the well-being of the physicians, the philosophy of the group, and how to take care of patients."

The Henry Ford Medical Group evolved into one of the nation's leading and largest group practices, now with more than 1,200 physicians practicing in more than 40 specialties.

"The self-governed, employed physician practice model of the Henry Ford Medical Group has been copied by many others because of our continued success, even through tough economic times," said Dr. Gregory L. Barkley, former chair of the Board of Governors and a nationally renowned epileptologist.

“ *As a practicing physician, you can certainly have a major impact on your patients in a very positive way, but you're probably talking two, three thousand people at the most. When you're training physicians, each of them will, in turn, take care of two to three thousand patients, so you have a much broader impact on a large scale than you would if you were simply in solo practice or in a small group practice.*”

Dr. Eric Scher
CHAIR OF THE DEPARTMENT OF MEDICINE
AND VICE PRESIDENT OF MEDICAL EDUCATION[1]

STRENGTHENING THE ACADEMIC MEDICAL CENTER

As far back as 1915, Henry Ford Hospital had instituted a robust medical education program. Drs. Frank Sladen and Roy McClure had developed residency programs in Medicine and Surgery as one of the first steps in developing a hospital.[2] Connections with Johns Hopkins University had proven invaluable, as the vaunted teaching hospital had served as a pipeline for Henry Ford Hospital in residents and new staff.

As the new CEO of Henry Ford Health System at the start of the 1990s, Gail Warden envisioned a vertically integrated health system in which all components of care—hospitals, medical clinics, pharmacies, home health care, medical products, etc.—functioned efficiently to serve the patient. Part of Warden's vision focused on revitalizing Henry Ford Hospital as an academic and research medical center. Unlike many of its peers, Henry Ford Health System did not own a medical school. However, Henry Ford Hospital explored affiliations with the University of Michigan as far back as 1937, and in the 1990s had agreements for the rotation

Henry Ford Health System and the Detroit Medical Center's Children's Hospital of Michigan announce a joint initative to prevent childhood disease through improved immunizations for the children of Detroit. Gail Warden is pictured at the podium during the press conference. *(From Henry Ford Health System. ID:101494_592.)*

of medical students at the hospital from the University of Michigan, Case Western Reserve University, and Wayne State University. In addition, it had put the pieces—and personnel—in place to continue to grow and refine its status as an academic medical center with a 980-bed teaching hospital, education and research, and strong residency and fellowship programs.

Dr. Eric Scher (center) with residents, Henry Ford Hospital. *(From Henry Ford Health System. ID:scher_1854.)*

"The care of the patient was always first and foremost," said Dr. John Popovich, who spent his third year of medical school training at Henry Ford Hospital, where he would later serve as CEO. "And then we educated so that we could create the learning environment where students could best take care of patients. We investigated to learn things that were new ways of being able to educate as well as to treat patients. That hierarchy is not necessarily the same in all institutions. But that was a hierarchy here, and it's the one that was lived by doctors. Those are the ones who created the environment, and they were the people that young physicians looked up to and wanted to emulate."[3]

Aligning with Universities

The largest single-campus medical school in the United States—Wayne State University—sits less than two miles from Henry Ford Hospital. With that proximity, there have always been frequent interactions. Physicians and scientists changed jobs between the institutions. Students looked for work at the hospital. But a formal relationship was a long time coming.

The hospital had first aligned with the University of Michigan in 1937, when residents were given academic credit for working in the hospital laboratories.[4] The two institutions

1980

Drs. Fred Whitehouse and Dorothy A. Kahkonen are the first physicians in Michigan and the second in the country to administer human insulin to a patient with diabetes.

1980

The Department of Neurology acquires the first Topical Magnetic Resonance (TMR) unit in the nation. This device allows non-invasive exploration of the brain and other organs. The department also becomes one of the few NIH-funded stroke centers in the United States.

1982

Nephrology and Hypertension expands research in hemodialysis treatment, kidney transplantation, and diabetes-related kidney disease. Photo: Dr. Pedro Cortes, c. 1995.

renewed the relationship in 1969, sharing resources and developing a cooperative program.[5] That program eventually offered third- and fourth-year medical students training at Henry Ford Hospital, many of whom returned as house officers or staff, including Eric Scher, who would later become chair of the Department of Medicine and vice president of medical education for the health system.

In addition to the hospital's alignment with the University of Michigan, a relationship with Case Western University in Cleveland developed in 1992, and a formal alliance with Wayne State University occurred in the early part of the 21st century. Dr. Mark Kelley, former CEO of the Medical Group, was key in developing a more formalized relationship with Wayne State University.[6] "We have a lot of students coming to Henry Ford who now enter our residencies, and many of our faculty are actually grads of that school of medicine," Dr. Kelley said. "So I think that really sharpened up our academic game."

The benefits were mutual: "The reason Wayne could be so large is that it had amazing cooperation with all of its community hospitals, including Henry Ford," said Dr. John Crissman, former vice chair of pathology at Henry Ford Hospital and dean of Wayne State University Medical School.[7]

The alliance between the hospital and Wayne State has paid long-term dividends. "Over the years, we have assumed a larger role in the education of Wayne State medical students," said Dr. Henry Lim, chair of the dermatology department and senior vice president of academic affairs for the health system, who added:

Currently, we have about one-third of the class spending their third year, which is the clinical year, at the Henry Ford Hospital. It has been one of the most popular rotations for Wayne students. It is a very natural partnership for

Dr. Henry Lim (right), vice president of Academic Affairs and chief of Dermatology, with renowed dermatologist Dr. George Mikhail in 1995. *(Detail From the Conrad R. Lam Collection, Henry Ford Health System. ID=05-030.)*

1982

Dr. Oscar Carretero is awarded $3.7 million from the NIH to study the role of hormones in the development of blood pressure. This is the largest single research grant ever awarded to a Henry Ford Hospital researcher at the time.

1983

More than 500 physicians and scientists throughout the world gather at Henry Ford Hospital for the Third International Symposium on Bone and Mineral Metabolism. The event is chaired by Dr. Boy Frame.

Dr. Bruce K. Muma of the Department of Internal Medicine, c. 1980. *(From the Conrad R. Lam Collection, Henry Ford Health System. ID=10-001.)*

us. We have the same mission of wanting to educate the next generation of physicians, of having a strong medical school and a strong academic presence in Detroit, so that we can continue to take care of the population here.[8]

Another important agreement exists between Henry Ford Health System and the Children's Hospital of Michigan, which is affiliated with Wayne State University and part of the Detroit Medical Center. In 2002, Ford Hospital's pediatric residency program merged into Children's Hospital's pediatric program. Children's Hospital provides pediatric training and rotations for Henry Ford's specialty residency and fellowship programs, whereas Henry Ford Medical Group physicians provide Continuity Clinic rotations for Children's Pediatric residents as well as ambulatory pediatric rotations. In addition, Henry Ford Medical Group sponsors the heart and liver transplant programs at Children's Hospital for pediatric transplant patients and also provides pediatric urology services.

A Powerful Draw

As the hospital increased its academic ties, it put in place an important recruiting tool that would bring in numerous key leaders. Case in point: Dr. Bruce Muma, who came to the hospital on the Hematology Service during his senior year at Wayne State University in 1982.

"Because of my education at Wayne State University, I had rotated through most of the hospitals in southeast Michigan already, so I had a good sense of what the hospital was like, what the people were like, how people interacted with each other," said Dr. Muma, who has held several leadership positions, most recently chief medical officer of the Henry Ford Physician Network in 2013. "I have to say that I felt a difference right out of the gate at Henry Ford Hospital. I felt like there was a higher level of engagement, collaboration, and teamwork."[9] That feeling

1985

From the Conrad R. Lam Collection, Henry Ford Health System. ID=10-008.

The cerebral blood flow machine in Neurology (pictured) allows the study of blood flow in the brain to assess risk of stroke. Dr. K. M. A. Welch and Dr. James Ewing lead the research.

1985

Dr. Fraser Keith, assisted by Dr. Donald Magilligan, performs Detroit's first heart transplant. Within five years, 100 transplants are performed, with one of the nation's best survival rates. The program Lifeshare is launched to promote organ donation awareness.

was reinforced by the welcoming atmosphere he encountered:

> *For trainees and learners, the ability to participate in the care of patients is far greater than what you see in other hospitals. It really gets back to the culture of teamwork and collaboration, where everybody wants everybody to succeed and participate, and so the senior staff teachers are very welcoming. They want the residents, the interns, and the students to learn. At the end of that one-month rotation as a senior medical student, in my mind there wasn't any other place to go for my residency.*[10]

Dr. Marwan Abouljoud at a transplant news conference at Henry Ford Hospital in 1996. *(From Henry Ford Health System. ID:101494_444.)*

Dr. Marwan Abouljoud, director of the Henry Ford Transplant Institute and chief medical officer of the Henry Ford Medical Group, who also had his first encounter with the hospital during his residency, added:

> *When I came to Ford, it had a reputation for being a diverse program, a heavy clinical program that combined academic research with a hefty dose of great clinical care. And it wound up delivering just that. It was one of the best clinical programs, to the extent that when I left my training here, people were always surprised by the depth and scope of my experience and my technical skills. These skills were all carried over from Henry Ford as a trainee.*[11]

1987

Dr. Ronald T. Burkman becomes chief of obstetrics and gynecology at Henry Ford Hospital. A nationally recognized expert in women's health, Dr. Burkman helps advance scientific knowledge in fertility management, menopause, pelvic infection, and reproductive health. He serves as department chair until 1995 and as vice president of women's health for the health system.

1987

Dr. Gene Jackson and other Henry Ford and Yale researchers identify the location of a gene on chromosome 10, which is linked to hereditary medullary thyroid cancer.

1988

For the first time, nurse managers are given pagers to be reachable 24/7. Pictured are (from left) Marsha Montgomery, Lynn Daniels, Karen Kitchak, and Veronica "Ronnie" Hall in the medical critical care unit.

Dr. Theodore Parsons III,
Chair of the Department
of Orthopedic Surgery,
Henry Ford Hospital.
*(From Henry Ford Health
System. ID:Parsons_
Theodore_07CLAB.)*

The positive experience at Henry Ford Hospital influenced Dr. Aboujoud to the point that, though fellowships in Alabama and Texas followed, Detroit remained a draw. While some of the consideration was family—his wife's relatives lived in the area—"the motivation to come here was driven heavily by career aspirations and certainly flavored by the family set-up," he said. "I was a little bit biased as well because when I left Ford as a surgical resident, there is something that you develop working here. You're part of the collective that connects together through family-type relationships and friendships that in a way empower you and lift you. And sometimes when you're down, they help you out."[12]

Beyond the academic programs, Henry Ford Hospital also focused on continuing education and mentorship for physicians. "This is one of the many reasons I came here," said Dr. Mani Menon, chair of the Urology Department and director of the Vattikuti Urology Institute at Henry Ford Hospital. "There was a formal emphasis on mentorship. They told me that I could pick someone to be my mentor. So I said, 'Well, I would like Mark Rosenblum.' That was great because, as much as I was an innovator, I was simply following in Mark Rosenblum's footsteps. Mark had innovated it all. He'd been here for five years before, so he had already blazed a trail."[13]

As the hospital's reputation for medical education grew, academics also became a recruiting tool. In addition to drawing residents, it attracted experienced physicians who were interested in training others. Dr. Theodore W. Parsons III, chair of the Department of Orthopedic Surgery, was recruited to the health system, courted by the attitude toward academics. "I saw great opportunity here for a training program that had six residents per year, resources to educate them, and faculty that were interested in teaching—a real diamond in the rough," Dr. Parsons said. "Resident education is what really interests me in the practice of medicine. It's wonderful to see the transition of young physicians coming in, starting their careers, and, five or six years later, leaving as capable and qualified providers."[14]

1988

Dr. Nalini Janakiraman establishes the Bone Marrow Transplantation program, which becomes known as the premier center of its type in Michigan. Pictured are Dr. Janakiraman (left) with Dr. Robert Chapman in 1994.

From Henry Ford Health System. ID:101494_032.

1988

The Harold C. Johns Distinguished Nursing Lectureship is endowed by Mrs. Gail C. Johns.

1990

Henry Ford Health System enters a joint venture with Mercy Health System of Farmington Hills. Mercy includes the St. Joseph Mercy of Macomb Hospitals, which later become part of Henry Ford Health System.

Film Work in Medical Education

From its inception, Henry Ford Hospital had sought to make medical education available using the tools of the time. Its library was robust. But as filmmaking grew, it offered possibilities for extending the hospital's medical education throughout the country.

John Kroll, hired as a hospital photographer in 1948, first began producing motion photography, working alongside doctors such as Jack Guyton, Conrad Lam, D. Emerick Szilagyi, Joseph Ponka, Harold Schuknecht, and W. Earl Redfern—all pioneers in their fields. Kroll invented equipment and procedures to make photography safer for patients in the operating room.[1]

When Joe Madej succeeded Kroll in the 1970s, he pushed filmmaking to the next level. Working with Dr. Joseph Beninson on the film *Pressure Gradient Prophylaxis of Thrombosis,* Madej showcased Dr. Beninson's years of research on use of the Jobst Stocking, a form of compression hose. The film won the Golden Eagle Award, presented by the Council on International Nontheatrical Events.[2] Golden Eagles are awarded by a jury system that chooses the best films submitted.[3]

The hospital also produced *Minds of Medicine*, a local weekly television show. The episodes featured research and medical breakthroughs and went on to win several Emmy Awards.[4]

While not all of the films have earned such lofty awards, medical education through filmmaking has benefited other hospitals, community groups, and organizations, such as the Easter Seals Society.

This page: Joe Madej, Henry Ford Health System videographer, 1990. *(From the Conrad R. Lam Collection, Henry Ford Health System. ID=09-035.)* Inset: Dr. Joseph Beninson and his wife, Evelyn, accepting the Golden Eagle Motion Picture Award from the Council on International Nontheatrical Events, Washington, DC, 1979. *(From the Conrad R. Lam Collection, Henry Ford Health System. ID=09-034.)*

While Henry Ford Hospital concentrated on its academic endeavors, subspecialties grew as a byproduct. Neurology was a prime example. Dr. Stanton Elias, chair of Neurology, recalled his predecessor—Dr. K. M. A. Welch—and his emphasis on creating an academic neurology department:

> *He set out to recruit a group of neurologists who would be academically oriented in terms of providing teaching for medical students, residents, and for other departments as well as those who were interested in research. And we had a structure for neurology that we would be subspecialty-oriented. That is, we wanted to recruit individuals who had special expertise in certain branches of neurology that were then evolving so that, over the years, the department grew significantly.*

Barbara Rossman. *(From Henry Ford Health System. ID:Rossmann, 2012.)*

Since it was established by Dr. Welch in 1981, the Department of Neurology has grown to be nationally recognized for its subspeciality expertise in stroke, epilepsy, neuro-oncology, ALS, multiple sclerosis, and movement disorders.[15]

Dr. Mark Rosenblum, former chair of the Department of Neurosurgery, was also attracted to the health system's commitment to academics and research. When he arrived in 1992, he founded the department's Brain Tumor Research Center, later named in honor of David Hermelin. "I was really floored by the opportunity to build something like this. It was a major academic center and remained so, and it has grown even more now," said Dr. Rosenblum.[16]

From Henry Ford Health System. ID:HFMH_2008.

Henry Ford Macomb Hospital

Henry Ford Macomb Hospitals dates back to 1899, when it was first established as the St. Joseph Sanitarium and Bath House by the Cincinnati-based Sisters of Charity and Father J. A. Van Hoomissen of St. Peter's Catholic Church in Mt. Clemens, Michigan.[1] The hospital specialized in holistic healing using the area's mineral spring water and opened the area's first nurse training program in the early 1900s.

Through the years, "St. Joe's" grew to become one of the largest providers of health care in Macomb County. In 1975, St. Joe's opened a new 300-bed hospital in Clinton Township known as "St. Joe's West," and the original "St. Joe's East" in Mt. Clemens continued to thrive.

In 1990, the now-large organization St. Joseph Healthcare became a member of the Henry Ford Mercy Health Network, an innovative partnership between Mercy Health Services and Henry Ford Health System. Later, when Trinity Health System acquired Mercy Health, executive Barbara Rossman was appointed CEO of the renamed St. Joseph's Mercy of Macomb Hospitals.

"Strategically, years before we became fully owned by Henry Ford Health System, we had determined that to be successful and meet the community needs, as well as move to where the community would grow, we

Growth occurred throughout the hospital, aided by endowed chairs funded by the generosity of many philanthropic members of the community. "It gives the physicians a certain amount of money on an annual basis that they have to spend. It is not to pay their salary," Gail Warden said. "Their salary is being paid by the medical group and the system. It's to give them money to do other things, to build their department. It made a big difference in our ability to attract people into those key jobs."[17]

Aligning With Community Hospitals

In the early 1990s, conversations between Dr. Dennis Lemanski and Dr. Michael Opipari of Horizon Health System and Dr. David Leach of Henry Ford Hospital led to an important expansion of medical education. In 1995, the merger with Horizon Health System brought two osteopathic hospitals to Henry Ford Health System: Bi-County Community Hospital in the Macomb region and Riverside Osteopathic Hospital in the Downriver region.

Dr. Joanna Pease. *(From Henry Ford Health System. ID:pease_joanna_11c.)*

These hospitals worked with third- and fourth-year students from Michigan State College of Osteopathic Medicine and the Kirksville College of Osteopathic Medicine. This was in addition to residency programs.[18]

Although Henry Ford Health System closed Riverside Hospital, the osteopathic medical education program was brought to Wyandotte Hospital. Former CEO of Riverside Hospital Dr. Lemanski worked tirelessly to make the medical education integration successful. He noted: "We started very small, but the entire hospital made a very strong commitment to medical education. They did not say no to anything I asked because they knew medical education was that important. The medical staff could not have been more welcoming."

needed to have ambulatory sites throughout Macomb County, principally in the northern part," Rossman said. "So we positioned ambulatory sites throughout the county. And then we put primary care practices either within those sites or aligned around those sites to ensure that they met the needs of the community. It has served us very well."

Henry Ford Health System fully acquired St. Joseph's Mercy, which, in 2007, was renamed Henry Ford Macomb Hospitals. Regardless of owner or name, throughout all these years, the "St. Joe's" mission and values of caring for the community have remained intact.

"The translation of our values from Trinity Health to Ford was seamless," Rossman said. "There was an implicit trust that the medical staff and our employed staff had with us as an organization. ... They believed and trusted that they would be equally cared for and cared about through Henry Ford Health System, and it's proven to be true."

The osteopathic medical education program originally from Bi-County Hospital migrated to Henry Ford Macomb Hospitals a few years ago. First a private practice physician at Bi-County in 1986 and now the Chief Medical Officer of Henry Ford Macomb Hospitals, Dr. Joanna Pease commented: "The level of attention we have to quality outcomes is now far superior than what we used to have. I have learned so much about what it takes to really ensure that we are providing safe care and quality care. It is truly a focus for us and for the whole health system."

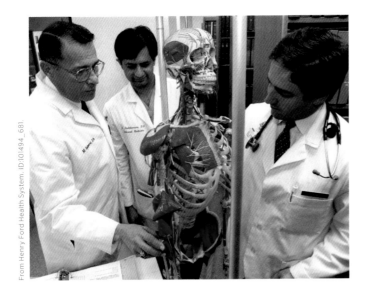

Above: Dr. Michael Opipari teaching residents, 1996. A clinician and educator for 41 years, Dr. Opipari served as vice president and chief medical officer of Horizon Health System, which included Bi-County Community Hospital. Horizon Health System merged with Henry Ford Health System in 1995.

Above right: Dr. Dennis Lemanski, former CEO of Riverside Osteopathic Hospital and currently senior vice president of Medical Education and Medical Staff Affairs, Henry Ford Wyandotte Hospital. Pictured in 1995.

As senior vice president of Medical Education and Medical Staff Affairs at Henry Ford Wyandotte Hospital, Dr. Lemanski works closely with the other medical education leaders at the health system.

"We are involved in providing office-based family medicine training for medical students and residents. And we're involved in discussions about what's going on in the Henry Ford Medical Group and what that large multi-specialty practice is doing," said Dr. Lemanski. "They willingly share with us best practices."[19]

Part of the Horizon Health System merger, Bi-County Community Hospital was located on the other side of metro Detroit in Warren. Its large osteopathic medical education program was later moved to Henry Ford Macomb Hospital in Clinton Township, under the direction of Dr. Joanna Pease. "In terms of the overall osteopathic profession, the future is bright because we have so many more students and also because the osteopathic profession is more focused on primary care, although not exclusively. That appears to be the wave of the future," said Dr. Pease.[20]

1990s

Dr. Michael Benninger (pictured, 1995) becomes chair of the Department of Otolaryngology-Head and Neck Surgery. He established the Center for the Performing Artist, the first of its kind in Michigan.

1992

The hospital begins a five-year study of Tamoxifen, a drug hoped to reduce the incidence of breast cancer in high-risk patients.

1992

Henry Ford Hospital and Case Western Reserve University School of Medicine in Cleveland announce an affiliation. The hospital will train Case Western Reserve medical students and develop a generalist residency training program.

Integral to educating medical students as well as residents and fellows is providing an in-depth learning experience across a large, diverse community.

In 1990, Henry Ford Health System entered a joint venture with Mercy Health Systems of Farmington Hills to expand health care services in metropolitan Detroit. This formed the Henry Ford Mercy Health Network, which included St. Joseph's Mercy of Macomb Hospitals in Clinton Township and Mt. Clemens as well as Mercy Hospital in Detroit (formerly Samaritan Hospital). Henry Ford agreed to manage Mercy Hospital. Gail Warden appointed Henry Ford Hospital adminstrator Brenita Searcy as Detroit Mercy Hospital's CEO. Searcy was the first African-American woman CEO at the health system.

From Henry Ford Health System. ID:101494_311.

Henry Ford Wyandotte Hospital

Wyandotte Hospital has served the Downriver community and southeast Michigan since 1926. Originally owned by the city of Wyandotte, the 379-bed acute care hospital first became affiliated with Henry Ford in 1988. The hospital acquired the osteopathic medical education program of Riverside Hospital when that hospital closed in the mid-1990s. Later, Wyandotte Hospital became fully integrated into the health care system.

Henry Ford Wyandotte Hospital staff and employees are proud of their commitment and service to their community. William Alvin, CEO of the hospital in the 1990s, recalled: "There was such a strong community identity to Wyandotte Hospital. ... You can never create the impression that [citizens'] community hospital was taken away from them by this big system, and that was a balance that we were constantly working with."[1]

James Walworth, the founding president of the Health Alliance Plan, was born at Wyandotte Hospital, lived in the community, and later became a board member. "I think what helped was the decision to put up a significant expansion, physical plant expansion, and service capacities at Wyandotte Hospital," Walworth said. "Ford's ability to create the funding for it and bring that into existence went a long way towards letting the community sense that 'our' hospital would in fact grow and prosper, even though it was part of the Ford system."

"The Heart and Vascular Institute is an example of where we have a great medical group partnership with private physicians,"

said Henry Ford Wyandotte Hospital CEO Denise Brooks-Williams. "We have patients whose care might start in Wyandotte, go downtown for a period of time, but then return to Wyandotte back into our care. We make it work by getting everyone to the table and planning how we want the care for those patients to unfold."

As a leader of the hospital's osteopathic medical education program and longtime clinician, Dr. Dennis Lemanski reflected:

I think that there is a very good working relationship and respect between hospital administration and the medical administration and the medical staff. The dedication of not just the medical staff but the whole hospital to 'We're going to be the best we can be,' and to show that we have good quality outcomes, that we're a safe hospital, that we provide care in a manner that we would like ourselves or our family to receive, that's what I'm most proud of. I'm honored to be affliated with this institution."[2]

Bill Alvin, Wyandotte Hospital CEO, 1996. *(From Henry Ford Health System. ID:101494_397.)*

Family medicine, which at that time had started its residency program at Henry Ford Hospital, gained the benefit of the health system's associations with the various community hospitals. For example, residents could acquire vastly different experiences at Grosse Pointe's Cottage Hospital and Detroit Mercy Hospital.

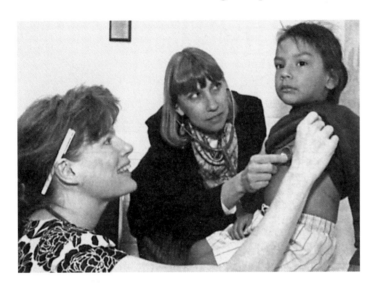

Drs. Susan Schooley (left) and Christine Jerpbak with a patient at the CHASS community center, 1992. *(From the Conrad R. Lam Collection, Henry Ford Health System. ID=10-004.)*

"We built a relationship with Mercy to establish a second base of operations for the Family Medicine training program. A core group of our faculty went into Mercy Hospital, established a practice in their ambulatory primary care network, and recruited residents to join us," said Dr. Susan Schooley, chair of the Department of Family Medicine, who added:

Like Henry Ford Hospital, these were patients who were sick and often arriving on the doorstep of the hospital, "crashing and burning" with lack of primary care, chronic illnesses that had become acute and emergent, and/or complications of diseases like diabetes and hypertension that had not been treated. This was an opportunity to train family physicians in the complexity of illness that was a mix of the biological problems that lack of treatment creates in a population, but also the very complicated psycho-social dimension that comes out of poverty and the lack of social resources and the difficulties that those combinations bring.[21]

Though always closely linked, the health system formalized a relationship between research and academics when, in 1990, academic programs combined with the Edsel B. Ford Institute for Medical Research. Together, they became the Henry Ford Health Sciences Center.

1992

From Henry Ford Health System. ID:101494_080.

Dr. Teresa Wehrwein is appointed director of the School of Nursing.

1992

Dr. Mark Rosenblum becomes chair of Neurosurgery. Under his leadership and in collaboration with Dr. Stanton Elias, the departments of Neurology and Neurosurgery become continuously ranked as the top in Michigan by *US News & World Report*.

1993

Henry Ford Health System receives a grant from the John A. Hartford Foundation of New York City to improve geriatric patient care. Nancy Whitelaw, Ph.D. of the Center for Health System Studies conducts the project, which is implemented by the Henry Ford Center for Seniors and the Metro Medical Group.

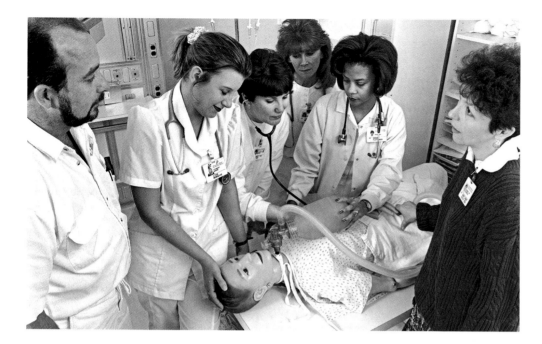

Henry Ford Hospital School
of Nursing students, 1996.
*(From Henry Ford Health
System. ID:101494_645.)*

Responding to Changing Needs

Henry Ford Health System made sure that its physicians and other staff had access to continuing education. In many cases, this was through accredited courses, seminars, and meetings, and later, online programs. But as medicine shifted, the health system morphed to ensure physicians were on top of the changes.

In 1993, in response to health insurance changes, the health system offered the Managed Care College to assist health personnel in better caring for patients while using clinical resources effectively. The Managed Care College was part of the Metro Medical Group, Health Alliance Plan's physician-owned group, which was integrated into Ford's medical group in the 1990s. And during the early 1990s, nurses' education began to transform as well, which led to changes

1994

1994

1994

Henry Ford Health System launches the Fund for the Future, a six-year, $150 million campaign to fund endowed chairs and support research. William Clay Ford and his wife, Martha Firestone Ford, are honorary co-chairs.

The Metro Medical Group joins the Henry Ford Medical Group to enhance customer service, and nine Metro Medical Group sites are renamed Henry Ford Medical Centers. The Metro Medical Group's Managed Care College becomes part of the Henry Ford Health Sciences Center.

From Henry Ford Health System. ID:20141016_0001.

Dr. Jan Rival receives an Outstanding Teacher Award from the University of Michigan. Henry Ford Hospital presents the Jan Rival Outstanding Resident Award each year in his honor.

1995

The Horizon Health System, which operates Bi-County Hospital in Warren and Riverside Hospital in Wyandotte, merges with Henry Ford Health System. This brings osteopathic medical education to the health system.

1996

After 71 years and more than 4,900 graduates, the Henry Ford Hospital School of Nursing graduates its last class of 89 students.

1996

Dr. Lester Weiss of Genetics is profiled in *Time* magazine for his research in telemedicine technology.

in one of the hospital's longest-running programs. In 1925, Henry Ford Hospital had launched the School of Nursing and its related Clara Ford Nurses Home. The program offered a registered nurse diploma for its graduates. However, by the early 1990s, that model had fallen out of favor, as nurses nationally were encouraged to pursue undergraduate and graduate degree programs.

"Nursing as a profession was saying, 'You shouldn't just be getting a diploma, you should be getting your degree,'" said Dr. Teresa Wehrwein, director of Henry Ford Hospital School of Nursing from 1992 to 1996. "We worked very hard with the nurses in the last few years of the program to encourage them to move as quickly as possible to earn their baccalaureate degree so they could move their career forward."[22]

The hospital's School of Nursing closed in 1996, though it continued to train nurses. It formed a partnership with Oakland University and conducted research. And when the health system aligned with Wayne State, the partnership included a nursing component.[23]

As the health system had grown its academic role, it had become one of the nation's largest medical education programs across the spectrum, with allopathic medical education at Henry Ford Hospital and the osteopathic medical education programs at community hospitals.

Opposite: Henry Ford Hospital's School of Nursing last graduating class, Masonic Temple, Detroit, 1996. *(From Henry Ford Health System. ID:101494_617.)*

Above: Teresa Wehrwein (left), director of the School of Nursing, and Dorothy Fox (center) with student nurses at Henry Ford Hospital in 1994. *(From Henry Ford Health System. ID:101494_081.)*

1996

From Henry Ford Health System. ID:101494_404.

Henry Ford Hospital nurse Mary Kravutske with patient, 1996. Mary becomes a longtime nurse leader and administrator in Nursing Development and Research.

1998

The Department of Emergency Medicine becomes the first to introduce an electronic medical record at the hospital.

1998

The Kresge Foundation awards Henry Ford Health System a $1 million grant for the School-Based Health Initiative, a project focused on improving the health care of children and adolescents in Detroit.

Eleven

" *What Henry Ford Hospital does is provide a social return on investment. Its nonprofit status is maximized at a level of quality and commitment to the community, a commitment to diversity, a commitment to excellence, to academics, and to research. That is a unique commitment within Metro Detroit and within the nation in terms of how it has been leveraged.*"

Dorothy (Dottie) Deremo
FORMER CHIEF NURSING OFFICER, HENRY FORD HEALTH SYSTEM[1]

Investing in Community and Quality Improvement

1980s
1990s

BUILDING ON THE VISION

HENRY FORD HOSPITAL
September 30, 1996

Cornerstone Ceremony
officiated by
Dennis W. Archer
Mayor City of Detroit

Henry Ford HEALTH SYSTEM

AS THE HEALTH SYSTEM GREW WITH NEW MEDICAL SATELLITES AND PARTNERSHIPS with community hospitals in the suburbs across the 1980s and 1990s, Henry Ford Hospital continued its commitment to the people of Detroit and to its mission of advancing clinical care, research, and education. These latter decades of the 20th century yielded new diseases, new social problems, and an increasing number of those who could not pay for care. Health care was under pressure to reduce costs while improving quality. Handling this delicate balance required application of business principles that were sweeping through the broader business world.

While Henry Ford Health System grappled with these issues, the father of the modern quality movement came to Detroit to advise the auto industry. To credit Dr. W. Edwards Deming as the architect of the health system's commitment to quality would ignore the individuals on staff who were already thinking this way. But those individuals were savvy

Cornerstone for the Henry Ford II Pavilion. CEO Gail Warden (left), Mayor Dennis Archer (right), and Congressman John Dingell (right foreground), 1996. *(From Henry Ford Health System. ID:101494_587.)*

Dr. W. Edwards Deming
autographs his book
for Gail Warden and
Dr. Roger Smith, 1993.
*(From Henry Ford Health
System. ID:101494_002.)*

enough to capitalize on Dr. Deming's principles of quality to help move the health system into a prominent spot as a leader in health care quality.

Henry Ford Health System could not ignore the challenges outside its doors, either. While it worked to improve quality, it simultaneously reinforced its commitment to the community, creating programs to deal with some of Detroit's most vexing issues.

AIDS Hits Detroit

In 1981, a mysterious new disease appeared. By 1986, what would be known as acquired immunodeficiency syndrome (AIDS), caused by the human immunodeficiency virus (HIV), would disproportionately affect minority populations—specifically, in the United States, the gay male community and intravenous drug users.[2]

1980

Shiley and Deknatel
Laboratories recognize
Dr. Conrad R. Lam as one
of 10 pioneers of cardiac
surgery in the world.
During 51 years of service
at Henry Ford Hospital,
Dr. Lam performed more
than 8,500 operations.

1982

Henry Ford Hospital obtains
Michigan's first Digital Video
Subtraction Angiography
(DVSA) technology.
This latest advancement in
radiology computer equip-
ment allows physicians to
determine if blood vessels
are functioning properly.

1982

From Henry Ford Health System. ID:101494_518.

The Department
of Emergency
Medicine receives
independent
status as a Level 1
trauma center
under the lead-
ership of Dr. Michael Tomlanovich (pictured).
He was appointed chair when emergency
medicine became its own department in 1980.

Dr. Evelyn Fisher of the division of Infectious Diseases saw the first AIDS patients at Henry Ford Hospital in 1981-1982. "We didn't have any drugs for HIV until four years after I saw my first patient," said Dr. Fisher. "We had some medicines for the infections, but some of the major ones we didn't have medicine for yet. So we became part of a trials network, a nationwide consortium to work on trying to find the best treatment the fastest that we could."

Dr. Fisher, Dr. Norman Markowitz, social worker Madelyne Markowitz, and nurse Kevin Frasier served as the first core team to help the AIDS patients at Henry Ford Hospital. With no treatment for the virus, patients were dying. Dr. Fisher led the prevention movement first into the gay community, visiting gay bars to educate about transmission and prevention and to help raise money to create and distribute AIDS education pamphlets. "In the Michigan community, we were the ones who started off seeing the most patients and trying to educate people about it, and get other people involved in it from early on," said Dr. Fisher.

Dr. Evelyn Fisher with patient, c. 1980s. *(From the personal collection of Linda Makohon.)*

David W. Benfer, then the hospital's CEO, witnessed firsthand how AIDS was affecting his community. The office of the CEO was on the second floor of the main hospital building, and the inpatient Infectious Diseases Unit was at the end of that floor. On his experience working near the unit and seeing patients infected with AIDS, Benfer commented:

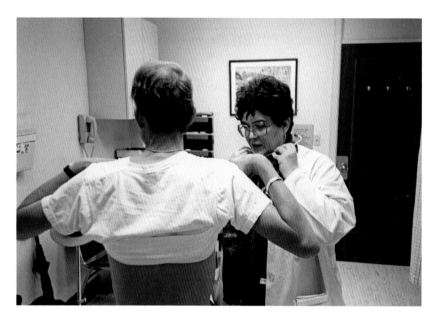

I tended to walk around a fair amount, and that was always one of my stops. It became apparent that we were seeing a significant rise in the population of HIV-infected patients,

1983

Drs. P. C. Shetty of Diagnostic Radiology and Raymond Littleton of Urology perform percutaneous nephroscope extraction, a new procedure for the treatment of kidney stones.

1983

Dr. Fareed Khaja of Cardiovascular Medicine is featured throughout the country for the clinical study of streptokinase, which works to restore blood supply to the heart muscle.

1987

Drs. Heung Oh and Daniel Reddy perform the first pancreas transplant at Henry Ford Hospital.

Dr. Evelyn Fisher, Division
of Infectious Diseases, 1990.
*(From the Conrad R. Lam
Collection, Henry Ford
Health System. ID=07-011.)*

and there didn't seem to be any kind of progressive community continuum that was really making a difference. Folks would be coming out of prisons infected; they couldn't get access to primary care. They couldn't get access to dental care, they couldn't get access to housing. There was that general discrimination against the HIV population because there was so little known about it by the general public.[3]

Benfer called CEOs from other hospitals in the area to discuss possible solutions. "One hospital couldn't take it on," he said. "We needed a way to get community support for this." Benfer asked each CEO for $10,000 with another $10,000 to be pledged at some point in the future. Out of that meeting, the AIDS Consortium of Southeastern Michigan was born. "It was a time when, even though hospitals competed, they were willing to take on community challenges, and this clearly was one of them," Benfer said. "This is an example of how Ford, kind of behind the scenes, tried to take a leadership role in improving community health in its market."[4]

The Infectious Diseases division took on a leadership role in the treatment of the disease with Drs. Fisher, Norman Markowitz, and division head Louis Saravolatz becoming recognized leaders in the treatment of HIV/AIDS.

It was not the first time Henry Ford Hospital had filled this leadership role—and it would not be the last.

Improved Outcomes for the Tiniest Patients

Like Dr. Fisher, Dr. Richard Smith saw a problem that needed solving. While a medical student at Howard University in Washington, DC, Dr. Smith saw how haphazard prenatal

1987

Dr. Fareed Khaja and
Dr. Alain Cribler perform
the first valvuloplasty, a
catheter-based proce-
dure that unblocks the
valve to improve blood
flow to the heart.

1988

Dr. Martin F. Mozes joins
the Henry Ford Hospital
staff as the head of
Transplantation. That same
year, he performs a liver
transplant on a Detroit-area
patient at the University of
Illinois, with follow-up care
at Henry Ford Hospital.

1989

Dr. Raymond Monto retires
from Henry Ford Hospital
after 50 years of service.
He held the position as
the chief of Hematology
from 1947 to 1978.

care in the underprivileged areas of the district resulted in one of the highest infant mortality rates in the world. "Women were given vouchers where they could call a cab if they were in labor, and the cab would drop them off at the loading dock," Dr. Smith said. "You ran out there as a student, delivering babies in taxicabs and on the loading docks, and I saw babies die. They'd come in with dead babies. You said: 'There's got to be a better way. There's got to be a way to improve health care.'"[5] Exploring this problem in the hopes of finding a solution is what ultimately led Dr. Smith into obstetrics and gynecology.

As a third-year student in training at Wayne State University, Dr. Smith worked with a nurse and social worker to develop a model of care. As a resident, he set up a teen pregnancy clinic with funding from the March of Dimes. The outcomes were so striking that he published the results. At a national conference, Dr. Smith met Dr. Bruce H. Drukker, Henry Ford Hospital's chair of Obstetrics and Gynecology. Dr. Drukker quickly sold Dr. Smith on the idea of coming to Henry Ford with its team approach to medicine. "I liked the concept—collaborative teams working together," Dr. Smith said. "It worked out fine because we were in the process of writing a new grant with the March of Dimes and so was Henry Ford. So, the March of Dimes said, 'Why don't we do a combined grant here?' It was a large grant at that time because they were interested in developing a national model for prenatal care for teenagers, and that's what we did."[6]

Dr. Richard Smith with his patients (women left and center), 2013. He delivered both generations of mother and infant. The infant pictured was Dr. Smith's 8,000th delivery. *(From Henry Ford Health System. ID:97052_rm1_4994.)*

1989

The Division of Infectious Diseases is awarded a federal grant of $4.5 million for a community-based, five-year study on AIDS treatment. The grant was awarded through the new clinical trials network, Community Programs for Clinical Research on AIDS (CPCRA).

1989

Dr. Robin C. Buerki, executive director of Henry Ford Hospital from 1951 to 1964, is inducted into the Health Care Hall of Fame by *Modern Healthcare*.

1990

Henry Ford Health System implements the quality management process to improve the quality and safety of health care. CEO Gail Warden and vice president Vin Sahney are among the first in the country to bring quality improvement to health care.

City Year Detroit students at Hart Plaza, Detroit, 1999. *(From Henry Ford Health System. ID:101494B_313.)*

Dr. Smith built a team devoted to teen pregnancy, including a social worker, a clinical nurse specialist, and a psychologist for support. "This became our clinic, our model. We developed this model and took it around the country," Dr. Smith said. "People began to follow it because we had good outcomes: tremendously reduced infant mortality, reduced repeat pregnancy rates, and reduced complications that are associated with young mothers having babies. The other thing we did as a result of our study was to show that providing this type of care does reduce cost."[7]

Michigan created a new model for prenatal care out of Dr. Smith's work. He also testified before Congress, which established the National Commission to Prevent Infant Mortality. "Our initial little clinic was here at the Clara Ford Pavilion in a room that used to be a nurses' lounge. We know how to innovate things at Henry Ford Hospital, and we continue to do that," Dr. Smith said.[8]

Community Partnerships with Detroit

Much work was being done by Henry Ford physicians, nurses, social workers, and others to help battle HIV/AIDS, teen pregnancies, and the underserved communities of Detroit. When Dennis Archer was elected mayor in 1994, he focused on expanding business in Detroit, including the health care business. Archer said:

1990

Led by CEO Gail Warden, the conference, "Urban Health Care: Solutions for the 1990s" is held at Ford Hospital. Its proceedings are published in the *Henry Ford Hospital Medical Journal*.

1990

The first Quality Day conference is held at Henry Ford Health System. This later grows into the Quality Expo, an annual event that highlights quality improvement projects across the health system.

From Henry Ford Health System. ID:101494_605.

1990

Dr. V. Ramesh Babu of Medical Genetics is awarded a five-year grant from the National Cancer Institute to research biogenetic and molecular genetics of bladder cancer.

One of the clear strengths that we had was what I call the other "big three."

Typically when you say, "the big three," you're talking about Ford, Chrysler, and General

Motors. The other big three, in my view, were Henry Ford, Detroit Medical Center, and

St. John Hospital. I was frustrated that many people were leaving this region, and they

would go to other hospitals outside the state of Michigan.[9]

One way to support the city's medical centers was obvious to Archer. "We were in the process of building two new stadiums," Archer recalled. "We were talking about the World Series and other kinds of events coming in, the Super Bowl, the NCAA Basketball Final Four, all those kinds of things. We wouldn't be able to have that unless we had hospitals

Henry Ford Health System Influences National Health Care Quality

As Henry Ford Health System moved to quality improvements, it found a hungry national audience. Dr. Vinod Sahney, then vice president of planning and marketing, first began meeting with Dr. Donald Berwick, then vice president of quality-of-care measurement at Harvard Community Health Plan and Dr. Paul Batalden, vice president for medical care at Hospital Corporation of America. The three had all been involved in applying W. Edwards Deming's principles for quality improvement to their own organizations.

The Institute for Healthcare Improvement (IHI) grew out of those informal discussions, originally designed to share ideas between the three organizations. "We applied for a grant from Hartford Foundation, and they gave us $1.2 million, and they basically said, 'Why don't you set up an organization and disseminate these ideas widely?'" Sahney remembered.

That became the first conference of IHI, and the three founders still were not sure of the interest. "We didn't know if 100 people would show up or 200, so we said 250," Sahney said. "Two weeks before, we already had 300, but the rooms couldn't accommodate that. The halls were not big enough, so we sold out."[1]

As IHI grew, it instituted the IHI Saving Lives Campaign, which intended to reduce levels of hospital-acquired infections or medical harm caused by adverse drug reactions or surgical complications. IHI set a goal to save 5 million lives. With the participation of hospitals around the country, the institute accomplished that in two years.[2]

Henry Ford Health System CEO Gail Warden was an avid supporter of IHI, including speaking at that first sold-out conference. He was named chair of the American Hospital Association in 1995 and was appointed by President Bill Clinton to the Federal Advisory Commission on Consumer Protection and Quality in the Health Care Industry.[3]

"One of the sets of recommendations that came out of that was that the National Quality Forum be created," Warden said. "It was an interesting time because some of the people that were involved with that are now in high places, namely Kathleen Sebelius (who served in the Obama Administration as Secretary of Health and Human Services). She was on the committee with me. And Nancy-Ann Min DeParle,"[4] head of the White House Office of Health Reform during the implementation of the Affordable Care Act.[5]

Warden also worked with the Institute of Medicine—an arm of the National Academy of Sciences—on lowering medical errors. Warden was part of IOM's Committee on the Quality of Health Care in America, which authored two important documents that explored reducing—and eliminating—medical errors: *To Err Is Human* and *Crossing the Quality Chasm*.[6]

Above: Dr. T. Jann Caison-Sorey, Hutchins Middle School, Detroit, 1994. *(From Henry Ford Health System. ID:101494_019.)*

Opposite: Dr. Sudhaker Ezhuthachan (right) and Christine Newman, R.N., Neonatal Intensive Care Unit (NICU), 1995. The NICU at Ford Hospital is state-of-the-art for the care of premature infants and those born with critical medical issues. *(From Henry Ford Health System. ID:101494_206.)*

with the kind of qualifications that would allow us to be able to serve the public. So it is absolutely vital that we have the best care that we can offer."

Mayor Archer also focused on education, opting to import the City Year program to Detroit. First a success in Boston, City Year places its corps members in city schools to help students overcome challenges not only inside but also outside school. The goal is to keep students in school and to help them graduate.

While talking to hospital leaders about this initiative, Mayor Archer met Warden, who volunteered Henry Ford Health System to be a champion for City Year. "It's a very unique program," said Archer. "I meet parents all of the time who talk to me about their son or daughter having joined City Year, how it's evolved, not just here but in other places throughout the country. It's a remarkable program that has done so much good here in the City of Detroit. Gail was a person who made that happen."[10]

One of the gaps between what students needed and what schools could provide lay firmly in health care. Henry Ford Health System joined with Detroit Public Schools, the Detroit Health Department, and the Michigan Department of Public Health to launch a series of clinics in the city. In all, the school-based health initiatives created 13 centers in inner city elementary and middle schools.[11]

The hospital's commitment to providing care to Detroit's underserved communities generated a significant amount of uncompensated care. Gary Valade, a Board Trustee since 1994 and later the system's board chair, recalled: "That number was manageable for a while, but over the years it grew higher and higher. I think we were pretty well committed to be here and to help the city in any way that improved its viability."[12]

1992

The Helping Hands Fund begins as part of the Henry Ford Health System Community Giving Campaign. The fund is designed to provide financial assistance to eligible Henry Ford Health System employees and volunteers in need. The 1992 campaign raises more than $342,000.

1992

The Department of Philanthropy announces $14 million in donations that will be used to establish the proposed cancer center as well as eight endowed chairs. That brings the number of endowed chairs to 23 at that time.

1992

The Medical Information Management System (MIMS) ushers in electronic record-keeping at the hospital. Photo: Paper medical records, c. 1994.

From Henry Ford Health System. ID:101494_084.

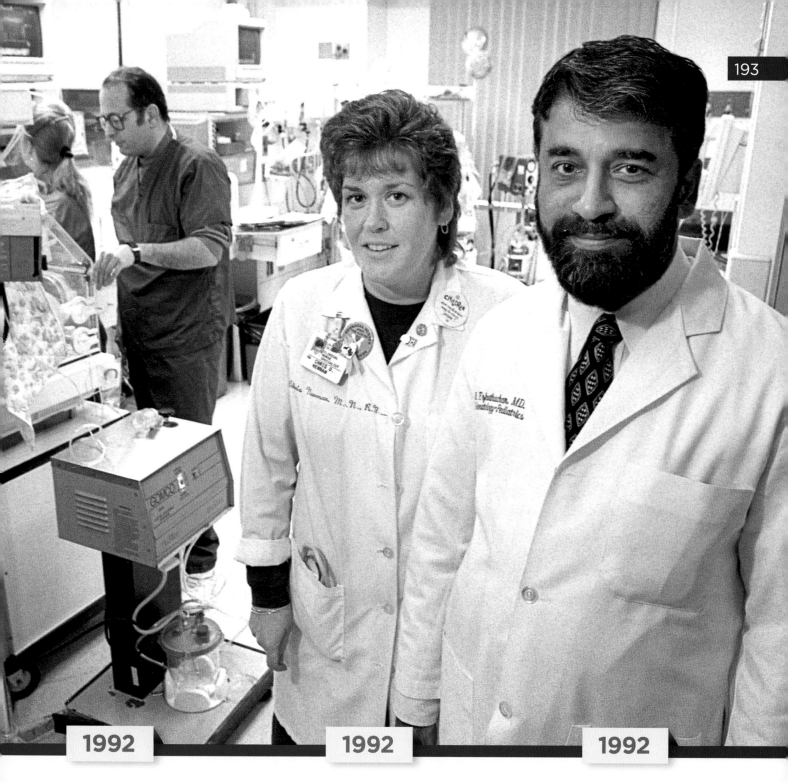

1992

1992

1992

Dr. Alexander Dlugi establishes the Henry Ford In Vitro Fertilization Program, one of six of its type in the US. Dr. Dlugi introduces a multidisciplinary approach to in vitro fertilization.

Under Radiation Oncology Chair Dr. Jae Ho Kim, radiosurgery technology becomes available at Ford Hospital. In partnership with Dr. Mark Rosenblum of Neurosurgery, radiosurgery is first used for the treatment of tumors located deep in the brain.

Henry Ford Hospital and Baxter Health Care Corporation begin a pilot project to recycle plastic and intravenous materials. Henry Ford Hospital's nurses Teresa Rybezynski, R.N., and Margaret Fox, R.N., lead the project.

During this time, uncompensated care spiraling toward $100 million and beyond challenged the health system staff to keep the organization in the black. "The challenge was offsetting that with other revenues and expense reductions," said David N. McCammon, a former Board of Trustees member. "It was always tough to make a good return and tough to get the money to finance your projects because you had that start with all the uncompensated care, which is still the case today."[13]

The Highest of Standards

Despite the financial difficulties that coincided with Henry Ford Health System's commitment to providing excellent care regardless of a patient's ability to pay, the system's quality level of care was maintained.

Businesses also faced this issue. The Japanese influence in manufacturing was keenly felt among Detroit automakers. Dr. W. Edwards Deming was the man behind the Japanese commitment to quality, and he was sought by Ford Motor Company to help improve its ability to do more with less.

"Deming insisted that he would only be a consultant if the top management of Ford Motor Company took his five-day course on the topic of quality," said Dr. Vinod Sahney, former senior vice president at the health system. "His main thing was, 'Quality must be led by senior management. It cannot be delegated out below, and if senior managers don't pay attention to quality, it'll never improve because if you delegate it to some department, people don't pay attention.'"[14]

Dr. Sahney, too, was hearing of Dr. Deming's principles and asked if he could take his course. "I became convinced that these ideas he was advocating were even more applicable in health care than in industry because in health care we have a lot of 'tribes,'" Dr. Sahney

1993

Dr. Thomas Royer is appointed senior vice president for Medical Affairs and the chairman of the Board of Governors of the Henry Ford Medical Group.

From Henry Ford Health System. ID:101494_620.

1993

Dr. W. Edwards Deming, developer of Total Quality Management principles, visits Henry Ford Health System leaders and trustees to discuss quality management techniques.

1993

Henry Ford Health System and the Virginia Park Community collaborate with the National Bank of Detroit to construct 45 single-family homes called the Virginia Park Estates (pictured, 1995).

From Henry Ford Health System. ID:101494_303.

said. "The nursing tribe, the pharmacy tribe, the neurosurgery tribe. Everybody is in their own fiefdom, and they don't really work together."[15]

Soon after taking the course, Dr. Sahney formed a team that traveled to 3M in Minneapolis, Motorola in Chicago, and Polaroid in Massachusetts. "They were all early adopters of Deming's ideas, but all in manufacturing, not health care," Dr. Sahney said.[16]

As Dr. Sahney sought health care examples, he connected with Dr. Donald Berwick, then vice president of quality-of-care measurement at Harvard Community Health Plan, and Dr. Paul Batalden, vice president for medical care at for-profit hospital chain Hospital Corporation of America, to exchange ideas. Out of that relationship grew the Institute for Healthcare Improvement.

Vinod Sahney, Ph.D., 2003. Detroit skyline view from 17th floor of the Clinic Building, Henry Ford Hospital. *(From Henry Ford Health System. ID:0048 2.)*

The interest in Deming's principles—and in quality improvement altogether—was coalescing. Quality was a major interest of Warden, the health system's CEO. Warden had long been an advocate for improving the quality of health care. Putting ideas to paper, Dr. Sahney and Warden wrote "The Quest for Quality and Productivity in Health Services," the first article of its type for the health care industry.[17]

The health system's commitment to quality paid off in both the short and long term. In 1989, Dr. Wilmer M. Rutt developed clinical guidelines through the Center for Clinical Effectiveness—one of the first such centers in the country.[18] In 1993, Henry Ford Health System and the Institute for Healthcare Improvement formed the Group Practice Improvement Network. Through shared learning, the 58 multi-specialty groups worked to improve the quality and value of medical group practices. The next year, 1994, the National Committee for Quality Assurance awarded Henry Ford

1993

The Health Alliance Plan becomes the first HMO in Detroit to receive full accreditation from the National Committee for Quality Assurance.

1993

From Henry Ford Health System. ID:101494_607.

Twenty-five quality improvement teams take part in the annual Quality Expo. In the coming decade, the number of quality improvement projects featured at the Expo grows 80 to 100 each year.

1994

The Henry Ford Health System receives the first National Quality Award for Health Care Integration from the National Committee for Quality Assurance.

Health System the first National Quality Award for Health Care Integration.[19] Along the way, the health system had put in place standards that would soon draw national attention.

Henry Ford Health System kept one idea at the center: improving patient outcomes. That coincided with the patient-focused care movement—an initiative that is standard in health care today. The quality push also brought new approaches to long-held beliefs, including the implementation of patient-focused care, as Steve Velick, former CEO of Henry Ford Hospital, explained:

Stephen H. Velick, CEO of Henry Ford Hospital, 1994. *(From Henry Ford Health System. ID:101494_052.)*

> *It was a total restructuring of how care was given, not only from a care delivery but from a facility renovation perspective. Care ought to revolve around the patient, and we needed to make things easier for staff, so we had to restructure the physical plant. The old central nursing station and supply room at one end of a unit really was somewhat of a waste of time for staff and inconvenient for patients because nurses weren't close. Back then we really were just beginning to talk about quality improvement and the importance of data measurement. My proposal was to do some measurement and create key indicators that would demonstrate that these changes were better from an efficiency standpoint. It was clear from patient satisfaction that they were better. … This was really one of the first times that a patient would have a nurse and an aide, and that nurse and that aide were principally responsible for that patient. They weren't rotating all over the place. So the patient knew their nurse, and physicians knew the nurses.[20]*

That simple philosophy—that the patients should have the same team of nurses and providers throughout their hospital stay—was somewhat revolutionary at the time. And it required a restructuring of the entire hospital, which brought on the need for renovations. Velick added:

1994

From Henry Ford Health System. ID:101494_004.

The Josefina B. Magno Endowed Chair in Hospice Care is established. A leader in hospice care at Henry Ford Health System, Dr. Magno (pictured) has been called the creator of the modern hospice movement in the US.

1994

The patient-focused care model led by nurses at Henry Ford Hospital is implemented. Interdisciplinary care teams include a registered nurse, care partner, patient support partner, pharmacist, and administrative support partner. The same team works with individual patients throughout their stay.

1995

Modeled after Leadership Detroit, established by the Greater Detroit Chamber of Commerce in 1979, the program Leadership Henry Ford Health System is created to promote understanding of system structure, strategy, and culture among staff leaders.

I had to physically show people that, in the semi-private rooms, in order to get somebody into the bed by the window from a stretcher, you had to move the bed by the door. So the sizes of the rooms were an issue. And if we wanted to appeal to the entire community base, we needed more private rooms. Plus we had an outdated emergency room. We had ORs that were outdated, and the alignment of services really left a lot to be desired. That was a major undertaking for the system from a capital standpoint and from a resources standpoint, where up to that time capital and investments had been put into ambulatory care sites. So the ambulatory system had grown significantly. But the inpatient facility needed more than refreshing.[21]

Construction of the West Annex, later renamed the Henry Ford II Pavilion, 1996. *(From Henry Ford Health System. ID:101494_648.)*

The concept of patient-focused care would set the hospital on a course for a multi-million dollar makeover and the addition of the West Annex.

New ways of thinking—whether focused on patients or quality innovations—were in keeping with the health system's long commitment to innovation. While many of those innovations had occurred in the practice of medicine, as the business of health care began to shift, new approaches to management were also needed.

"Henry Ford Hospital is in a really unique situation in that it is not university-based, and yet it is recognized in that academic environment as a place where innovation can occur and where innovation in health care delivery can occur, as well as new therapeutics," said Dr. W. Douglas Weaver, former division head of cardiology and medical director of the Heart and Vascular Institute. "This place wouldn't be special if we didn't have special people who along

1995

Steve Velick begins a customer service improvement initiative centered around quality management, process, and organizational performance.

1995

Gail Warden becomes chairman of the American Hospital Association.

1995

From Henry Ford Health System. ID:101494_339.

The Henry Ford Center for Senior Independence, designed to assist the elderly with independent living, opens.

Henry Ford Hospital
QUALITY LEADERSHIP FORUM

← CAFETERIA

1995

1996

Construction of the east entrance at the Clinic Building, Henry Ford Hospital.

Dr. Evelyn Fisher wins the Michiganian of the Year award from the *Detroit Times* for her work with AIDS patients.

Left: Dr. W. Douglas Weaver, then chief of cardiology and medical director of the Heart and Vascular Institute, 2012. *(From Henry Ford Health System. ID:92077_hvi_033.)*

Opposite: Quality Expo at Henry Ford Hospital, 1994. For more than 20 years, this annual event has showcased more than 80 quality improvement projects undertaken each year throughout the health system. *(From Henry Ford Health System. ID:101494_110.)*

the way have really made significant contributions to medicine. It's one thing to be very satisfied with the health care you get, but professionals judge professionals by the other contributions. So if you want to be known as a major center, not only do you have to take care of your patient population, but you've got to be doing other things that have national recognition so that your peers also believe and invest in the organization."[22]

One thing was for sure: Henry Ford Health System was being recognized for its outstanding care and its leadership on the national stage.

1996

1997

1998

Nurses (from left) Dottie Deremo, Cleo Stewart, Teresa Wehrwein, and Dorothy Fox at an annual Nursing Alumni meeting.

From Henry Ford Health System. ID:101494_540.

President Clinton appoints Gail Warden to the Health Care Quality Commission.

Dr. C. Edward Coffey, chair of Psychiatry, makes international news when his study of the male versus female brain was published in the *Archives of Neurology.* The MRI study showed that the male brain shrinks faster than the female brain.

Twelve

What's wonderful about working in a hospital that is patient-centered is our research labs are just a corridor away from the clinic, which has a tremendous motivating impact on doing research. A lot of the work that we've done over the years has been translated to the clinic. To do translational research, you have to understand what's going on at sometimes a gene or molecular level, but the goal is really to alter treatment, to improve management of patients."

Dr. Michael Chopp
SCIENTIFIC DIRECTOR OF THE HENRY FORD NEUROSCIENCE INSTITUTE[1]

COLLABORATIVE CARE AND BENCH-TO-BEDSIDE RESEARCH

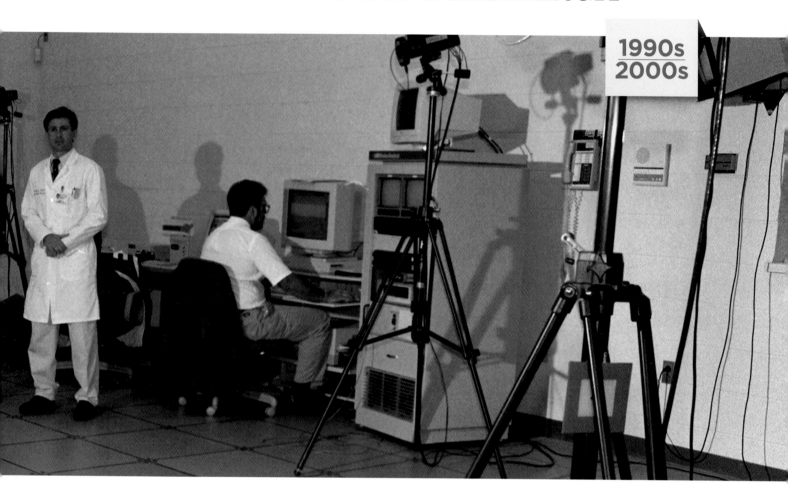

1990s
2000s

As a health system, Henry Ford had a distinct advantage: Operating in multiple locations within urban and suburban areas brought access to a large, diverse patient base. That advantage offered Henry Ford increased opportunities to sharpen its research capabilities and deliver the latest techniques and treatments to patients.

The national reputation, honed for decades, grew as well. Some of the system's physician researchers and bioscientists were at the top of their fields. National multi-center studies were conducted at Henry Ford Hospital, allowing its physicians to affect the broader world of disease and disorders. Henry Ford Hospital and Henry Ford Health System had moved into areas of excellence that would be formally recognized by national accrediting bodies.

At the core of it all, though, was a commitment to bench-to-bedside research, taking the research out of the lab and into the patient experiences. "For me, it was really never much of a choice between being in a medical group or academic setting versus a private practice or

Dr. David Fyhrie (second from left) and Dr. Scott Tashman (third from left) performing research in the Herrick-Davis Motion Analysis Laboratory, Department of Orthopedic Surgery, 1993. *(From Henry Ford Health System. ID:101494_643.)*

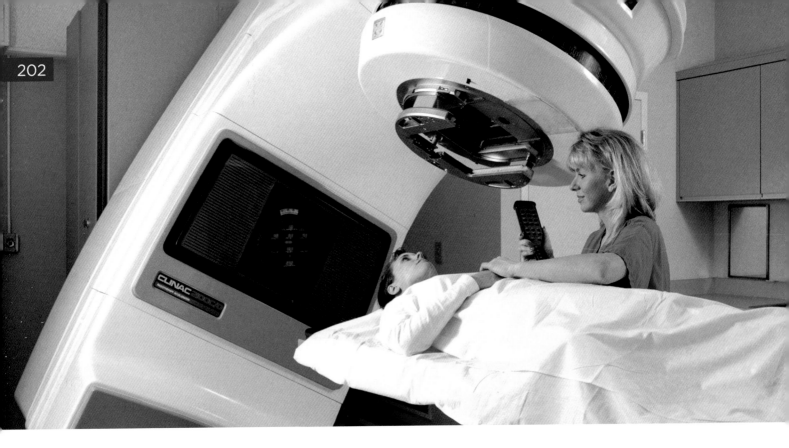

Linear accelerator, Department of Radiation Oncology, 1996. *(Detail From Henry Ford Health System. ID:101494_657.)*

community setting in that sense," said Dr. Benjamin Movsas, chair of the Department of Radiation Oncology. "I feel very passionate about research and trying to always figure out what we can do to further help our patients. I also enjoy teaching a lot, so it seemed like the right setting for me."[2] Radiosurgery of the brain and spine was developed at Henry Ford Hospital in the 1990s, with spine radiosurgery first performed in 2001. From the leadership of Dr. Jae Ho Kim to Dr. Movsas, the Radiation Oncology Department has stayed at the forefront of the field.

The Way Medicine Should Work

Since the very beginning, Henry Ford Hospital's unique arrangement with its physicians had created a team approach. As the health system grew, adding more hospitals and

1990

The Henry Ford Health Care Corporation is renamed the Henry Ford Health System.

1990

The William T. Gossett Parkinson's Disease Center, led by Dr. Jay Gorell (pictured), is established in the Department of Neurology.

From Henry Ford Health System. ID:101494_702.

1990

Dr. Clarence S. Livingood, former chief of Dermatology, becomes the first physician in Michigan to be awarded the American Medical Association's Distinguished Service Award.

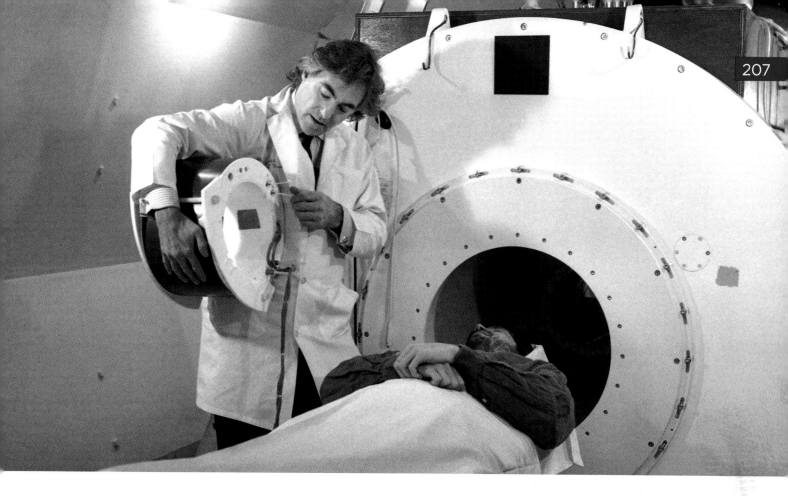

In 2003, Dr. Chopp and colleagues landed the first NIH Program Project in the US on neurorestoration research to further study brain injury due to stroke or head trauma.[16]

In many ways, the organization of Henry Ford Health System created an ideal situation for physicians and researchers to align. Dr. Mark Rosenblum, former chair of the Department of Neurosurgery, noted:

The Medical Group is set up as probably the most ideal arrangement of physicians and scientists who team together to manage, to investigate, and to develop new treatments for diseases of all types that we have. We're all employed. We all have only one responsibility.

Neurology chief Dr. K. M. A. Welch with patient in 3-Tesla magnet, 1996. *(From Henry Ford Health System. ID:101494_454.)*

1994

From Henry Ford Health System. ID:101494_166.

Dr. Kimberly Brown joins Henry Ford Hospital as medical director of liver transplantation. She becomes chief of the Division of Gastroenterology/Hepatology in 2003.

1994

Dr. Michael Seidman from the Department of Otolaryngology establishes the Henry Ford Tinnitus Center, one of only four in the US. Photo: 1997.

From Henry Ford Health System. ID:101494_703.

1994

From Henry Ford Health System. ID:101494_075.

The Comprehensive Epilepsy Center is established by neurologists Drs. Gregory Barkley (left), Brien Smith (right), and neurosurgeon Kost Elisevich.

Above: Neuroscientist
Dr. Michael Chopp, 1995.
*(From Henry Ford Health
System. ID:101494_653.)*

Right: (from left) Neuro-
oncologist Dr. Tom Mikkelsen,
brain tumor patient Kirk Dyer,
and then-chief of neurosurgery
Dr. Mark Rosenblum, 1994.
*(From Henry Ford Health
System. ID:101494_222.)*

That's to do the best that we can for the patient and, if we're lucky enough, to develop new treatments. If you get the right people in the same room focused on the same problem, sometimes coming at it from different avenues—for example, neurologists and neurosurgeons dealing with not only brain cancer but stroke or Parkinson's disease or epilepsy—we team together. It's absolutely fundamental to the patients' best interest. It really defines team medicine.[17]

Centers of Excellence

As understanding of disease and disorders grew, accrediting bodies began recognizing Centers of Excellence—a national designation that specifies that an institution has met a certain level of care. In 2013, eight programs at the health system had earned this designation: Bariatric Surgery, Cancer, Heart and Vascular, Neuroscience, Organ Transplantation, Orthopedic Surgery, Urology, and Wellness. Many of these centers could not have achieved this level of recognition without philanthropic support.

1995

Davida F. Kruger of the Division of Endocrinology and Metabolism is appointed president of education and health care for the American Diabetes Association. A certified nurse practitioner in diabetes, Kruger is a principal investigator on numerous diabetes research projects. She has written widely on diabetes care and is the recipient of numerous awards for excellence in research and distinguished service.

1995

The Fordsmen Club reunites: First row (left to right): Felton Petty, Ernest Slaton, Charles Robinson, and Fletcher Jefferson. Back row (left to right): Virgil Waters, Lee Gooden, and George Smith.

From Henry Ford Health System. ID:101494_293.

Brain tumor research expanded in 1992; researchers at Henry Ford have since identified 40 genetic markers related to brain tumors.[18] Much of this growth came as research received philanthropic support to establish the Hermelin Brain Tumor Center.

The center was named after David Hermelin, US Ambassador to Norway, who was treated by Drs. Mark Rosenblum and Tom Mikkelsen. After his diagnosis, Hermelin's family and friends raised $10 million for brain tumor research at the hospital.[19] Established in 1998, the Hermelin Brain Tumor Center received more than $30 million in research funding in its first decade and has led the initiation of new therapies as a founding member of the National Cancer Institute's brain tumor consortium, as well as many other clinical trials. Concerning Hermelin's legacy, Dr. Rosenblum said:

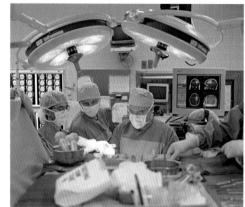

Brain tumor surgery at Henry Ford Hospital. Second from left: Dr. Kost Elisevich. Center: Dr. Mark Rosenblum, 1999. *(From Henry Ford Health System. ID:101494B_570.)*

> *David Hermelin was this phenomenal, enthusiastic person who contributed to the well-being of so many people. He was a very generous philanthropist as well. This man had such an unbelievable attitude. He took it on himself, his wife Doreen, and his family to see what we could do to make an impact and leave a legacy. As he would say, "It's my brain tumor center."* [20]

While Hermelin did not survive his brain tumor, "he still kept a positive mental attitude, so that was very important," Dr. Rosenblum said. "He would tell jokes and do magic for people in the radiation therapy waiting room while other people were waiting to have radiation therapy. It was the most remarkable thing you've ever seen in your life."[21]

Others in the community came forward to help with cancer research, too. Rajendra and Padma Vattikuti donated $20 million to support urological disease research.[22] The Vattikutis came to learn about what was being done with prostate cancer research at Henry Ford Hospital via their relationship with Dr. Vinod Sahney.

1995

From Henry Ford Health System. ID:101494_379.

The Heart and Vascular Institute conducts myriad research under the direction of Drs. Sidney Goldstein of Cardiology (left) and Daniel Reddy (right) of Vascular Surgery.

1995

From Henry Ford Health System. ID:101494B_58.

The Magnetoencephalography (MEG) Laboratory is established to pinpoint where seizures occur in the brain. Pictured, from left: Dr. Gregory Barkley and Dr. Norman Tepley, 1999.

Dr. Mani Menon, chief of the Urology Department, said:

> *I was interested in developing a minimally invasive technique for the treatment of prostate cancer, and that took me through a long route into robotics. … The prostate sits in a deep cavity in the human body. It's surrounded by a maze of veins. It's a bloody operation done the conventional way. And surgeons simply had a tough time learning it. With robotics, we now have the advantage of 3D visualization, of advanced optics. One way in which I thought that surgeons could learn is by simply taking the images and projecting them on a screen in 3D so people could see what the surgeon was doing. So we needed to create an operating room that would allow us to do that. We got the regulatory approval, and this is what has allowed me to train hundreds of surgeons. Every week, we'd have five or six people coming to see what we were doing.*[23]

Dr. Mani Menon with surgical robot. *(From Henry Ford Health System. ID:101494B_721.)*

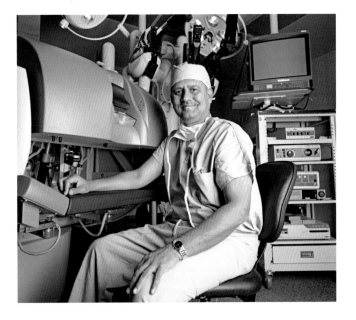

Since its inception, the Vattikuti Urology Institute—under the direction of Dr. Menon—has performed more robotic-assisted prostate surgery than any other center in the world. Through Dr. Menon's and his team's global efforts, more than 1.5 million men with prostate cancer have undergone robotic prostatectomy in at least 30 countries.

A Changing World

Medicine was changing significantly in the 21st century, especially with the new practice of minimally invasive surgery, such as robotics, which made recovery easier on patients.

1995

1995

1996

Henry Ford Hospital Nursing Conference is led by (from left) Teresa Wehrwein, Dottie Deremo, and Ken Stanton.

From Henry Ford Health System. ID:101494_377.

From Henry Ford Health System. ID:101494_373.

Mrs. Marion Lam (center) at the opening of the Conrad R. Lam Archives at Henry Ford Health System.

A cross-racial living kidney transplant between two friends is performed at Henry Ford Hospital. This is the first of its kind in Michigan.

Dr. Paul Edwards, Distinguished Cornelius McCole Chair of the Department of Ophthalmology, detailed how cataract eye surgery improved with the advent of the robots. "Previous to that, we would make a large incision and express the central part of the cataract as a whole, but now we are able to make little holes in the eye and, with a needle-like device, go in, and the needle-like device vibrates, and as it vibrates it shaves the cataract up into little pieces."

Ford Family Legacy of Giving Continues

Many new advances that were developed at Henry Ford emerged from research that was supported by the philanthropic community in metropolitan Detroit and nationally. Henry Ford Health System maintained its long association with the Ford family, who continued to make significant contributions.

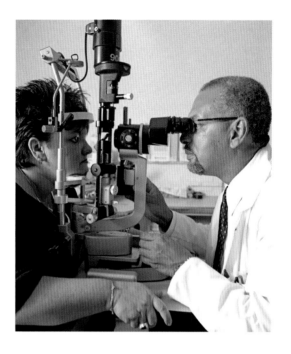

Dr. Paul Edwards. *(From Henry Ford Health System. ID:101494B_754.)*

As the honorary co-chairs of the Henry Ford "Fund for the Future," a major fundraising initiative launched in 1994, William Clay and Martha Ford committed $6 million. Josephine (Dody) Ford, in memory of her late husband Walter B. Ford (from another Ford family), donated $4 million to establish a cancer center at Henry Ford Hospital. In 1998, Josephine donated $10 million to the cancer center, which was renamed in her honor.

"She was clearly very influenced in a positive way by the care that [Walter] received and made a major donation to the Henry Ford Health System. This established the cancer center," said Dr. Robert Chapman, director of the Josephine Ford Cancer Institute. He added:

The economic impact on the health care system in terms of the cancer patients we treat has tripled, and we continue to grow both in a business sense but also in terms of the scope

1996

The first successful transplant of the Acorn CorCap Cardiac Support Device is conducted at Henry Ford Hospital. The surgery is performed by cardiothoracic surgeon Dr. Robert Brewer. Dr. Barbara B. Czerska, director of the Heart Failure Program, provides medical care for the patient.

1996

Joyce Farrer, R.N., a longtime administrator of the Department of Emergency Medicine, participates in "Take our Daughters to Work" Day.

From Henry Ford Health System. ID:101494_441.

1997

Dr. Donald M. Borsand shows the architectural rendering for the supervision center planned in Roseville.

From Henry Ford Health System. ID:101494_756.

and the quality of care that we're able to offer patients who pass through our doors. The difference between a cancer institute and individual divisions of medical oncology or surgical or radiation oncology is that the cancer institute provides an infrastructure that brings all of that together. It allows all of the different disciplines to feed off of each other and perform optimally, while bringing in both supportive care services and research on top of the basic platform of clinical services.[24]

Dr. S. David Nathanson.
(From Henry Ford Health System. ID:101494_412.)

Breast cancer research and treatment has benefited greatly from the cancer team approach. Dr. S. David Nathanson from surgical oncology research, Dr. Maria Worsham from pathology and otolaryngology research, and Dr. Christine Cole Johnson from public health sciences

research each studied the genetics of breast cancer and development of new diagnostic tests. In the 1990s, Dr. Nathanson started the multidisciplinary breast cancer clinic with tumor board results, patient education, and specialty consultation for patients at one visit. As part of a national clinical trial, Dr. Nathanson was among the first to use sentinel node biopsy as a diagnostic tool for breast cancer, which later became a standard of care nationwide. The research team of Drs. Worsham, Cole Johnson, and Usha Raju designed a test to determine the risk of breast cancer recurrence, which was available only at Henry Ford Hospital in 1998. This breast cancer gene test was approved by the US Food and Drug Administration.

1997

1998

1998

From Henry Ford Health System. ID:101494_619.

Scientist Dr. Hajimi Hayashi of Immunopathology receives a Distinguished Career Award from Henry Ford.

Josephine Ford, granddaughter of Henry Ford and Henry Ford Hospital Board of Trustee member, donates $10 million to support cancer research at Henry Ford. The Josephine Ford Cancer Center is named in her honor.

The Benson Ford Endowed Chair in Transplantation is established at Henry Ford Hospital.

Lung cancer and pulmonary diseases were another major research effort undertaken at Henry Ford Hospital. The Division of Pulmonary and Critical Care Medicine, led by Drs. Paul Kvale, John Popovich, and Michael Eichenhorn, as well as Dr. Bill Conway, achieved national recognition via participating in NIH multicenter national trials to advance treatment for patients with these debilitating lung diseases. The Division also became one of few in the US to offer interventional pulmonology therapies, led by Dr. Michael Simoff.

By 2014, the Josephine Ford Cancer Institute had 12 different types of tumor boards—multidisciplinary teams that evaluate and discuss personalized treatment plans. Research is a significant aspect of the institute; in 2014, more than 200 cancer research trials had been conducted.[25]

Lynn Ford Alandt, Henry Ford's great-granddaughter and daughter of Benson and Edith, along with her husband Paul, donated $5 million in 2004 for the first electromagnetic navigation suite in Michigan. The Paul & Lynn Alandt Catheterization & Electrophysiology Center is the site of innovative cardiac therapies today at the Edith and Benson Ford Heart and Vascular Institute.

With so many advances in research, Henry Ford Hospital and Henry Ford Health System's impact on the broader field of medicine was no doubt being felt. But the health system would move into an era of ensuring that performance excellence occurred with every patient encounter, no matter which Henry Ford facility was involved.

Walter Buhl Ford II and Josephine Clay Ford. *(From the Conrad R. Lam Collection, Henry Ford Health System. ID=12-003.)*

1998

Henry Ford Health System is awarded a grant from the state of Michigan. The African-American Initiative for Male Health Improvement (AIMHI) program was created to concentrate on diabetes, stroke, and eye disease. Dr. Kimberlydawn Wisdom of the Medical Treatment Effectiveness Program in Diverse Populations (MEDTEP) takes the lead in the partnerships with the community organizations.

1998

Nancy Schlichting joins Henry Ford Health System as senior vice president.

1999

Friends and family of David Hermelin, former US ambassador to Norway, donate $10 million for brain tumor research. The Hermelin Brain Tumor Center is named in his honor.

Thirteen

" *The difference between people who are really successful and people getting by is successful people can execute the plan. We have a disciplined approach. It's very deliberate in terms of what we're going to do and how we monitor it, so we are continuing to stay on point in terms of execution.*"

Anthony Armada
FORMER CEO, HENRY FORD HOSPITAL[1]

Culture of
Performance Excellence

2000
Present

Henry Ford Health System's Pathology and Laboratory Medicine Service Line received the prestigious ISO 15189 accreditation in June 2013 as the largest integrated laboratory system in the US. *(From Henry Ford Health System. ID:76193_jjg_9634.)*

ALL THE PIECES OF THE QUALITY AND PERFORMANCE IMPROVEMENT PUZZLE WERE IN hand. But before Henry Ford Health System could fully realize its potential, it had to fit those puzzle pieces together seamlessly. It would do so with a new leadership team in place, a new hospital in the suburbs, and a renewed commitment to its Detroit home base.

Toward the end of the 1990s, the system dealt with new financial challenges, especially as Henry Ford Hospital grappled with crippling amounts of unpaid care. The world of health care was changing, too. Increasing its emphasis on quality initiatives and the kind of improvements that showcased the staggering pace of medical change had not necessarily resulted in improved financial outcomes. But Henry Ford Health System forged ahead by realigning its components and creating a vision that would earn the respect of its peers.

Third Time's a Charm

Gail Warden had met Nancy Schlichting while Warden was chair of the American Hospital Association (AHA). He began mentoring her, asking about her career plans, and providing advice on her future. When a position as Henry Ford's chief administrative officer opened up, he thought of Schlichting. She interviewed and was offered the job, which she turned down. "It was just not the right time for me," Schlichting said.[2]

It was actually the second time she had declined an offer at Henry Ford. She previously had been recruited as CEO of St. Joseph's Mercy Hospital, at that time operating as a joint venture of Henry Ford and Mercy Health System. That also had been a wrong fit.[3]

Despite declining the jobs, Schlichting knew plenty about Henry Ford. She had met Stan Nelson while he was Henry Ford CEO and in AHA leadership. She had also visited the Fairlane Medical Center during her AHA fellowship position. "I met Dr. Bruce

From left, Gail Warden and Nancy Schlichting. *(From Henry Ford Health System. ID:gail&nancy0051.)*

Steinhauer on that visit and had a chance to learn about the vision of the Henry Ford Health System, how unique it was in terms of its structure and its accomplishment," Schlichting said. "And then, when I worked in Ohio, I came back to Henry Ford because of the learning lab that was offered for really understanding all the dimensions of the health system. Long before I ever thought I'd work here, I had been here twice."[4]

The third time Schlichting was offered a position—this time as senior vice president—the

2000

The Health Alliance Plan Internet Referral Program, which provides immediate access to medical services, is honored by the US government. The program's website is placed in the Smithsonian Institution's permanent information technology collection at the National Museum of American History.

2000

From Henry Ford Health System. ID:101494_014.

The Henry Ford Center for Senior Independence becomes the first Program of All Inclusive Care (PACE) site in the state of Michigan. Longtime geriatric specialist Dr. Gwendolyn Graddy-Dansby (pictured, 1995) is director.

timing was right. She took on the role in 1998 and a year later was promoted to chief operating officer. "I always felt like it was a bit of an arranged marriage with these amazing mentors that I had," Schlichting said. "The decision to come to Detroit actually was very disappointing to my mentor in Akron, who wanted me to succeed him when he retired. So while that didn't work out, coming to Henry Ford has been by far the best decision I've ever made in my career."[5]

Schlichting's career at Henry Ford took off. By 2001, she had assumed the additional responsibilities as president of Henry Ford Hospital, which was in serious need. The financial pressures, particularly at the flagship hospital, led to rounds of layoffs as the facility tried to regain its financial footing. Not only were providers cutting payments, but the urban center struggled with uninsured patients.

"The hardest thing I've done since I've been at Henry Ford was to lay off about 600 people from Henry Ford Hospital in January of 2002," Schlichting said. "The only thing good that came out of it was we got back on our financial footing. We turned around the institution in terms of its operations, and, ultimately, we brought a lot of the people back that we had to lay off. But that was a very difficult time. One of the drives for everything we do, even in today's environment, is to never repeat that situation."[6]

The financial turnaround allowed the hospital to put in place benchmarks that would show "where opportunities are," said Tony Armada, who succeeded Schlichting as Henry Ford Hospital CEO. "We started a monthly operating review that looked at all of the aspects of operations in a very disciplined way, and that was one of those takeaways from the for-profit industry."[7]

The turnaround at Henry Ford Hospital was swift, with the hospital operating in the black within a few years. But it also put in place key pieces that would shape the hospital—and the health system—for many years to come.

2000

Radiofrequency ablation is offered for patients with liver cancer. Dr. Marwan Abouljoud (pictured left, with US Senator Carl Levin), surgical director of the Liver Transplant Program, pioneers this minimally invasive technique.

2000

The hospital's anticoagulation program receives American Medical Group Association recognition for its breakthrough improvements in patient care. Dr. Scott Kaatz of Internal Medicine is director of the program.

2001

Raj and Padma Vattikuti donate $20 million to support prostate cancer research and education. Named in their honor, the Vattikuti Urology Institute at Henry Ford is led by Dr. Mani Menon, who soon becomes known as the "father of robotic surgery" for his global influence on the research and use of robotic prostatectomy to treat prostate cancer.

Leadership Development

When system CEO Gail Warden decided to retire and the search began for his successor, Schlichting quickly made her way to the top of the list. Robert Riney, then the chief human resources officer, commented on the selection of Schlichting as system CEO:

Bob Riney and Nancy Schlichting. *(From Henry Ford Health System. ID:87257_bob_nancy_2011.)*

Nancy is clearly smart as a whip. She's articulate, and she's a very warm and genuine person, but she's also incredibly strategic. I've been in a lot of search committees because of my HR background. Watching her was really like watching art in its greatest form because she knew how to engage all members of the search committee and tell a story that was inspirational, aspirational, and pragmatic about the evolution of Henry Ford Health System.[8]

Unlike Warden, who had a varied background that included health plans, Schlichting's experience had primarily been in hospitals. Prior to accepting the position as CEO of the health system, Schlichting needed to make sure the Board of Trustees recognized that her strengths were different from those of her would-be predecessor:

One of the key questions I asked the board was: "Do you want me to be exactly like Gail?" Because Gail and I are very different in our backgrounds and in our experiences. I was relieved when they said, "No, you have to do the job in the way that you want to do it." So I've always tried to build connectivity with the people that deliver care into my world.

2001

Nancy Schlichting becomes the first woman CEO of Henry Ford Hospital.

2003

Dr. John Ferrara, Dr. Jeffrey Genaw, Dr. Arthur Carlin, and Wanda Szymanski, R.N., develop the Bariatric Surgery Center.

2003

Michigan Governor Jennifer Granholm appoints Dr. Kimberlydawn Wisdom as the state's first surgeon general. Dr. Wisdom serves on committees with the US Department of Health and Human Services and the National Institutes of Health.

On my worst days, I go visit patients because that gives me a constant reminder of the importance of what we do, and it continues to inspire me.[9]

Schlichting, who was the first woman CEO of Henry Ford Hospital, became the first woman CEO of Henry Ford Health System in 2003. Other key positions needed to be filled. Riney became chief operating officer and Jim Connelly chief financial officer. Other important leaders at the time were Dr. Mark Kelley, CEO of the Henry Ford Medical Group; and Dr. William Conway, chief quality officer. Armada was recruited to be CEO of Henry Ford Hospital.

"[Nancy] has shown a great propensity to think out of the box and take in leaders that might not have come through stereotypical pathways in health care, including myself," said Riney. "She constantly helps create the environment to make people love and fall back in love with the place they work."[10]

Schlichting also quickly became involved in the city leadership. "She is eloquent in terms of her vision," said Dave Bing, Detroit mayor from 2009 to 2013. "She knows exactly where she wants the hospital to go, she knows what it's going to take internally to get everybody on the same team to complement her vision, and … she's one of the few females who are

Focused on Wellness

Dr. Kimberlydawn Wisdom had spent most of her career at Henry Ford Health System when she was tapped by Governor Jennifer Granholm to be Michigan's surgeon general in 2003—the first person to hold that position in the state. When it was time for her to transition back to Henry Ford, she wanted to focus on community health and wellness as well as health disparities.

As senior vice president of community health and equity, chief wellness officer and chief diversity officer of the health system, Dr. Wisdom is today one of the leading proponents of the health care industry's shift toward disease prevention. She noted:

It's very clear now that we need to move upstream to address wellness. Our data shows us nationally that there are many chronic conditions that are entirely preventable, and if we address those or approach those conditions from a wellness perspective, we can

prevent them. We can be a healthier city, healthier state, healthier country, and compete globally. It's an opportunity to begin to create a virtual center where we can speak with one single voice in terms of all the wellness offerings that we have across the health care system. It's also an opportunity to help people understand that wellness is a lifelong journey that we want everyone to experience, and not a destination to be achieved by only a few.[1]

In 2011, President Barack Obama appointed Dr. Wisdom to serve on an advisory group on prevention, health promotion, and integrative health. The group advises the president's Cabinet on health promotion and disease prevention.[2]

leading one of our major organizations here in the city. So I think that, as young women in particular are looking at their futures, all they've got to do is look at Nancy. She's a great role model."[11]

Mayor Dave Bing at the CHASS Southwest ribbon cutting, 2012.

A Common Strategy

By 2005, with new leadership in place and Henry Ford Hospital realigned, it was time to bring the health system together in a way that would raise the bar throughout. The integration meant ensuring that patients who sought care at any Henry Ford facility would receive the same high-quality level of care. That meant standardizing care protocols across the health system as well as developing a shared culture of performance excellence among the more than 20,000 employees.

"A lot of our work has been not necessarily mergers or acquisitions but more about creating a synergy, an alignment through collaborative planning and program development approaches," said William Schramm, senior vice president of business development. "It's helping the organization achieve a desired business model, which is a compilation of the products and services in the portfolio. How do you leverage those various products and services to sustain the enterprise over the long term? It really is looking at both inside and outside the organization, how we continue to bring together the right pieces and the right approach to sustain the organization."[12]

2003

Nancy Schlichting becomes CEO of Henry Ford Health System, the first woman to hold that position. She appoints Bob Riney executive vice president and chief operating officer.

2003

Linda Harden, R.N., receives the People's Choice Award—Michigan Registered Nurses, Detroit News/Free Press.

2004

Henry Ford Health System receives the Foster G. McGaw Prize. The annual award is given to an organization committed to programs and services that promote health and well-being in the community.

Building a health system that will operate with strength for the long term has meant ensuring that the culture permeates all operations, whether as a new enterprise or an acquisition, as Armada noted:

> *Henry Ford has always had a very strong culture. The common denominators for an organization to become highly reliable and high-performance are in the leadership and in the engagement of people. If you can create a culture where leaders lead, it builds trust within the environment, and everyone then feels that they understand why they do what they do. That's when the engagement of the people starts to occur. And I believe that's when you actually transform cultures from average to good, from good to great, from great to best.*[13]

Henry Ford Health System's culture was about to be challenged with its plans for expansion. The idea had always been to build a hospital in West Bloomfield. That's one of the reasons why Henry Ford purchased significant acreage in the 1970s when it placed a clinic there. However, securing a certificate of need had been nearly impossible. Darlene Burgess, vice president of corporate and government affairs, recalled:

> *The formula that the commission was using basically said that the area where we wanted to build a hospital currently had adequate hospital access. The reason was the planning area went all the way over almost to Brighton. What it ignored was the fact that, early in the history of that area, most of the*

West Bloomfield Hospital construction, 2008.
(From Henry Ford Health System. ID:DSC_0037.)

2004

Francine Parker is appointed president and CEO of the Health Alliance Plan (HAP). She started with HAP in 1978 and was a leading force for its continual growth.

2004

A nurse-led rapid response team is implemented at Henry Ford Hospital. Results show reduced mortality rates.

2005

Henry Ford Health System breaks ground on the $310 million, 300-bed Henry Ford West Bloomfield Hospital.

Construction of the Henry Ford West Bloomfield Hospital, 2008. *(From Henry Ford Health System. ID:RM1_2490.)*

hospitals were built on the east side of that planning region, whereas the population grew over time to the west side. So in areas like West Bloomfield and Canton and those other communities on the west side, there were no hospitals. We weren't able to get the commission to recognize that basic flaw in their planning formula.[14]

Rather than continue to fight the commission, Henry Ford Health System took its issue to the Michigan legislature in 2002. "In five weeks, we had a law that allowed us to expand the clinic we had at that location into a 300-bed hospital," Burgess said.[15] This decision was reached despite heavy opposition from competing hospitals, some health plans, and the business community. Ultimately, Henry Ford West Bloomfield Hospital was approved and planning began.

2005

Henry Ford Health System joins the Institute for Healthcare Improvement's 100,000 Lives Campaign, which implements proven health care improvement techniques to reduce medical errors and save lives.

2005

The Henry Ford Medical Group designs an insignia to reflect the professional standards of the medical staff.

2005

Dr. Emanuel Rivers of Emergency Medicine is inducted into the Institute of Medicine for his research on sepsis, which was published in the *New England Journal of Medicine*.

Merging Hospital Functions

At the same time the health system was building the new hospital in West Bloomfield, the system began to focus on how to deliver quality care on a consistent basis. That meant merging some hospital functions—never an easy task, especially when it meant job loss. However, standardizing would bring cost savings, greater efficiencies, and improved results for patients.

Take pathology, for instance. Each facility had its own laboratory services and private pathology group. Dr. Richard Zarbo, senior vice president for Pathology and Laboratory Medicine, said:

There was no means of standardizing across the system, being able to do things in a standardized fashion so that patients saw the same reference ranges, for instance, or even had the same quality on a pathology report. This was a total frustration to me, as I was chair of the College of American Pathologists Quality Committee. I helped set the standards for what is quality, and what is quality assurance. All of those laboratories reported to administrators of each medical center. Nothing was standardized.[16]

Dr. Richard Zarbo (right) of Pathology in 2004. *(From Henry Ford Health System. ID:48514_dscf0109.)*

Integration was no simple process. It took several years until the disparate lab services were integrated into one. "In 2008, I brought a plan to Bob Riney, and I told him I wanted to integrate all of the community hospitals' lab services into one corporate entity, one service

2006

2006

Dr. Ron Davis, director of the Henry Ford Health System Center for Health Promotion and Disease Prevention, is elected president of the American Medical Association.

From the Conrad R. Lam Collection, Henry Ford Health System. ID=09-044.

The Emergency Department expands to include a lobby area and 27 additional bays for patient care. From left, Drs. Richard Nowak, Michael Tomlanovich, and Enrique Enriquez of Emergency Medicine, c. 1990.

line," Dr. Zarbo said. "I told him, 'We have to act because there are private practice contracts that are going to come up for renewal, and if we renew them, it'll never happen in my lifetime. But if you allow me to do this now … I can do that.'"[17]

Dr. Zarbo then had to make his case to hospital administrators at each of the facilities and to persuade the existing pathologists to join the Henry Ford Medical Group. "That allowed us, over a four-year period of time, to consolidate all non-emergent testing from those hospitals into core laboratories on the Detroit campus," Dr. Zarbo said.

Practically speaking, it meant around-the-clock results, where previously some of the suburban hospitals had more limited hours. Dr. Zarbo added:

Cytogenetics Laboratory,
Dr. Daniel Van Dyke (left)
and Nancie Petrucelli, 1999.
*(From Henry Ford Health
System. ID:101494b_277.)*

It's rapid response testing, and it allowed us, by feeding volume into these core laboratories, to reduce our costs back to the hospitals by 20 percent in four years. We have worked at that day in and day out in a maniacal fashion. We are probably one of the models for the nation of what a core laboratory operation is like.[18]

The result is a laboratory system that operates by principles of lean management, frequently adopted by manufacturing to encourage continual improvement. Henry Ford Health System had found a way to take the best business principles and apply them to health care.

Nursing also experienced the same desire to integrate services—and to ensure that quality was standard across the system, said Connie Cronin, former chief nursing officer first at Wyandotte Hospital and then for the health system. "It's important that you have your own identity, but there's a point where you have to work together," Cronin said. "There have to be some similarities across all of the system. Otherwise, you're not a system.

2007

The Henry Ford Health System No Harm Campaign is launched with a goal to reduce mortality by 25 percent within three years. The system-wide initiative to improve patient safety and reduce medical errors will go on to win a quality award in 2011.

2007

MetaVision iMD software is implemented to bring electronic documentation to adult ICUs and NICUs.

2007

Henry Ford Health System launches the $250 million ENVISION Campaign to raise funds to expand facilities and enhance clinical programs and research. The campaign exceeded its goal in 2013, garnering 65 gifts of $1 million or more.

You're just a group of places. I saw that as an opportunity to really get nursing together, all the leadership of nursing, and work together for some very specific goals."[19]

Topping that list of goals were quality and safety standards. "It's all about the quality of care that we can deliver to our patients, and it's all about providing safe care," Cronin said. "Deeply ingrained in any nurse, as in any physician, is the desire to provide safe, quality care. So the challenge was, how do we define quality, and how do we measure it?"[20] The same continual measurement and improvement would take hold throughout the system.

Nurses in Board Room, Henry Ford Hospital, 2001. *(Detail From Henry Ford Health System. ID:101494b_676.)*

Veronica (Ronnie) Hall, currently chief nursing officer for the health system, said, "The Corporate Nurse Executive Council meets monthly to continue to standardize clinical protocols, policies, and procedures, even job descriptions. We look at what will benefit all of the nursing across the system. This is how we move things forward, by looking at what's currently happening and being planned in each of the communities."[21]

Aligning All Parts of the System

The quest for performance excellence needed to be part of the health system's culture at every level. That meant each new board would become engaged with the system's goals. "Nancy Schlichting talked about the mission, vision, and values of the system. She talked about what each entity brought to the table in terms of its services and how it added value to the system as a whole," said Edith Eisenmann, vice president and chief governance officer.[22]

2008

Dr. John Popovich leads development of the Henry Ford Physician Network. The network includes Henry Ford Medical Group and independent practice physicians at the Henry Ford Health System sharing adoption and use of clinical protocols for high-quality care.

2008

From Henry Ford Health System. ID:menon0889.

The Vattikuti Urology Institute nears 4,000 robotic procedures, more than any other hospital in the world. Dr. Mani Menon (center) is pictured with residents.

Dr. John Popovich, 1999.
(From Henry Ford Health System. ID:101494b_575.)

In 2005, Schlichting selected the Baldrige performance criteria for the health system to follow. The engagement of the board members was evident when, in 2007, the system Board of Trustees made health care quality its top priority for the system. That led to the launch of the No Harm Campaign, a system-wide sharing of best clinical practices and a new way to help align the Medical Group and independent practice physicians at Henry Ford.

An important focus of integration across the health system involved the relationship between the Henry Ford Medical Group and the health system's independent practice physicians. The Henry Ford Physician Network was introduced to remove the barriers to coordination of patient care across providers. It was an idea that had been kicked around for decades—back to Gail Warden's earliest days at the system. Dr. John Popovich, president and CEO of Henry Ford Hospital, noted:

[Gail] saw that times were changing, in which hospitals had to be able to integrate their clinical staff, especially the physicians. They could be separate groups, but they had to really work as a team. He saw that becoming increasingly important, which today is the basis of what we consider to be the integrated health system, with networks that are physician-led and have physicians in more prominent positions of organizational leadership. All good ideas always come around.[23]

The Henry Ford Physician Network was an answer to that good idea, offering physicians—whether practicing privately or in the Henry Ford Medical Group—access to collaborative practices to improve quality while lowering cost.

2009

The Henry Ford Hospital Intensive Care Unit expands to more than 240 beds, becoming the largest ICU in Michigan. The medical and surgical ICUs are staffed by specialist intensivist physicians and critical care nurses.

2009

Henry Ford Hospital is Michigan's first to participate in a domino donor kidney transplant in which eight patients receive a new kidney from eight unrelated donors at four hospitals in four states. Performed at Henry Ford Hospital, Johns Hopkins Medical Center in Baltimore, INTEGRIS Baptist Medical Center in Oklahoma City, and Barnes-Jewish Hospital in St. Louis, the surgeries begin the largest series of kidney paired donations ever.

2009

The Henry Ford West Bloomfield Hospital opens to the public. The $360 million, 730,000-square-foot hospital is the second one built in the history of the health system.

It was not always an easy sale. Dr. Popovich "spoke to these physicians and listened to their concerns, validated them, didn't defend them, and had undertaken many steps to change them," said Dr. Charles Kelly, president and CEO of the Henry Ford Physician Network. He added:

> *We got together with a consultant group to talk about how we could change this hub-and-spoke feeder hospital system that we've built into one that could be envisioned as more of a partner with its private physicians. Many models were examined. But in the end, the decision was made that developing an aligned physician network based on [Federal Trade Commission] guiding principles, around clinical integration that was physician-led, would be the most successful approach. The whole idea is that you're aligning all of your physician groups, whether it be in private practice or employed practice, to one goal, essentially delivering superior quality, so it can never be a bad strategy. But you also have an eye on efficiency, and so the business model really is one of creating a narrowed network of physicians committed to high performance. That is what will differentiate you in the marketplace and serve as a strategy for growth.[24]*

The Henry Ford Physician Network includes all Henry Ford Medical Group physicians and those independent practice physicians who elect to belong—a total of 1,900 physicians. "We excelled in our performance with our learning lab contract as the result of our outcome measures," Dr. Kelly said. He added:

Dr. Charles Kelly, CEO, Henry Ford Physician Network. *(From Henry Ford Health System. ID:96119_RVA_6200.)*

> *We actually bent the cost curve. That was really a key success factor for us because with that data and that success, we could go to other purchasers of health care essentially with, "Here's what we did with our employees. Let us do it for you." That is a very convincing*

2010

Dr. John Popovich becomes the first physician CEO of Henry Ford Hospital since Dr. Robin C. Buerki in the 1950s.

2010

Henry Ford Hospital receives the American Hospital Association's McKesson Quest for Quality Prize.

2010

Primarily funded by an anonymous donor, the intraoperative MRI is installed within Henry Ford Hospital's operating rooms to obtain a more precise and accurate image of the brain during neurosurgical procedures. Dr. Steven Kalkanis (pictured in the iMRI suite) is appointed chief of Neurosurgery in 2014.

From Henry Ford Health System. ID:83147_rva_7351.

message to someone who is providing health care to their employees to see such success. So there
were not only savings but enhancement of quality, and that satisfies both sides of the
value equation.[25]

Perfect Depression Care

Henry Ford Health System's commitment to improving health care delivery was on pace
with a national movement to improve results. In 2001, while Warden chaired a task force at
the Institute of Medicine (IOM), a groundbreaking study—*Crossing the Quality Chasm*—was

released. The IOM report "pointed out how good the people are in health
care in this country and how much progress we're making scientifically
around health care on the one hand," said Dr. C. Edward Coffey, former
CEO of Behavioral Health Services. "On the other, it pointed out that all
that hard work and dedication and knowledge is not being translated into
measurably better care at the bedside. That gap between what's possible on
the one hand and what patients were receiving on the other is the chasm
that was referred to in the title of the report."[26]

Inspired by the report, and the blueprint it offered to improve health
care, "It was obvious that this was a path forward for us, that if we could
find a way to leverage this information in this document, we might be able

Dr. C. Edward Coffey, 1999.
(From Henry Ford Health
System. ID:101494b_576.)

to improve health care substantially and reconnect to the values that got us into the business in the first place," Dr. Coffey said.[27] "We decided to use the IOM's Chasm Report
as a model for not just improving our depression care, not just making it better by 2 or
3 or 10 percent, but by dramatically transforming the care and eliminating errors, making
it as perfect as possible."[28]

2010

The NanoKnife, which sends
out quick, short electri-
cal pulses to kill tumors, is
offered as a tool for hard-
to-reach surgical areas
by Dr. Vic Velanovich,
longtime chief of the
General Surgery Division.

2010

Dr. Marwan Kazimi and
Dr. Marwan Abouljoud
perform the first intesti-
nal transplant in Michigan
at Henry Ford Hospital.
The 11-hour procedure
includes transplant of
the patient's small bowel,
stomach, and pancreas.

2011

From Henry Ford Health System. ID:Hall_Veronica_10C.

Veronica (Ronnie) Hall
is named chief nursing
officer for Henry Ford
Health System and
continues in her role as
chief operating officer
for Henry Ford Hospital.

Dr. Coffey took this concept to his staff. He asked: "What would truly effective depression care look like, and how would we know? We were struggling with this concept. It couldn't just be simply a reduction by some percent in depression symptoms, which is what everyone else has been doing for decades."[29]

A multidisciplinary group grappled with the idea of perfection. Dr. Coffey recalled:

A nurse said, "If we were truly effective at depression care, maybe nobody would die from suicide." The room got still and quiet. No one said anything for a couple of minutes, and then finally one of our more senior clinicians spoke up and said, "Well, that's crazy! If someone wants to kill themselves, we can't possibly stop it." And the department began to have a dialogue wherein, on the one hand, we knew that it might be true that if somebody really wants to do this, it may be impossible to stop them. But on the other, if zero is not our goal, what number must our goal be? How many suicides are we going to tolerate as a system?[30]

Out of that discussion, Henry Ford Behavorial Health Services moved to Perfect Depression Care, a promise to every single patient that he or she will not die from suicide. The goal was impressive, and the results were staggering. In the first four years of the program's implementation, the rate of suicide fell by 75 percent. Then, the department achieved its goal of no suicides and has maintained that for more than a decade.[31]

Behavioral Health Services team, c. 2000. *(From Henry Ford Health System. ID:Group.)*

The success of Perfect Depression Care led to the Joint Commission's Ernest Amory Codman Award, a health care award that recognizes excellence in performance measurement. Dr. Coffey added:

The fundamental essence of that culture is what we call a "just culture." It's a culture in which every single teammate is encouraged to swing for the fence, to hit a home run at each at-bat, but at

2011

2011

Bob Riney becomes president of Henry Ford Health System.

Henry Ford Health System is one of only four US recipients of the 2011 Malcolm Baldrige National Quality Award. The award is presented annually by the President of the United States to organizations that demonstrate quality and performance excellence.

the same time, to not be penalized if they swing for the fence and strike out. That's the essential role of

the leader. You have to create that balance between going for it and striving—reaching for the moon,

on the one hand, and yet not feeling paralyzed by fear if you don't succeed every single time.[32]

Saving Lives

Audacious goals were not limited to the psychiatry department. The Institute for Healthcare Improvement launched a campaign to reduce treatment-related infections. The campaign, called Saving Lives, set a goal in 2004 to save 100,000 lives. Henry Ford Health System contributed to that goal, saving 200 lives and $2.5 million annually. Out of that success came Henry Ford Health System's No Harm campaign.

Between 2008 and 2011, the campaign resulted in a 26 percent reduction in harm events and a 12 percent reduction in patient mortality. Most hospitals were reducing harm events between 1 and 2 percent at the time.[33] That success rate brought the 2011 John M. Eisenberg Patient Safety and Quality Award to Henry Ford Health System.

"[Physicians] were anxious to try anything like the No Harm campaign to improve the results—either quality results or customer satisfaction results," said Gary Valade, chair of the Board of Trustees during this time period, who added:

I think the attitude of the management team being willing to accept and test and try to

do the right thing—whether it was the right thing for getting reimbursement or not—they

always acted toward trying to do the right thing for the patient. That really impressed me,

and you can see it in the doctors. They're trying as hard as they can to make this the best place

that they can.[34]

2011	2011	2011

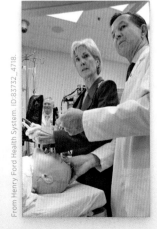

From Henry Ford Health System. ID:83732_4718.

Kathleen Sebelius, (left) US secretary of Health and Human Services, visits Henry Ford Health System. Dr. Scott Dulchavsky (right) demonstrates education techniques in the SIM Center.

Henry Ford Health System holds the 20th Annual Quality Expo.

Henry Ford Health System receives the John M. Eisenberg Patient Safety and Quality Award in Washington, DC. The system is recognized for its successful No Harm Campaign, which serves as a national model for improvement in patient safety.

Dr. William Conway kicks off the No Harm campaign. *(From Henry Ford Health System. ID:rm1_7887.)*

First, Do No Harm

As Henry Ford Health System worked to improve quality, it launched the No Harm campaign under the leadership of Dr. William Conway. The "No Harm" campaign was a Henry Ford Health System initiative that built upon the Institute for Healthcare Improvement's Saving Lives campaign.

"There were a lot of demands on health care for change and in all kinds of different directions," said Dr. Conway, the health system's chief quality officer at that time. In assessing changes the health system needed to make, it drew upon its Board of Trustees as representatives of their communities. "We were trying to figure out how to organize this retreat of the board, and the staff wanted to use the outline of the Institute of Medicine's six aims, which includes improved safety, efficiency, and effectiveness. It was impressive, the response of the board. They said, 'We can't imagine that going through a health care experience, you could be harmed. You really need to do something about that.' And this was almost a unanimous opinion of the board."[1]

The board suggested Dr. Conway and his team put together an aggressive program that included several lofty aims. The team developed a comprehensive measure of harms in hospitals—accidents related to medicines, infections, and poor care, among other things. From that, an approach was created to attack the root causes.

"Over three years, we reduced harm at about three times the rate that it was going down across the rest of the country, so it was a pretty successful program," Dr. Conway said. "It mobilized the entire organization. We had safety champions deployed in just about every department in the organization. Medicare has now adopted this approach. Instead of looking at what, in the past, would have been working on one project at a time, it meant taking on the entire topic of harm reduction in a more comprehensive way."[2]

Within three years, the campaign was estimated to have saved the health system $10 million.[3]

The World Notices

Riding high on the two major initiatives that had earned some of the highest honors in health care, Henry Ford Health System set its goals even higher: to land some of the top awards in business.

"Gail created a very strong appetite in the organization for awards and industry recognition," said Patricia Stoltz, formerly the director of Health Care Quality Improvement Education and Research at Henry Ford and later an examiner with the Malcolm Baldrige Quality Awards. "From my perspective, it was a cultural characteristic, and other organizations might not have it. I think that there was just a recognition among the very top leaders that this kind of visibility was an enhancement to the system in terms of its reputation."[35]

In 1999, the Baldrige Award—the nation's highest business honor—had begun assessing health care entities as part of its process. That drew the attention of Nancy Schlichting, who noted:

> There were a couple of goals that I had for the Baldrige work. One was just to get better in everything we do. I didn't think our operational performance was at the level that it needed to be. We weren't focused on our patients enough. We weren't focused on our employees enough. We weren't focused on our community enough, or our physicians. We had a lot of room for improvement. The other goal was, I wanted the system to get better. I wanted the integration of our work to get better.[36]

That last goal was one reason that Schlichting opted to have the entire health system—not just one business unit or facility—enter the Baldrige process. "One of the great strengths of Baldrige is that it pushes you to be more integrated, and so I was hoping we'd be a better

2011

The Transplant Institute at Henry Ford Hospital receives the Department of Health and Human Services Medal of Honor for Organ Donation for reaching a 75 percent organ donation rate for eligible donors. It is the second consecutive year that the hospital has received the honor.

2012

Dr. William O'Neill joins Henry Ford Hospital as director of the Center for Structural Heart Disease. Dr. O'Neill is internationally known as a leader in interventional cardiology.

system. I thought, 'If only one unit won, it wouldn't help the system,'" she said.[37] "It might spur jealously, which would not be good for the culture."

Schlichting had explored the Baldrige award before coming to Henry Ford and noted:

> *When I came here, I didn't think we were ready for it right away because we were going through all of our cost work, and it was very hard to get people focused on that framework at a time when we were doing pretty radical things to the overall structure of the organization. So it was actually a couple years after I became CEO that I worked with our team to really examine how we would integrate that work into what we were doing. I became very convinced that it was going to be an important ingredient in our success.*[38]

Henry Ford Hospital employees display the Malcolm Baldrige National Quality Award flag. *(From Henry Ford Health System. ID:89289_DSC_1484.)*

2012

The Detroit Institute of Ophthalmology, founded by Dr. Philip Hessburg, merges with Henry Ford's Department of Ophthalmology. A former staff member at Henry Ford Hospital, Dr. Hessburg developed the Hessburg-Barron Vacuum Cornea Trephine in 1974. He served as an adjunct professor at Henry Ford Hospital throughout his career and later rejoined the staff.

2012

Construction begins to transform the former Cottage Hospital in Grosse Pointe to a medical center with senior housing onsite. The new team approach for the care of older adults is a unique partnership between Henry Ford Health System, the American House Senior Living Communities, and REDICO.

Nancy Schlichting
(center right) and Bob
Riney (right) accept the
Malcolm Baldrige award in
Washington, DC, 2012. *(From
Henry Ford Health System.
ID:90523_baldrige029.)*

Dr. Bill Conway, then chief quality officer for the health system, added:

It meant an overhaul of the entire operation, moving to a fully integrated health care delivery system where patients could move seamlessly across sites of care. We spent about six months studying different methodologies for quality management in the organization. We looked at Lean; some organizations were exclusively using that. We looked at ISO techniques, and then we looked at the Baldrige standards and chose that predominantly because it emphasized standardization and integration across the entire enterprise. At the

2013

Henry Ford Health System implements a no-nicotine hiring policy and enhances its existing policies that prohibit the use of tobacco at facilities.

2013

Dr. William O'Neill, medical director of the Center for Structural Heart Disease, performs the world's first cardiac transcaval procedure. This method uses a catheter-based approach to implant a new heart valve.

time that we won, we were the largest, most complicated, more academic organization in
health care to ever win the Baldrige Award.[39]

The health system first began discussing the Baldrige journey—and the revolution that it would involve—in 2006. "That was way ahead of its time," Armada said. "But it also focused us to look at things in a disciplined and systematic way. I believe the effort of starting that dialogue allowed the system to act like a system as opposed to individual hospitals."[40]

By 2011, Henry Ford Health System was ready to compete at the national level, having earned the award at the state level in 2007. The very process of participating in Baldrige required that same level of coordination and involvement that the award was designed to showcase. Schlichting commented:

> *When the Baldrige examiners came to Henry Ford, 1,200 people participated in that*
> *work. I remember that after we announced that we had won, I talked to a security guard,*
> *who told me he was the first person that greeted the Baldrige examiners when they arrived.*
> *I said, "Well, then you won the Baldrige Award for us because, obviously, you created an*
> *amazing first impression." I asked him what he told them, and he said, "You know, I told*
> *them that every day I try to do the very best job for our staff and our patients." I said,*
> *"Then you won the Baldrige Award." So the fact that everyone feels the pride of that work …*
> *It's not like one business unit accomplishment. It's the entire health system.*[41]

Henry Ford Health System had undergone significant changes—including new leadership and an integration of all of its parts. And the world had noticed.

2013

2013

From Henry Ford Health System. ID:Carretero_8164.

Dr. Oscar Carretero (pictured, right), of the Hypertension and Vascular Research Division, is awarded his fifth Program Project grant from the National Institutes of Health. He is the first scientist at the health system and among the few in the US to reach this research award milestone.

Dr. Scott Dulchavsky, chief of surgery at Ford Hospital, is inducted into the Space Technology Hall of Fame. He is recognized for training astronauts to use ultrasound technology on the International Space Station.

Fourteen

" *There are many stories about the resiliency of this organization. If you look at history, things have never been easy for this organization. There have always been challenges. And in many ways I think it's a good thing. I think it's one of the reasons that we're so unique. We attract that underdog mentality that says there's a greater cause and it's not going to be easy, but we're just going to keep pushing and pushing.*"

Bob Riney
PRESIDENT AND CHIEF OPERATING OFFICER,
HENRY FORD HEALTH SYSTEM[1]

CULTURE OF COLLABORATION, INNOVATION, AND COMMUNITY

2000 Present

HENRY FORD HEALTH SYSTEM HAD JUST EARNED THE MOST COVETED PRIZE IN business when it was honored with the Malcolm Baldrige Award in 2011. The win was a bright spot in a community that had been financially struggling for more than a decade. Detroit was on the verge of bankruptcy, operating in the red for a number of years. Making matters worse, during the Great Recession that surfaced in the third quarter of 2008, the city—specifically the automotive industry—was hit particularly hard.

Since the turn of the century, Detroit had seen drastic changes that mounted with each passing year. The city's population had decreased significantly since its heyday with suburbs taking on a much larger—and more affluent—demographic. In the effort to expand its footprint and retain its customer base, Henry Ford Health System reacted by growing services to patients in the suburbs, all the while remaining committed to helping rebuild Detroit's core.

Dr. Scott Dulchavsky and Nancy Schlichting at the Henry Ford Innovation Institute's opening night, 2012. *(From Henry Ford Health System. ID:85650_4801.)*

Henry Ford West Bloomfield Hospital. *(From Henry Ford Health System. ID:Pond_2500.)*

West Bloomfield: A New Kind of Hospital

Henry Ford Health System would build no ordinary hospital after it won the hard-fought battle to obtain a certificate of need that would allow it to expand its West Bloomfield facility.

"It was an opportunity for us to get into a marketplace where we knew we could create strategic advantage, but, to Nancy's credit, she wanted to create something different at West Bloomfield," said Tony Armada, former CEO of Henry Ford Hospital.[2]

That "something different" began when Nancy Schlichting hired Gerard van Grinsven, the area general manager and vice president of the Ritz-Carlton Hotel Company. When van Grinsven, who knew Schlichting from her frequent visits to the Dearborn hotel's

2000 | **2000** | **2000**

Gail Warden, hospital president and CEO, co-authors a landmark Institute of Medicine report called *To Err is Human*, outlining methods for hospitals to reduce and to report medical errors. The report earns Warden an invitation to the White House.

Drs. Marwan Abouljoud and Atsushi Yoshida perform Michigan's first adult living donor liver transplant at Henry Ford Hospital.

Dr. S. David Nathanson, surgical oncologist, pioneers the use of sentinel node biopsy for the detection of breast cancer in the lymph system. The procedure inserts blue dye and radioactive solution near the breast tumor to track the pathway of malignant cells.

restaurant, had a job offer in the health care industry, he sought Schlichting's advice. After he detailed the job offer, Schlichting told him to forgo the position and instead come to work for Henry Ford Health System. Van Grinsven recalled the conversation:

Gerard van Grinsven. *(From Henry Ford Health System. ID:VanGrinsven_Gerard_06C.)*

I said, "Well, in what capacity, Nancy?" She said, "I don't know yet." So I went in for advice, left with a job, but didn't know what the job entailed. And then a month later, she called me back to the corporate offices, and I met with her and Bob Riney. They offered me, a guy who had never worked in health care, the job of president and CEO of a brand new hospital sitting on 160 acres of wetlands and woodlands, which wasn't built yet. [3]

The selection of van Grinsven as president and CEO was no accident. It was the kind of outside-the-box thinking that encompassed the West Bloomfield project, which would provide convenient care for the growing suburban population. "The growth was in the suburbs," said

Henry Ford West Bloomfield: Serving the Whole Body

From its very beginnings, West Bloomfield would be a different kind of hospital—one that focused on wellness related to mind, body, and spirit. The hospital provides the expected services: women's, orthopedics, cancer care, emergency facilities, and surgeries, among others. It also includes a full complement of wellness services, including a demonstration kitchen and the nation's first hospital-based organic greenhouse. The Vita Wellness Center offers everything from acupuncture to yoga. And Henry's, the hospital's dining facility, offers 24-hour room service.[1]

Every aspect of the hospital was designed with four filters, according to Gerard van Grinsven, the hospital's first CEO:

The first filter is quality and safety. The second is compassionate care. Everything we do, it has to embrace compassion. Studies have shown it will help the healing of our customers. The third filter is memorable experiences. How can we make every experience for the patient, family member, or community member a positive, memorable experience? Then the fourth is

efficiency. How can we do it in a way that we are cost-effective?[2]

Prototype rooms took community input. Environmentally friendly construction processes were in place. Traditional medicine met complementary therapies. Patient rooms were private and welcomed family members—including in intensive care.[3]

Within the hospital's first year, more than 1,300 babies were born there, and 30,000 patients received treatment in the hospital's Emergency Department. Patient satisfaction scores reached the 99th percentile within three months of opening.[4]

From Henry Ford Health System. ID:91502_dsc_6379.

Allan Gilmour, former chief financial officer and chair of the Board of Trustees. "It was necessary to go where the patients were. In general, health care is local. We need to go to a place within five or 10 miles of home at the most. As Henry Ford Health System has grown, this is exactly what it's doing, going to where people live and where people need care."[4]

The new hospital would not only offer top-notch care, but also act as a community center focused on wellness—a place where citizens could come without visiting a doctor or a patient. "Very early on, we decided that we were positioning ourselves as a community center for well-being and not as a traditional hospital," said van Grinsven. "So we created four filters. These were our moral compasses in how we were going to make decisions, based on the design of the hospital, based on the processes we were going to create for our customers, that, all the time, every decision would go through those four filters."[5]

From left: Douglas McClure (son of first surgeon-in-chief Dr. Roy McClure and longtime Trustee), his wife Marjorie, and Allan Gilmour. *(From Henry Ford Health System. ID:101494_336.)*

Using those filters meant larger rooms in the Emergency Department with doors that offered more privacy. It meant Vita, a wellness institute. It meant nutritious foods in the cafeteria and a 90-seat auditorium with a demonstration kitchen. "That meant we had to postpone the opening by six months, and we had to go to the board and ask for more money," van Grinsven said. "We could show that through this approach, our cash flow performance would significantly improve. That was not embraced by all, and it took a lot of hard work to convince everybody that this was the right thing to do, and so we did, and the results speak for themselves."[6]

The emphasis on the new facility created a bit of sibling rivalry with the main hospital downtown. "I had all these people say, 'Everyone downtown will just flock to West Bloomfield to work,'" Schlichting said. "I said, 'No, they won't,

2001

From Henry Ford Health System. ID:101494b_693.

Scientist Dr. Hani Sabbah holding the "Acorn" heart device. The Acorn CorCap cardiac support device offers an innovative treatment for heart failure.

2004

The Henry Ford Transplant Institute is established at Henry Ford Hospital with Dr. Marwan Aboujloud as director.

2005

Dr. Carl Pesta becomes Speaker of the House of the American Osteopathic Association. A longtime physician of Henry Ford Bi-County Hospital, Dr. Pesta also served as the hospital's medical director.

because if they want to work in an environment like that, then they would already be working in an environment like that. They came to Detroit because this is where they want to work.'"[7]

In fact, for some of the physician staff, the opposite was true: doctors did not want to go to West Bloomfield. "It got us out of our comfort zone as downtown doctors practicing exclusively at Henry Ford Hospital," said Dr. Mark Kelley, then CEO of the Henry Ford Medical Group. "This new facility helped us grow our inpatient service in a new region. We learned a lot from launching a new community hospital open to private physicians. We built better relations with outside doctors and also grew full inpatient and outpatient services for a new population of patients. The lessons will help us meet the challenges of health reform."[8]

Serving the Community Needs

Henry Ford Medical Group CEO Dr. Mark Kelley (front seat), administrator Paul Szilagyi (back seat), and Board of Governors' manager Jan Arntfield (back seat), in Ford Model T, Greenfield Village, Six Clinic Conference, 2004. *(From Henry Ford Health System. ID:47657_dscf0065.)*

Henry Ford Health System has always served a diverse patient base, including patients without access to quality care and the affluent. In the late 1980s, Dr. Michael Benninger, former chair of the Otolaryngology-Head and Neck Surgery Department, created the Center for Performing Artists at Henry Ford Hospital. "Detroit was a remarkable market for performing voice care," Dr. Benninger said. "Our patients were a combination of the latter years of Motown and a new generation of pop and rock artists such as Madonna and Bob Seger. At the time, our relationship with the Michigan Opera Theater also began."[9]

2005

The Paul and Lynn Alandt Catheterization and Electrophysiology Center opens. The center features the first electromagnetic navigation suite in Michigan.

Pictured, from left: Dr. W. Douglas Weaver, Paul and Lynn Alandt, Nancy Schlichting, and Dr. Claudio Schuger.

2006

Henry Ford Health System is awarded $5 million to reduce disparities in cancer care. Henry Ford Hospital is the only health system in the Midwest awarded funds from the Centers for Medicare & Medicaid Services.

2007

St. Joseph's Mercy of Macomb Hospitals become fully owned by Henry Ford Health System and renamed Henry Ford Macomb Hospitals.

While performers were treated in the physicians' offices, many would also be treated on-site for performances as needed. "When big-name performers came to town, we would often be asked to come on-site just to be there in case there were problems," Dr. Benninger said. "For opening night of any new opera, either Dr. Glen Gardner or I would make sure we were at the opera house in case something happened."[10]

"Anything can happen" said Chair of Otolaryngology Dr. Kathleen Yaremchuk. She treated opera legend Luciano Pavarotti during a performance in Detroit. And she treated a chimp

Evening reception at the Six Clinic Conference, 2004, from left: Dr. Jonathan Schwartz, Tom Groth, Dr. Michael Benninger, Tom Nantais, and Dr. Kathleen Yaremchuk. *(From Henry Ford Health System. ID:47657_dscf0076.)*

with an earache at the Detroit Zoo. "To me, this is really a learning organization. It's a university of sorts because having a health plan, you can learn about insurance; being with a hospital, you learn about Joint Commission and what's responsible for credentialing. The Medical Group is much like a private practice opportunity, so you learn how to manage the operating room, how to manage other physicians' schedules and that kind of thing; and research is available as well. Whatever you're interested in, you have the opportunity to pursue it here."[11]

The interests of many of the health system's employees include helping those in need. During the past several decades, physicians have worked in both the Cabrini Clinic and the Community Health and Social Services Center (CHASS). CHASS found its role as a safety net becoming even more important as the economy waned. "Our slogan that's been around for a while now is, 'When others can't, we can,'" said Dr. Felix Valbuena, Henry Ford staff physician and chief medical officer of CHASS. "All of the other major health systems around the city send us patients you are

2007

Henry Ford Health System opens the Center for Simulation, Education, and Research. The $5 million, 12,000-square-foot educational facility allows healthcare professionals to practice their skills using medical simulators.

2007

Led by pharmacy director Ed Szandzik, a pharmacist-directed anticoagulation service (PDAS) is implemented at Henry Ford Hospital. This innovative program improves monitoring and safety of patients on anticoagulants.

2008

Henry Ford Health System Nursing receives the Education and Training Award from the Michigan Health Council for implementing an accelerated nursing degree program with Henry Ford Community College.

Ricardo Guzman (at podium), CHASS CEO, 2004. *(From CHASS and Henry Ford Health System. ID:47696_chass0052.)*

uninsured, who maybe don't qualify for insurance with the hope that we're going to see them here at CHASS and get them into Henry Ford."[12]

As Detroit found itself with a more financially disparate population base, Henry Ford Health System maintained its commitment to quality patient care to serve both ends of the spectrum.

Continuing to Innovate

A culture of exploration remains deep within the DNA of the Henry Ford Health System. Good questions that evolved into research have brought numerous innovations through Henry Ford physicians and scientists.

Dr. Emanuel (Manny) Rivers used his backgrounds in microbiology, public health, and emergency medicine to advance understanding of sepsis, an illness brought on by a severe

2008

The Henry Ford II West Pavilion at Henry Ford Hospital—a $35 million expansion—opens to the public.

2009

Mort and Brigette Harris establish the Harris Stroke Center at Henry Ford to support advanced stroke therapies and research.

From Henry Ford Health System. ID:73888_harris.

2009

Henry Ford Health System initiates the Healthcare Equity Campaign. The campaign raises awareness about the disparities of health that exist and provides tools to improve cross-cultural communication and collaboration.

response to bacteria. Dr. Rivers' sister-in-law was struck by severe sepsis after an insect bite. She nearly had to have her arm amputated. "When I saw that as a disease, the light bulb went off," said Dr. Rivers, who added:

Dr. Emanuel Rivers. *(From Henry Ford Health System. ID:85946_RVA_3980b.)*

> *I'm an emergency physician, I'm an ICU physician, and also I'm an internal medicine physician. And so when you apply a research methodology to early detect, treat rapidly, and then prevent the complications that may occur downstream, it was just a combination of all of the things that I was trained to do. When all these things came together, that's where the light bulbs went off.*[13]

Dr. Rivers developed a study that explored how various treatments could change the outcome of sepsis. His research, published in *The New England Journal of Medicine*, was widely adopted, and he became the first Henry Ford physician inducted into the Institute of Medicine in 2005.[14]

Pioneering research has meant collaboration with other researchers around the country and globally. The Medical Group's physicians and scientists participate in NIH-sponsored national consortia and clinical trials across nearly every disease set: heart disease, lung disease, diabetes, brain cancer, prostate cancer, and so on. More than 1,800 clinical trial therapies were available to patients in 2013 alone.

In cardiac care, Dr. William O'Neill, who witnessed a fatal heart attack while a medical student at Henry Ford Hospital, joined the staff in 2012 and has pioneered treatment in valve disease through the hospital's Center for Structural Heart Disease. "We built on techniques, so that the valve implants were kind of an off-shoot of balloon valvuloplasty," said Dr. O'Neill. He has been a pioneer in the interventional cardiology field for decades and was recruited to Henry Ford Hospital by CEO Dr. John Popovich. Dr. O'Neill commented:

2010

Henry Ford Hospital introduces Air Med 1 aeromedical helicopter service, providing transportation to the critically ill and trauma patients within a 150-mile radius in Michigan and Ontario.

2010

Henry Ford Health System and Wayne State University sign a five-year affiliation agreement to provide greater academic opportunities for medical students.

2011

Henry Ford Health System, the Detroit Medical Center, and Wayne State University launch the Live Midtown program to encourage employees to purchase or rent homes in the Midtown Detroit area. Financial incentives are provided for qualified applicants.

2011

The Henry Ford Innovation Institute opens in the renovated education building at Henry Ford Hospital's campus.

We're not only doing these new procedures, but we're doing a cold-blooded analysis of the outcomes and the efficacy. We try new things, and if the new things don't work, then we stop doing them. That's really the important thing about an academic institution—the scientific rigor that tells you that this is a good therapy, a safe therapy, an effective therapy, as opposed to it's dangerous or ineffective. We have to be able to quickly recognize when a treatment is ineffective or dangerous.[15]

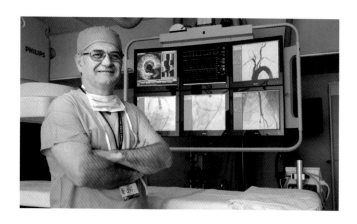

New procedures developed by Henry Ford physicians or by others elsewhere can be taught safely at the Center for Simulation, Education, and Research, which allows physicians, nurses, and other health professionals—students and staff alike—to hone their skills and learn new techniques in a risk-free environment. The 12,000-square-foot "Sim Center" is fully accredited and the most advanced facility of its kind in Michigan.

Dr. William O'Neill, director of the Center for Structural Heart Disease, Henry Ford Hospital, 2013. *(From Henry Ford Health System. ID:91679_rva_4121.)*

The spirit of innovation became more formalized with the launch of the Henry Ford Innovation Institute in 2011. While the Institute brings together experts across different industries to find new solutions to the most vexing medical issues, one of its first inventions was a new type of hospital gown, which functions more like a wrap-around robe than the previous backless gown.

The health system's commitment to innovation has not gone unnoticed. In 2013, Henry Ford Health System ranked seventh for most innovative companies in southeast Michigan. And in 2014, CEO Nancy Schlichting was selected by Detroit Mayor Mike Duggan to lead the committee charged with developing the Innovation District in Detroit.

Improving Lives a World Away

Henry Ford Health System's roots were clearly in Detroit, and its branches had spread across southeastern Michigan. However, the good work being done throughout the health system just begged to be shared.

Dr. Scott Dulchavsky began to apply methods developed at Henry Ford through United Nations programs that would "train somebody in Sub-Saharan Africa how to quickly diagnose a problem pregnancy that would result in a death if that individual didn't walk for five days to reach an extended health care facility," Dr. Dulchavsky said. In 2011, the program was in 68 countries.[1] "That's an empowering technology," Dr. Dulchavsky added. "It came from a very constrained environment and was co-opted very effectively to that. We're looking at commercialization of that now."[2]

The program has developed at-risk pregnancy textbooks that are now available in Brazil, China, Japan, and Nicaragua. "We're also working with the manufacturers of ultrasound on how to make the machines of the future more intuitive," Dr. Dulchavsky said. "That's the kind of innovation we're trying to promulgate here in the Innovation Institute, to take something we're doing in one way, modify it a little bit, or a lot, to fulfill the need for others across the globe."[3]

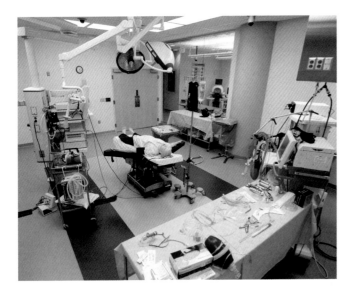

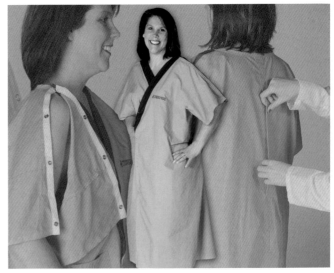

Above left: Center for Simulation, Research, and Education, Henry Ford Hospital, 2010. *(From Henry Ford Health System. ID:sim_jjg_5240.)*

Above right: The new hospital gown developed by a multidisciplinary team at the Henry Ford Innovation Institute, 2013. *(Detail From Henry Ford Health System. ID:94867_HFiiGown_carousel.)*

Chief of Surgery Dr. Scott Dulchavky was instrumental in developing both the Innovation Institute and the Simulation Center, as was Dr. Popovich, who in 2010 was the first physician to be named CEO of the hospital since Dr. Robin Buerki took on the position in the 1950s.

A Vital Part of Detroit

The city of Detroit—and the main hospital itself—would not be left behind as Henry Ford Health System spread its wings into new communities and new arenas. Under Schlichting, the health system "has really been about making sure that both the underserved and maybe the little less needy get the same quality of access to care," said Denise Brooks-Williams, president and CEO of Henry Ford Wyandotte Hospital. "She's fiercely committed to making sure that the Detroit community thrives, not just from a health care perspective but from a total perspective."[16]

2011

From Henry Ford Health System. ID:76369_rva_4706.

Dr. Tamer Ghanem of the Department of Otolaryngology performs the first image-guided transoral robotic procedure for a patient with throat cancer.

2012

The first class of 24 students graduates from the Henry Ford Early College (HFEC). The college, located in One Ford Place, began six years prior with a goal of preparing students for the medical field. HFEC is a public early college high school.

2012

The Clara Ford Nursing Excellence Award is established. The award recognizes nurses who embody the vision of Henry Ford Health System.

That was no easy task as Detroit faltered, even filing bankruptcy in 2013. "The system had great potential, but Detroit was on the decline," said Dr. Mark Kelley. "I saw this opportunity to use health care to help rebuild Detroit. I saw this happen in Boston and Philadelphia in the 1970s. It is now happening in Detroit. Health care, anchored by education and research, has gone from being perceived as a problem to being promoted as an economic engine for urban growth."[17]

That has been aided by a significant investment in Henry Ford Hospital and the surrounding area. Henry Ford Health System, along with the Detroit Medical Center and Wayne State University, launched a program to offer incentives for employees to live in Midtown.[18]

Henry Ford Hospital helicopter flying over downtown Detroit, 2013. *(From Henry Ford Health System. ID:11111_dsc_8646b.)*

The program offered more reasons to live there as well with a $500 million mixed-use development in the Midtown area. The project was expected to draw another $500 million in outside funding. The first tenant was Cardinal Health Systems, which brought additional jobs for its new distribution facility.[19]

Henry Ford also expanded its commitment to Virginia Park, a housing development for people with low and moderate incomes. The program, a coalition that includes the health system and the city, stretches back to 1975. In 2009, Virginia Park received a $275,000 grant to begin construction on Philadelphia Court, which would provide 65 new units.[20]

"Henry Ford has been very integral in helping revitalize the city of Detroit," said former Detroit Mayor Dave Bing. He added:

2013

Henry Ford neurosurgeons perform the first minimally invasive brain surgeries in Michigan, one for epilepsy and the other to treat a brain tumor. Dr. Steven Kalkanis (pictured, center), Dr. Ian Lee, and Dr. Jason Schwalb perform the surgeries.

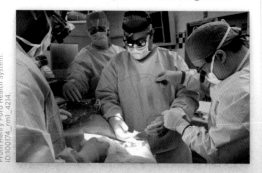

2014

Dr. Mani Menon, director of the Vattikuti Urology Institute, receives the Hugh Hampton Young Award at the annual meeting of the American Urological Association. The award is given to an individual for outstanding contributions to the study of genitourinary tract diseases. Dr. Menon was honored "for innovation in robotic surgery, changing the field of surgical therapy for prostate cancer and improving the quality of life for many patients."

2014

Dr. William O'Neill and his interventional cardiology team at Henry Ford Hospital reach a medical milestone, performing the 25th successful transcatheter valve replacement. Henry Ford is the only hospital in the US performing this unique procedure.

Henry Ford Health System has invested in a lot of community projects, and the kind of commitment that they've made most recently to look at the development around the hospital itself is enormous. They don't go out and beat their chest about what they are doing and how important they are to the community. But without them, I think the revival would really probably flounder. The future of both downtown and Midtown is well-entrenched ... and that's because institutions like Henry Ford have made commitments to invest and develop—not only just in hard dollars, but in human capital. That's the differentiation between them and a lot of other folks: how they look at people and how important people are as an investment.[21]

The investment was not just within the area but also at Henry Ford Hospital. In 2010, the hospital completed a $310 million expansion that included the Henry Ford II West Pavilion, which added 40 private rooms that enable patients' families to stay overnight. The expansion also included new lab facilities, expansion of existing operating rooms, and upgrades to the physical systems.[22]

The Electronic Medical Record at Henry Ford

With the growth of the medical satellite centers since the 1970s and the expansion of the health system since the 1980s, one medical record per patient soon became unwieldy. For patients who may be seen at many different locations at Henry Ford, this required a fleet of trucks transporting patient charts around southeast Michigan. The process worked, most of the time, but not having a patient chart at every single visit led to the development by Henry Ford information technologists of the Medical Information Management System (MIMS). MIMS was a remote terminal program created as a window to view patient laboratory data. MIMS was released in 1989 and rapidly expanded to include information from other data systems, including anatomic pathology, radiology, and dictated clinic notes. At that time, few health systems in the country had created a way for ambulatory teams to access this data remotely.

MIMS was given a graphical interface in 1992 and spread throughout the system under the name CarePlus. This homegrown electronic medical record (EMR) eventually allowed direct entry of data such as vital signs, notes, and immunizations. CarePlus was widely lauded and received a gold medal from the Smithsonian Institute for Innovation in Computing in 1997.

By 2003, CarePlus had outgrown its platform and needed a major update. With no suitable outside vendor, the health system's IT team designed CarePlus Next Generation (CPNG), a web-based EMR. This EMR had the same functionality as the original CarePlus but was more scalable and had significant additional capabilities for registries, problem lists, and shared inboxes among groups of patient care teams. CPNG went live in March 2011.

Because of government regulatory demands for health systems to implement a fully functional, officially credentialed EMR with computerized provider order entry, Epic Systems Corporation was engaged to become the EMR for Henry Ford Health System, with CPNG serving as a repository for the 20 years of previous data. The health system's hospitals, medical centers, employed practices, and portions of the Henry Ford Physician Network were all live on Epic by June 2014. Epic's leadership considered the experience at Henry Ford Health System to be one of the best installations in its history, an accomplishment undoubtedly due in large part to the health system's early leadership in the development and adoption of EMR for its patients.

Under Dr. Popovich's leadership as CEO, the hospital now has the largest intensive care unit complex in Michigan and an air-ground ambulance service for emergent complex care. With roots as a medical student at the hospital, Dr. Popovich holds a special passion for its people. He said: "The people who make up this organization are what make me most proud. I'm proud of what we do not only as a health care provider but what we do in the city. We represent what's good and right about health care, and we represent what's good and right about organizations that are participants in urban environments that are distressed. I'm proud to be part of an organization that has that type of social consciousness and awareness."

This investment in the core of the organization has boosted the hospital and the people who work there. "It is our flagship," Schlichting said. "We now have a beautiful facility that is what the staff deserves in terms of the care that's provided there, and it has become a real hallmark of the turnaround of Detroit. The fact that we now attract patients from all over the world to that facility raises our confidence as an organization."[23]

Above left: Edsel Ford II with bust of his father Henry Ford II at the opening of the Henry Ford II West Pavilion. *(From Henry Ford Health System. ID:101494B_424.)*

Above: Exterior view of the Henry Ford II West Pavilion. *(From Henry Ford Health System. ID:RAY_1836.)*

2014

Neuroscientist Dr. Michael Chopp receives the 2014 Abraham White Distinguished Science Award for his discovery of the role of a protein in the treatment of brain injuries and neurodegenerative diseases.

2014

CEO Nancy Schlichting receives the TRUST award from the American Hospital Association's Health Research & Educational Trust affiliate. The award recognizes individuals who have made significant and lasting contributions to health care.

2015

Henry Ford Hospital celebrates its 100th birthday.

Fifteen

"*We're an organization of people who are never satisfied. We're all a bit restless. We all want to see things improve, and that's a great quality. I think we will be a much better organization five years from now, 10 years from now, maybe 100 years from now. You can't even envision what this organization could be. But I really believe very strongly that we will constantly improve what we do.*"

Nancy Schlichting
CEO, HENRY FORD HEALTH SYSTEM[1]

HENRY FORD HEALTH SYSTEM:
IT'S ALL ABOUT THE PEOPLE

Henry Ford Health System employees. *(From Henry Ford Health System. ID:102760_RVA_3477.)*

Henry Ford Hospital marks a full century of service in 2015. From a vision of a hospital in Henry Ford's mind to a large, integrated health system with national reach and international influence, these 100 years have transformed not only how diseases are diagnosed and treated but also how health care is delivered to people. Although it looks far different than it did in 1915, Henry Ford Health System rests on bedrock that has not changed: a commitment to quality care for patients regardless of their ability to pay, an affection for the city of Detroit and all the communities it serves, and a willingness to solve the unsolvable.

"One of the great aspects of Henry Ford Hospital is our diversity," said CEO Dr. John Popovich. "Our employees and patients represent 12 or more different languages and come from all parts of the world. We have the opportunity to serve and learn from a population that represents the cultural tapestry of the city of Detroit and southeast Michigan. This is why we provide multicultural care where the comfort for each patient is based on that individual's specific needs and cultural requirements."

A Continued Commitment to Serve

Denise Brooks-Williams joined Henry Ford Health System in 2013 as president and CEO of Wyandotte Hospital. As a leader, she attended one of the health system's banquets marking employee anniversaries. It was eye-opening.

"I don't think I've been in an organization that had so many 45- and 35-year recipients," said Brooks-Williams. She added:

> *I sat at a table with a couple who were talking about their next 30 years. People are very passionate about the organization, long-tenured staff, and they're still highly committed to serving in this area. People are excited about what the future of health care looks like and how they can be a part of it. That's very attractive, and it makes my job easier because people are not afraid of the changes that are coming.*[2]

Thomas Nantais, chief operating officer of Henry Ford Medical Group, is at the opposite end of the spectrum from newcomer Brooks-Williams—with 30-plus years of service—but he too finds the longevity of employees to be a strength. "The service awards banquet is an amazing feat," he said. "At one time, I had counted a family of four generations that worked here. A high school girl was an intern, her mother was a nurse, her grandmother worked in dietary, and the great-grandmother was a volunteer. It's not uncommon to have two or three or even four generations working here."[3]

"If nurses are here more than three or four years, they tend to become what we call lifers," said Veronica (Ronnie) Hall, chief nursing officer of the health system and chief operating officer of Henry Ford Hospital. "The glue that keeps us together is the collaboration of our physicians, the support of our allied health, the really strong presence of a nurse practice, and a voice in clinical practice—the teaming that we have is incredible. I think our fast-moving pace, high-complex knowledge base, and feeling like a part of an accomplishment—that's what keeps the nurses here."

Through the years, the growth can be attributed to the focus on people—both those served by the health system and those who serve in it. "Continuing to focus on each person in the organization, not only each patient but also each employee, physician, and volunteer, and making sure they feel valued, that's part of how you build a culture that allows people to feel like they're an important part of our success," Nancy Schlichting said. "I call it taking care of the people who take care of people."[4]

Opposite:

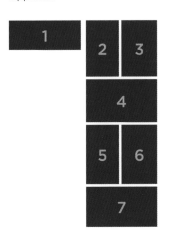

1. From left: Robert and Nancy Vlasic, and Brigitte and Mort Harris.
2. Valerie and David McCammon.
3. Raj and Padma Vattikuti.
4. From left: Benson Ford, Jr., Eleanor Ford, William Clay Ford, Jr., Lynn Ford Alandt and Paul Alandt.
5. Gary and Margaret Valade.
6. Edsel Ford II and Cynthia Ford.
7. From left: Dr. Mark Rosenblum, William Davidson, David Hermelin, Dr. Tom Mikkelsen, Eugene Applebaum, 1999.
(From Henry Ford Health System. ID:101494_369, mccammon, vattikuti, RHB_008b, valade062, 44426_0092, 101494b_329.)

A Philanthropic Legacy: 100 Years of Giving

Henry Ford Health System was established through the generosity of Henry, Clara, and Edsel Ford. The Ford Family has made an indelible impact on Henry Ford Health System, contributing multiple millions of dollars together and individually.

Alongside the Ford Family, thousands of individuals, corporations, and foundations have contributed to Henry Ford Health System to make a difference in the life of another.

In 2007, the ENVISION Campaign launched, with $270 million raised by 2013 for the expansion of facilities and the enhancement of clinical programs and research. The Henry Ford philanthropic community grew to nearly 80,000 donors, with 65 giving $1 million or more to help transform patient care.

Nowhere else was "giving begins at home" more evident than with Henry Ford employees. Since 2007, employee giving increased to more than $3 million a year in 2013. This was unequaled by any other organization in the US.

Across 100 years, five generations of the Ford Family, the Hermelin Family and friends, Rajendra and Padma Vattikuti, Mort and Brigitte Harris, the Vlasic Family, Ford Motor Company, and the W. K. Kellogg Foundation top the list of more than 120 donors that have contributed more than $1 million each. These families and foundations, as well as the employees, have changed the face of Henry Ford Health System with their philanthropic gifts.

Above: The Henry Ford Innovation Institute. *(From Henry Ford Health System. ID:hfii_jjg_9273.)*

Above right: Henry Ford Hospital. *(From Henry Ford Health System. ID:hfh_7469.)*

The demands are high, but time and time again, Henry Ford Health System employees have shown they are up to the task.

In many ways, the health system's focus on people has been one of the key reasons it has endured, said Barbara Rossmann, president and CEO of Henry Ford Macomb Hospitals, which celebrated its own centurial birthday in 1999. She cited a research study that examined organizations with a history of more than 100 years:

> *The success of those organizations was really dependent upon the commitment they made to the people that they worked with within the organization. As the organization evolved over time, the commitment to help retool and invest in their employees so they could transition into new aspects within their organization was vital. For Henry Ford Health System, I see that's been true. Our commitment through the years to people—and helping transition people as the needs for our delivery have changed—is what makes us sustainable as an organization.[5]*

And it is not just a commitment at the top or to those whose titles denote leadership positions. "They are an institution that excels and demands excellence across the board," said Dave Bing, former Detroit mayor. He added:

> *The care that you get from people down in that organization is very, very impressive. It's easy to look at the top and say they're the ones who are making a difference. I think leadership starts at the top, but it permeates throughout your organization. I don't care if it's*

somebody sweeping the floor. They do it to the best of their ability, and I think they're glad

that they're part of the family. You don't find that in a lot of places.[6]

Serving in a Time of Change

The Patient Protection and Affordable Care Act, passed by Congress in 2010, will cause a sea change in how health care facilities operate once fully enacted. But health care has long been changing and evolving, from the advent of health maintenance organizations to this current iteration. "We're at one of those critical points in history where we're on the threshold of major changes," said Dr. Bill Conway, CEO, Henry Ford Medical Group. He also noted:

> *One thing that's reassuring about Henry Ford is, if you look back on our history, we have always figured out the answers. When HMOs became popular in this country, we were on the cutting edge. Quality emphasis was introduced; we were there. In this new era, we'll figure this out. I think there will be two things that will be evident. One is, we'll look back and realize that we were a big part of the rebuilding of Detroit. And we will be one of the organizations that defines the new pathway to delivering American health care.*[7]

Seated, from left: Robert Riney, president and chief operating officer, Henry Ford Health System; Nancy Schlichting, CEO, Henry Ford Health System; Sandra Pierce, chair, system Board of Trustees. Standing, from left: Dr. William Conway, CEO, Henry Ford Medical Group; Joseph Schmitt, senior vice president of finance, Henry Ford Health System; Dr. John Popovich, CEO, Henry Ford Hospital; James Connelly, CEO, Health Alliance Plan. *(From Henry Ford Health System. ID:jjg_0517 leadership.)*

Although the types of service may change as medical knowledge progresses, the vision does not. "We believe we are here to transform communities and people through health and wellness, one person at a time," Schlichting said. "Our vision is not fully embraced by many in health care but is completely aligned with what health care organizations should be doing now and in the future."[8]

Growing in Size and Knowledge

Henry Ford Hospital began with just 48 private patient rooms. In a century, the organization has grown a health system that includes nearly 2,000 hospital beds, 1,200 staff physicians, and a wide variety of delivery systems.[9] Future growth is certain, but its direction is unclear.

No matter how large it grows, however, Henry Ford Health System will continue to make an impact on the national stage—just as it has throughout its history. "If you look at the influence that clinical leaders from Henry Ford have had on the national scene, I don't think any other system would, quite frankly, size up equally," said Bob Riney, president and chief operating officer of Henry Ford Health System. "You go through every prestigious group, both administrative and clinically, and you see Henry Ford leaders as previous presidents. That says something about the caliber of the organization and the kind of leaders it produces."[10]

Henry Ford at 100

One thing is for certain: The future will not find Henry Ford Health System standing still. Riney said:

> Much in life is cyclical, and it's the constant focus on continuous improvement and never settling. It really makes a great organization. As our founder Henry Ford 100 years ago said: "Detroit doesn't need another hospital. It needs a hotel for sick people." What are we doing today across the industry? We're working harder to create a concierge-type environment in our hospitals. Fifty years from now, my guess is we'll still be working on that because it's an iterative process. You're constantly learning new needs and new ways to meet those needs because our patients aren't static. They evolve. Their needs evolve. As we look at the next 100 years of this system, we're going to find that we are continually going back to the future and then inventing things that will become a new part of the future.[11]

Henry Ford Hospital.
(From Henry Ford Health System. ID:hfh_night_13.)

Throughout its history, Henry Ford Health System has endured a depression, several recessions, two World Wars and a few smaller ones, a prosperous Detroit and a bankrupt one. It has seen medicine change and the expectations of health care evolve. But as the health system enters its second century, it does so buoyed by the people who come to work every day, devoted to caring for those who are sick and to helping others prevent illness. It does so firmly embracing its past while looking forward—confidently—to the future.

"Anyone working in the health care industry already has an innate passion for wanting to make a difference in people's lives," said Sandra Pierce, chair of the health system's Board of Trustees. "Henry Ford Health System is not only nationally but internationally recognized for its leadership; for its physicians and the advancements made in many of the specialist fields; for its heritage of accomplishment regardless of the obstacles; for its balance sheet that is as solid as any; for the academics and research grants that are among the top in the country; for its integrated system; and for being part of the community that created the middle class, that actually put the world on wheels, and that is in the midst of not only surviving but thriving. Who wouldn't want to be part of this story?"

WHAT IS AND WILL BE HENRY FORD HOSPITAL

IN 1915, THERE WERE HOSPITALS FOR THE RICH AND others for the poor, but Henry Ford Hospital aimed to provide top-quality health care at prices working people could afford. Top practitioners agreed to work as a salaried group. The entire staff, all carefully selected, then brought its individual talents to bear in carrying out treatment with the goal of returning health to patients and patients to their community.

Henry Ford loved machines; he was possessed by a need to know how things worked and then do them better than they had been done before. His hospital was, in a very real sense, his new machine, and innovation was central to its functioning.

The essence of Henry Ford Hospital, distilled since it was founded 100 years ago, became this venerable institution's driving, sustaining force. The soul of Henry Ford Hospital has always resided by design in the men and women whose primary focus was on a single goal, which has never changed in the century since: The patient was and would remain paramount.

All hospital tasks, from housekeeping to medical practice, were focused on healing that patient.

Although the professional skills of the physicians were revered, everyone knew that without each member of the team, the best care could not be provided. Just as any step in Ford's famous assembly line affects every other, the importance of all team members to the production of health care became a fundamental part of Henry Ford Hospital and the Henry Ford Health System culture.

The depth of employee commitment to this hospital and organization isn't often seen at a secular institution. It's exemplified by those with long tenures, many working for more than 40 or 50 years.

From inception, Henry Ford Hospital was a learning institution with education and research programs rivaled only by university facilities. The academic mission of the organization, especially of what came to be called the Henry Ford Medical Group, was the continuing education of staff physicians and the education of future generations.

Education led to questions needing answers, spawning research and innovation meaningful to patient care. Innovation in the medical care delivered throughout the decades at Henry Ford Hospital has often been in the implementation of new technology and the perfection of procedures to minimize harm and create quality results.

Henry Ford Hospital was one of the country's first general hospitals to include a psychiatric unit. It was the first to use purified heparin to treat blood clots. It was one of only a few US hospitals chosen as a national test location for penicillin. The first liquid oxygen tent was developed on site. The first food pump was created. The hospital was the first to use the multiple-lead electrocardiogram. For the first time in Michigan, and one of the first in the world, a Henry Ford surgeon performed a graft to correct an abdominal aortic aneurysm and established the state's first blood vessel bank. Michigan's first successful open heart surgery using the heart-lung bypass machine was performed at Henry Ford Hospital.

The drive to innovate continued through the years and produced the state's first hospital-based CT scanning center; pioneering work in coronary angioplasty; the first use in Michigan and the second in the US of human insulin to treat diabetes; metro Detroit's first heart, liver, and lung transplants; and many other firsts.

Even more innovation and ingenuity prospered at Henry Ford as the health system moved ahead in the 21st century. The system pioneered the valid concepts of brain neuroregeneration and use of robotics in surgery. Henry Ford Medical Group physicians saw robotic surgery as a technological enhancement for surgery with less invasiveness, a theme permeating the development of catheter-based technology to treat vascular and valvular heart disease, the use of image-guided neurosurgery, and stereotactic radiation therapy. In keeping with the founder's stated mission, this was innovation applied to the betterment of care, not to the development of products.

Few organizations have produced such dramatic innovations in care practice models. The creation of regional satellite facilities—multi-specialty ambulatory centers functioning as hospitals without beds—initially secured access to a population moving from the city of Detroit to the suburbs. These facilities eventually created the basis for a distributed regional care delivery network that would serve as a foundation of population management for a managed care population. As many hospitals became more focused on only the sickest of patients, these facilities led a change to broader, ambulatory care focused on restoration of health.

Integral to the care of patients being seen in different health facilities across southeast Michigan, Henry Ford Health System was one of the earliest adopters of electronic medical records under CarePlus. This was a homegrown program serving as the repository of all Henry Ford Medical Group patient histories. We did this in the 1990s because it made sense. The expansion to the multi-facility, multi-faceted, geographically diffuse Henry Ford Health System required it to provide the patient with the best possible care.

As the health system continued to grow with joint ventures, unique partnerships, as well as the acquisition and development of regional community hospitals, the physician workforce expanded to the private-practice community. The commitment to coordinated and integrated care, regardless of practice model, resulted in the development of the Henry Ford Physician Network—a virtual physician group practice.

Henry Ford Health System—its hospitals, medical centers, health centers, health insurance, behavioral health services, and Community Care Services for products related to eye care, home care, pharmacy services, and durable goods—is designed to provide the full continuum of health care in every region in southeast Michigan.

In Detroit, the employees of Henry Ford Hospital live and work in a community that has survived the toughest economic and social challenges of, perhaps, any city in America. Yet their sense of mission and values and their energy and optimism about the work they do and the lives they influence—their patients, families, colleagues, and the community they serve—continues to grow and deepen. That is its most enduring legacy of leadership and history.

After 100 years, Henry Ford Hospital and the complex health system it now leads remains as dedicated to the community as from the start.

We started as a hospital and a relatively small medical group. As we grew as an organization, we grew well beyond the confines of one hospital in Detroit to multiple hospitals, insurance, community care services, and multiple clinics throughout the entirety of southeast Michigan. Through it all, the flagship of this organization has always been Henry Ford Hospital, which sets the cultural tone for the organization. It creates the academic values of the organization and remains the tertiary quaternary epicenter of our institution. It carries the heart and soul of the organization on the Detroit campus.

Henry Ford Hospital is not only a great treasure for the Henry Ford Health System; it is one of the national treasures in American health care as well. It has been this for the last century, as it will be for the next.

John Popovich, M.D.
PRESIDENT AND CEO, HENRY FORD HOSPITAL

NOTES TO SOURCES

Introduction

1. *Time* magazine, December 13, 2010.
2. Henry Ford and Samuel Crowther, *My Life and Work* (Garden City, NY: Doubleday, Page & Co, 1922).

Foreword

1. Henry Ford and Samuel Crowther, *My Life and Work* (Garden City, NY: Doubleday, Page & Co, 1922).

Chapter One

1. "Henry Ford Quotations," *Benson Ford Research Center, The Henry Ford*, http://www.thehenryford.org/research/henryFordQuotes.aspx.
2. Major League Baseball, online, "World Series History: Recaps and Results" section.
3. Detroit Historical Society, online, "Industrial Detroit: 1860–1900" timeline.
4. *Ibid.*
5. "The First Model A Laid a Foundation for the Future," *Vehicle History, Ford Motor Company*, http://corporate.ford.com/our-company/heritage/vehicle-history-news-detail/670-model-a-1903.
6. General Motors company, online, "Creation: 1897–1909" article.
7. US Census Bureau, online, "Statistical Abstract of the United States: 2003" list.
8. Kofi Myler, "Detroit's population from 1840 to 2012 shows high points, decades of decline," *Detroit Free Press*, July 23, 2013.
9. US Census Bureau, online, "Statistical Abstract of the United States: 2003" list.
10. Patricia Scollard Painter, *Henry Ford Hospital: The First 75 Years* (Detroit: Henry Ford Health System, 1997), p. 13.
11. *Ibid.*
12. *Ibid.*
13. *Henry Ford Hospital: The First 75 Years*, p. 15.
14. *Ibid.*
15. *Ibid.*
16. "The Reminiscences of Mr. E. G. Liebold (Part I)," Accession 65, Owen W. Bombard Interviews series, *Benson Ford Research Center, The Henry Ford*, p. 70, http://cdm15889.contentdm.oclc.org/cdm/compoundobject/collection/p15889coll2/id/11506/rec/111.
17. Liebold reminiscences, p. 72.
18. *Henry Ford Hospital: The First 75 Years*, p. 20.
19. "The Rouge: A Timeline," *Ford Rouge Factory Tour, The Henry Ford*, http://www.thehenryford.org/rouge/timeline.aspx.
20. "Henry Ford's $5-a-Day Revolution," *Company Milestones, Ford Motor Company*, http://corporate.ford.com/our-company/heritage/company-milestones-news-detail/677-5-dollar-a-day.
21. "Henry Ford Explains Why He Gives Away $10,000,000," the *New York Times*, January 11, 1914.
22. *Ibid.*
23. *Ibid.*
24. Liebold reminiscences, p. 72.
25. Liebold reminiscences, p. 74.
26. *Ibid.*
27. Liebold reminiscences, p. 75.
28. *Ibid.*
29. "Mental Sequelae of the Harrison Law," *New York Medical Journal*, 102 (May 15, 1915) as reported in *The Consumers Union Report on Licit and Illicit Drugs* by Edward M. Brecher and the editors of *Consumer Reports* magazine, 1972.

30. Liebold reminiscences, p. 76.
31. Liebold reminiscences, p. 77–78.
32. "The Reminiscences of Dr. F. Janney Smith," Accession 65, Owen W. Bombard Interviews series, *Benson Ford Research Center, The Henry Ford*, p. 8, http://cdm15889.contentdm.oclc.org/cdm/compoundobject/collection/p15889coll2/id/15959/rec/187.
33. Smith reminiscences, p. 8–9.
34. *Henry Ford Hospital: The First 75 Years*, p. 80.
35. Liebold reminiscences, p. 85.
36. Liebold reminiscences, p. 121.
37. "Historical Highlights," *Edith and Benson Ford Heart & Vascular Institute, Henry Ford Health System*, http://www.henryford.com/body.cfm?id=40560.
38. Smith reminiscences, p. 4.
39. Liebold reminiscences, p. 122–123.
40. Smith reminiscences, p. 10.
41. Larry W. Stephenson, *Detroit Surgeons: 300 Years* (Grosse Pointe Farms, MI: Dorian Naughton Pub., 2011), p. 89.
42. Liebold reminiscences, p. 130.
43. Smith reminiscences, p. 11.
44. *Ibid.*
45. Smith reminiscences, p. 12.
46. Liebold reminiscences, p. 138.
47. *Ibid.*
48. Liebold reminiscences, p. 118.
49. Liebold reminiscences, p. 119.
50. Liebold reminiscences, p. 142.
51. Smith reminiscences, p. 10.

Chapter One Sidebar:
Dr. Frank Sladen: Henry Ford Hospital's First Physician-in-Chief

1. Melanie Bazil, "Frank J. Sladen, M.D.," *Lam Archives, Henry Ford Health System*, http://www.henryfordconnect.com/sladen.cfm?id=448.

Chapter One Sidebar:
Dr. Roy McClure: First Surgeon-in-Chief

1. "The Reminiscences of Dr. F. Janney Smith," Accession 65, Owen W. Bombard Interviews series, *Benson Ford Research Center, The Henry Ford*, p. 10, http://cdm15889.contentdm.oclc.org/cdm/compoundobject/collection/p15889coll2/id/15959/rec/187.
2. Larry W. Stephenson, *Detroit Surgeons: 300 Years* (Grosse Pointe Farms, MI: Dorian Naughton Pub., 2011), p. 89.

Chapter Two

1. "The Reminiscences of Dr. F. Janney Smith," Accession 65, Owen W. Bombard Interviews series, *Benson Ford Research Center, The Henry Ford*, p. 21-22, http://cdm15889.contentdm.oclc.org/cdm/compoundobject/collection/p15889coll2/id/15959/rec/187.
2. "The Reminiscences of Mr. E.G. Liebold (Part I)," Accession 65, Owen W. Bombard Interviews series, *Benson Ford Research Center, The Henry Ford*, p. 85, http://cdm15889.contentdm.oclc.org/cdm/compoundobject/collection/p15889coll2/id/11506/rec/111.
3. Liebold reminiscences, p. 85–86.
4. Liebold reminiscences, p. 102.
5. Frank J. Sladen, M.D., (unpublished memoirs, Accession 92.14, Conrad R. Lam Archives, Henry Ford Health System).
6. Smith reminiscences, p. 19.
7. Liebold reminiscences, p. 109.

8. Liebold reminiscences, p. 156.
9. Smith reminiscences, p. 17–18.
10. Smith reminiscences, p. 19.
11. "Tilting Devices for Hospital Beds," patent filing by Henry Ford, publication number US1517418 A, issued by the US Patent Office Dec. 2, 1924.
12. *Ibid.*
13. Moises Rivera-Ruiz, Christian Cajavilca, and Joseph Varon, "Einthoven's String Galvanometer," *Texas Heart Journal* 35, no. 2 (2008).
14. William Eyler, MD, interview by Jim TerMarsch, digital recording, 14 September 2012, Marsch Creative.
15. Seyed B. Mostofi, *Who's Who in Orthopedics* (London: Springer, 2005), p. 265.
16. Melanie Bazil, "Historical Collections," *Lam Archives, Henry Ford Health System*, http://www.henryford.com/body_nologin.cfm?id=39481.
17. "History of Medicine," *Department of Medicine, Henry Ford Health System*, http://www.henryford.com/body.cfm?id=58754.
18. Melanie Bazil, "Historical Collections," *Lam Archives, Henry Ford Health System*, http://www.henryford.com/body_nologin.cfm?id=39481.
19. Smith reminiscences, p. 18.
20. Max K. Kole, Shaun T. O'Leary, Ghaus M. Malik, and Mark L. Rosenblum, "Historical Perspective on the Department of Neurosurgery at the Henry Ford Hospital," *Neurosurgery* 48, no. 2 (2001).
21. "History of the Division," *Endocrinology, Diabetes, & Metabolism Fellowship, Henry Ford Health System*, http://www.henryford.com/body.cfm?id=50691.
22. Melanie Bazil, "Historical Collections," *Lam Archives, Henry Ford Health System*, http://www.henryford.com/body_nologin.cfm?id=39481.
23. William R. Eyler and Arlene W. Hipple, "In Memoriam. Howard Philip Doub, M.D.," *Radiology* 118, no. 3 (1976).
24. College of American Pathology, online, "CAP Outstanding Service Award Established in Honor of Frank W. Hartman" list.
25. Smith reminiscences, p. 20.
26. Smith reminiscences, p. 21.
27. Smith reminiscences, p. 20.
28. William F. Pletz, "The Railroad that Went No Place (But Eventually Made It)," republished on *Michigan Railroads*.
29. Smith reminiscences, p. 21.
30. *Ibid.*
31. Liebold reminiscences, p. 154.
32. "Doctors in Medicine 1916," *The Johns Hopkins University Circular*, vol. 37, p. 857.
33. Thomas J. Heldt, "The Functioning of a Division of Neuropsychiatry in a General Hospital," *American Journal of Psychiatry* 84, no. 3 (1927).
34. "1927 Sees Scientific Advances on All the Frontiers of Knowledge," Science Service as published in the *Catalina Islander*, January 4, 1927, p. 11.
35. John M. Dorsey, "In Memoriam. Thomas J. Heldt, 1883–1972," *American Journal of Psychiatry* 129, no. 6 (1972): 762.
36. *Ibid.*
37. *Carbondale Free Press*, May 28, 1924.
38. Patricia Scollard Painter, *Henry Ford Hospital: The First 75 Years* (Detroit: Henry Ford Health System, 1997), p. 57.
39. *Carbondale Free Press*, May 28, 1924.
40. Smith reminiscences, p. 25–26.
41. "The Reminiscences of Mr. E. J. Farkas," Accession 65, Owen W. Bombard Interviews series, *Benson Ford Research Center, The Henry Ford*, p. 366, http://cdm15889.contentdm.oclc.org/cdm/compoundobject/collection/p15889coll2/id/7759/rec/64.

42. Farkas reminiscences, p. 368.
43. Farkas reminiscences, p. 368–369.
44. Farkas reminiscences, p. 370.

Chapter Two Sidebar: No Smoking, Please

1. "The Reminiscences of Dr. F. Janney Smith," Accession 65, Owen W. Bombard Interviews series, *Benson Ford Research Center, The Henry Ford*, p. 13, http://cdm15889.contentdm.oclc.org/cdm/compoundobject/collection/p15889coll2/id/15959/rec/187.
2. Victoria Stagg-Elliot, "AMA Immediate Past President Ron Davis, MD, succumbs to pancreatic cancer," *Amednews*, published November 24, 2008.
3. Michigan Governor's office, online, "Michigan's Smoke Free Air Law" section.

Chapter Two Sidebar: Clara Ford: Henry's 'Great Believer'

1. "The Reminiscences of Mr. and Mrs. Clarence Davis," Accession 65, Owen W. Bombard Interviews series, *Benson Ford Research Center, The Henry Ford*, http://cdm15889.contentdm.oclc.org/cdm/compoundobject/collection/p15889coll2/id/4285/rec/49.
2. *Ibid.*

Chapter Three

1. Patricia Scollard Painter, *Henry Ford Hospital: The First 75 Years* (Detroit: Henry Ford Health System, 1997), p. 75.
2. American College of Surgeons, online, "Clinical Congresses of the American College of Surgeons," section.
3. *Henry Ford Hospital: The First 75 Years*, p. 57.
4. Dr. Scott Dulchavsky, interview by Jim TerMarsch, digital recording, 14 November 2012, Marsch Creative.
5. "Finding Aid for Ford Motor Company Iron Mountain Plant Records, 1950-1951," Accession 523, *Benson Ford Research Center, The Henry Ford*, http://www.dalnet.lib.mi.us/henryford/docs/FordMotorCompanyIronMountainPlantRecords_Accession523.pdf.
6. "The Reminiscences of Dr. W. H. Alexander," Accession 65, Owen W. Bombard Interviews series, *Benson Ford Research Center, The Henry Ford*, p. 14, http://cdm15889.contentdm.oclc.org/cdm/compoundobject/collection/p15889coll2/id/1229/rec/5.
7. Kingsford Charcoal Company, online, "Our Heritage" tab.
8. Alexander reminiscences, p. 6.
9. *Ibid.*
10. "The Reminiscences of Dr. C. F. Holton," Accession 65, Owen W. Bombard Interviews series, *Benson Ford Research Center, The Henry Ford*, p. 5, http://cdm15889.contentdm.oclc.org/cdm/compoundobject/collection/p15889coll2/id/6531/rec/87.
11. "Ford Motor Company's Brazilian Rubber Plantations," *Benson Ford Research Center, The Henry Ford*, http://www.thehenryford.org/research/rubberPlantations.aspx.
12. *Ibid.*
13. *Ibid.*
14. *Ibid.*
15. Greg Grandin, *Fordlandia: The Rise and Fall of Henry Ford's Forgotten Jungle City* (New York: Henry Holt & Company, 2009), p. 189.
16. Dr. Joseph Elliott, interview by Jeffrey Rodengen, digital recording, 11 September 2013, Write Stuff Enterprises, LLC.
17. *Fordlandia: The Rise and Fall of Henry Ford's Forgotten Jungle City*, p. 325.
18. Mary A. Dempsey, "Fordlandia," Michigan History, July/August 1994, republished on "Ford Motor Company's Brazilian Rubber Plantations," Benson Ford Research Center.
19. Arthur M. Woodford, *This is Detroit: 1701–2001*, Wayne State University Press, Detroit, 2001. p. 121.
20. *Ibid.*
21. *This is Detroit: 1701–2001*, p. 122.
22. *Henry Ford Hospital: The First 75 Years*, p. 60.

23. "Ford Undergoes Sudden Operation," *Associated Press* wire as reported in *Ludlington Daily News*, November 27, 1932.
24. "Ford On Way to Recovery," *Associated Press* wire as reported in *Milwaukee Sentinel*, November 29, 1932.
25. *Henry Ford Hospital: The First 75 Years*, p. 63.
26. "The Reminiscences of Dr. F. Janney Smith," Accession 65, Owen W. Bombard Interviews series, *Benson Ford Research Center, The Henry Ford*, p. 24, http://cdm15889.contentdm.oclc.org/cdm/compoundobject/collection/p15889coll2/id/15959/rec/187.
27. Smith reminiscences, p. 25.
28. Smith reminiscences, p. 25–26.
29. *Henry Ford Hospital: The First 75 Years*, p. 64.
30. "Cochrane Prepares for European Trip: Baker Takes Over," *Associated Press* wire as reported in *St. Petersburg Times*, September 10, 1937.
31. *Henry Ford Hospital: The First 75 Years*, p. 65.
32. "Toles Kayoes Adamick in 2," *Associated Press* wire as reported in *Milwaukee Journal*, September 29, 1938.
33. "Place Injured Detroit Fighter in Oxygen Tent," *Associated Press* wire as reported in *Meriden Record*, October 4, 1938.
34. *Henry Ford Hospital: The First 75 Years*, p. 65.
35. *Ibid.*
36. Conrad R. Lam, "Heparin Administration," *Annals of Surgery* 113, no. 6 (1941): 1085-1086.
37. Roy D. McClure, "Goiter Prophylaxis with Iodized Salt," *Science* 82, no. 2129 (1935).
38. Melanie Bazil, "Elizabeth M. Yagle, M.D.," *Lam Archives, Henry Ford Health System*, http://www.henryford.com/body_nologin.cfm?id=57537.
39. Blue Cross Blue Shield Blue Care Network of Michigan, online, "Our History" section.
40. *Henry Ford Hospital: The First 75 Years*, p. 67.

Chapter Three Sidebar: Elizabeth Moran: A Leader with Exacting Standards

1. *Ludington Daily News*, April 5, 1950.
2. *The SONAH* (Henry Ford Hospital School of Nursing and Hygiene yearbook, 1937) p. 32.
3. Wilma Gandy, interview by Jim TerMarsch, digital recording, 20 May 2013, Marsch Creative.

Chapter Three Sidebar: Edsel and Eleanor Ford: The Second Generation of Commitment to the Hospital

1. Frank J. Sladen, M.D., (unpublished memoirs, Accession 92.14, Conrad R. Lam Archives, Henry Ford Health System).
2. Ford R. Bryant, *Friends, Families, and Forays* (Detroit: Wayne State University Press, 2002), p. 286.
3. "The Reminiscences of Dr. F. Janney Smith," Accession 65, Owen W. Bombard Interviews series, *Benson Ford Research Center, The Henry Ford*, p. 26, http://cdm15889.contentdm.oclc.org/cdm/compoundobject/collection/p15889coll2/id/15959/rec/187.

Chapter Four

1. Dr. Richard Smith, interview by Jim TerMarsch, digital recording, 11 September 2013, Marsch Creative.
2. Patricia Scollard Painter, *Henry Ford Hospital: The First 75 Years* (Detroit: Henry Ford Health System, 1997), p. 69.
3. *Ibid.*
4. PBC Children of the Camps, online, "Internment History" article.
5. Jay Lindsay, "World War II-Era German U-Boat Found Off Coast Of Massachusetts," *Associated Press* report, July 27, 2012.
6. Detroit Encyclopedia, Detroit Historical Society, online, "Arsenal of Democracy" article.
7. *Ibid.*
8. *Henry Ford Hospital: The First 75 Years*, p.68.
9. *Henry Ford Hospital: The First 75 Years*, p. 71.
10. *Henry Ford Hospital: The First 75 Years*, p. 72.

11. *Ibid.*
12. The US Cadet Nurse Corps, online, "History" tab.
13. Lucile Petry, "The Public Health Significance of the U.S. Cadet Nurse Corps," *American Journal of Public Health* 33, no. 11 (1943): 1353.
14. "The Public Health Significance of the US Cadet Nurse Corps," p. 1354.
15. *Henry Ford Hospital: The First 75 Years*, p. 72.
16. National Academy of Sciences, online, "History" section.
17. Dr. Howard Markel, "The Real Story Behind Penicillin," *PBS Newshour*, September 27, 2013.
18. Melanie Bazil, "Milestones of Henry Ford Hospital," *Henry Ford Health System*, http://www.henryford.com/body.cfm?id=47720#1941-1945.
19. "The Real Story Behind Penicillin."
20. *Henry Ford Hospital: The First 75 Years*, p. 75.
21. "Postwar World to Be Healthy, Says Surgeon," *Miami News*, February 24, 1943.
22. Roy D. McClure, Conrad R. Lam, and Harvard Romence, "Tannic Acid and the Treatment of Burns: An Obsequy," *Annals of Surgery* 12, no. 3 (1944).
23. GE Healthymagination Challenge, online, "The Scarf Technique: A Rediscovered Approach To Early Detection Of Breast Cancers," article.
24. Sharon R. Kaufman, *The Healer's Tale: Transforming Medicine and Culture* (Madison, WI: University of Wisconsin Press, 1993), p. 37.
25. "Historical Highlights," *Edith and Benson Ford Heart & Vascular Institute, Henry Ford Health System*, http://www.henryford.com/body.cfm?id=40560.
26. Frank W. Hartman, Vivian G. Behrmann, and Roy D. McClure, "The Oxyhemograph," *American Journal of Surgery* 78, no. 6 (1949).
27. *Ibid.*
28. "Gas conditioning apparatus," patent filing by Frank Hartman, publication number US2277547 A, issued by the US Patent Office March 24, 1924.
29. William S. Haubrich, "Ormond of Ormond's Disease," *Gastroenterology* 132, no. 3 (2007): 838.
30. *Ibid.*
31. "Science Takes Center Stage," *Henry Ford Health System*, http://www.henryford.com/body.cfm?id=47718.
32. Dottie Deremo, interview by Jeffrey Rodengen, digital recording, 25 June 2013, Write Stuff Enterprises, LLC.
33. Nathan Bomey, John Gallagher, "How Detroit Went Broke," *Detroit Free Press*, September 15, 2013.
34. *Henry Ford Hospital: The First 75 Years*, p. 80.
35. *Henry Ford Hospital: The First 75 Years*, p. 78.
36. "Historical Collections," *Lam Archives, Henry Ford Health System*, http://www.henryford.com/body_nologin.cfm?id=39481.
37. *Henry Ford Hospital: The First 75 Years*, p. 79.
38. "Registry of Students," University of Michigan Official Publication, 1941–1942.
39. Conrad R. Lam and Magda Puppendahl, "The Pyruvic Acid Method of Burn Slough Removal," *Annals of Surgery* 121, no. 6 (1945).
40. Melanie Bazil, "History of Women in Medicine - Questions & Answers," *Lam Archives, Henry Ford Health System*, http://henryford.libguides.com/content.php?pid=276314&sid=3780371.
41. *Ibid.*
42. *Ibid.*
43. *Ibid.*
44. *Henry Ford Hospital: The First 75 Years*, p. 81.
45. *Henry Ford Hospital: The First 75 Years*, p. 82.
46. *Henry Ford Hospital: The First 75 Years*, p. 72.
47. *Henry Ford Hospital: The First 75 Years*, p. 81.
48. *Henry Ford Hospital: The First 75 Years*, p. 82.
49. *Henry Ford Hospital: The First 75 Years*, p. 83.
50. *Henry Ford Hospital: The First 75 Years*, p. 83–84.
51. *Henry Ford Hospital: The First 75 Years*, p. 84.
52. Michael S. Nussbaum, "The Gavel Box," *Surgery* 150, no. 4 (2011).

Chapter Four Sidebar: Dr. Edward Quinn: Infectious Diseases Pioneer

1. Dr. Norman Markowitz, interview by Jim TerMarsch, digital recording, 24 March 2014, Marsch Creative.

Chapter Four Sidebar:
Dr. Conrad Lam

1. Melanie Bazil, "Conrad R. Lam, M.D.," *Lam Archives, Henry Ford Health System*, http://www.henryford.com/body.cfm?id=39487.
2. "Historical Highlights," *Edith and Benson Ford Heart & Vascular Institute, Henry Ford Health System*, http://www.henryford.com/body.cfm?id=40560.
3. Hardin-Simmons University Hall of Leaders, online, "Conrad R. Lam, MD" article.

Chapter Four Sidebar:
The Growth of Cardiovascular Services

1. "Historical Highlights," *Edith and Benson Ford Heart & Vascular Institute, Henry Ford Health System*, http://www.henryford.com/body.cfm?id=40560.
2. *The Encyclopedia of Cleveland History*, online, "F. Mason Sones Jr., MD" article.
3. Melanie Bazil, "Conrad R. Lam Lectureship," *Lam Archives, Henry Ford Health System*, http://www.henryford.com/body_nologin.cfm?id=57064.

Chapter Five

1. Roger F. Smith, "D. Emerick Szilagyi, MD – An Appreciation," *Journal of Vascular Surgery* 13, no. 1 (1991).
2. "Science Takes Center Stage," *Henry Ford Health System*, http://www.henryford.com/body.cfm?id=47718.
3. American Board of Medical Specialties, online, "ABMS Bios" section.
4. *Ibid.*
5. American College of Hospital Executives, online, "Career Development" section.
6. "ABMS Bios."
7. American College of Healthcare Executives, online, "Past Chairmen" list.
8. "ABMS Bios."
9. Patricia Scollard Painter, *Henry Ford Hospital: The First 75 Years* (Detroit: Henry Ford Health System, 1997), p. 90.
10. "ABMS Bios."
11. Henry Ford Health System, outline.
12. *Henry Ford Hospital: The First 75 Years*, p. 90.
13. *Henry Ford Hospital: The First 75 Years*, p. 91.
14. "Science Takes Center Stage."
15. *Henry Ford Hospital: The First 75 Years*, p. 85.
16. *Henry Ford Hospital: The First 75 Years*, p. 86.
17. *Henry Ford Hospital: The First 75 Years*, p. 87.
18. Dr. William Eyler, interview by Jim TerMarsch, digital recording, 4 September 2012, Marsch Creative.
19. *Ibid.*
20. "Raymond Craig Mellinger, MD," *Grosse Pointe News*, March 4, 2013.
21. Melanie Bazil, "Historical Collections," *Lam Archives, Henry Ford Health System*, http://www.henryford.com/body_nologin.cfm?id=39481.
22. Charles Turner, David Burr, Web Jee, et al. "Tribute to Harold M. Frost, M.D.," *Journal of Musculoskeletal & Neuronal Interactions* 4, no. 4 (2004).
23. American Society for Bone & Mineral Research, online, "ASBMR Harold M. Frost Young Investigator Award" article.
24. A. J. Desmond & Sons, online, "John Rankin Caldwell, MD" obituary.
25. *Henry Ford Hospital: The First 75 Years*, p. 93.
26. Obits for Life, online, "George Mikhail, MD" obituary.
27. Michael Hoskins, "Meet Dr. Whitehouse: Historical Endo Extraordinaire," *Diabetes Mine*, http://www.diabetesmine.com/2012/03/meet-dr-whitehouse-historical-endo-extraordinaire.html.
28. Dr. Melvin Block, interview by Jeffrey Rodengen, digital recording, 25 June 2013, Write Stuff Enterprises, LLC.
29. *Ibid.*
30. "Henry Ford Hospital Dermatology History," *Henry Ford Health System*, http://www.henryford.com/body.cfm?id=51822.
31. "History of the Division," *Department of Medicine, Henry Ford Health System*, http://www.henryford.com/body.cfm?id=60327.
32. *Henry Ford Hospital: The First 75 Years*, p. 104.
33. *Michigan's TV & Radio Broadcast Guide*, online, "History of Michigan TV Broadcasting" timeline.
34. *Henry Ford Hospital: The First 75 Years*, p. 98.
35. Eyler interview.
36. *Ibid.*
37. *Ibid.*
38. *Henry Ford Hospital: The First 75 Years*, p. 108.
39. "History of HAP," *Health Alliance Plan of Michigan*, http://www.hap.org/corporate/history.php.
40. Center for Medicaid and Medicare Services, online, "CMS Programs Key Milestone" section.
41. "Population Change in Metro Detroit," *Detroit News*, July 19, 2007.
42. Wilma Gandy, interview by Jim TerMarsch, digital recording, 20 May 2013, Marsch Creative.

Chapter Five Sidebar:
Dr. Jack Guyton: Mathematics and Medicine

1. A. Edward Maumenee, "Jack S. Guyton, MD," *Transactions of the American Ophthalmological Society* 86 (1988).
2. *Ibid.*
3. Patricia Scollard Painter, *Henry Ford Hospital: The First 75 Years* (Detroit: Henry Ford Health System, 1997), p. 93.
4. *Ibid.*
5. "Jack S. Guyton, MD"
6. *Ibid.*
7. Stephanie Shapiro, "Is There a Doctor in the House?" *Hopkins Medicine Magazine*, Winter 2013.
8. "Cornelius McCole Obituary," *Times Leader*, June 24, 2008.
9. "Is There a Doctor in the House?"
10. "Jack S. Guyton, MD"

Chapter Five Sidebar: Dr. Clarence S.
Livingood: Father of Dermatology

1. Donald M. Pillsbury, Marion B. Sulzberger, and Clarence S. Livingood, *Manual of Dermatology* (Philadelphia: WB Saunders, 1942).
2. American Academy of Dermatology, online, "Livingood Award and Lectureship" article.
3. Rep. Carolyn Cheeks Kilpatrick, "The Example Of Superb Public Service: Dr. Clarence S. Livingood Of Grosse Pointe, Michigan," Speech to the US House of Representatives, July 29, 1998.
4. "Detroit Institute for Children Medical Director to Receive Prestigious CATCH Award," Detroit Institute for Children, press release, issued October 9, 2013.
5. Melanie Bazil, "Clarence S. Livingood, M.D.," *Lam Archives, Henry Ford Health System*, http://www.henryford.com/body.cfm?id=51822.

Chapter Five Sidebar: Dr. Richmond Smith:
Endocrinology Leader

1. "History of the Division," Endocrinology, Diabetes, & Metabolism Fellowship, *Henry Ford Health System*, http://www.henryford.com/body_program.cfm?id=50691.
2. Dignity Memorial, online, "In Memory of Raymond C. Mellinger, MD" obituary.
3. Dr. William Eyler, interview by Jim TerMarsch, digital recording, 14 September 2012, Marsch Creative.

Chapter Six

1. Dr. Richard Smith, interview by Jim TerMarsch, digital recording, 11 September 2013. Marsch Creative.
2. Cassandra Spratling, "King's 1963 Walk to Freedom still inspires Detroit," *USA Today*, June 19, 2013.
3. Walter P. Reuther Library, Wayne State University, online, "Detroit's Walk to Freedom" article.
4. Walter Douglas, interview by Jim TerMarsch, digital recording, 13 September 2012, Marsch Creative.
5. Dennis Archer, interview by Jim TerMarsch, digital recording, 17 July 2013, Marsch Creative.
6. Vivien T. Thomas, *Pioneering Research in Surgical Shock and Cardiovascular Surgery* (Philadelphia: University of Pennsylvania Press, 1985).

7. Wilma Gandy, interview by Jim TerMarsch, digital recording, 20 May 2013, Marsch Creative.
8. Douglas interview.
9. Patricia Scollard Painter, *Henry Ford Hospital: The First 75 Years* (Detroit: Henry Ford Health System, 1997), p. 115.
10. Dottie Deremo, interview by Jeffrey Rodengen, digital recording, 25 June 2013, Write Stuff Enterprises, LLC.
11. Gandy interview.
12. Lee Gooden, interview by Jim TerMarsch, digital recording, 29 May 2013, Marsch Creative.
13. Joan Daniels, interview by Jim TerMarsch, digital recording, 14 November 2013, Marsch Creative.
14. *Henry Ford Hospital: The First 75 Years*, p. 115.
15. *Henry Ford Hospital: The First 75 Years*, p. 116.
16. *Ibid.*
17. Deremo interview.
18. Douglas interview.
19. New Detroit, online, "Our History" section.
20. Deremo interview.
21. Gooden interview.
22. *Ibid.*
23. Dr. Bruce Steinhauer, interview by Jim TerMarsch, digital recording, 2013, Marsch Creative.
24. Gandy interview.
25. Smith interview.
26. Dr. John Popovich interview by Jim TerMarsch, digital recording, 14 September 2012, Marsch Creative.

Chapter Six Sidebar:
Walter E. Douglas Sr.:
Committed to the Community

1. Walter Douglas interview by Jim TerMarsch, digital recording, 13 September 2012, Marsch Creative.
2. *Ibid.*

Chapter Six Sidebar:
A Diverse Community Emerges

1. Randy Walker, interview by Jim TerMarsch, digital recording, 14 February 2013, Marsch Creative.

Chapter Six Sidebar:
Lee Gooden: Problem Solver

1. Lee Gooden, interview by Jim TerMarsch, digital recording, 29 May 2013, Marsch Creative.

Chapter Six Sidebar:
Wilma Gandy: Ward Clerk to Advocate

1. Wilma Gandy, interview by Jim TerMarsch, digital recording, 20 May 2013, Marsch Creative.
2. *Ibid.*
3. *Ibid.*

Chapter Six Timeline:

1. *Traverse City Record-Eagle*, 2 April 1969, Page 19, http://www.newspapers.com/newspage/1490213/.

Chapter Seven

1. Dr. Robert Chapman, interview by Jim TerMarsch, digital recording, 12 July 2013, Marsch Creative.
2. Joe Carlson, "Healthcare Pioneer Nelson Dies at 86," *Modern Healthcare* 42, no. 32 (2012): 4.
3. Stan Nelson, interview by Jim TerMarsch, digital recording, 2013, Marsch Creative.
4. *Ibid.*
5. *Ibid.*
6. *Ibid.*
7. National Conference of State Legislatures, online, "Certificate of Need: State Health Laws and Programs" section.

8. Ann Saphir, "The Visionary Who Built A Better Ford," *Modern Healthcare*, February 8, 1999.
9. Nelson interview.
10. *Ibid.*
11. *Ibid.*
12. *Ibid.*
13. *Ibid.*
14. Steve Velick, interview by Jim TerMarsch, digital recording, 5 February 2013, Marsch Creative.
15. Nelson interview.
16. *Ibid.*
17. *Ibid.*
18. Melanie Bazil, "Theresa Jones, R.N.," *Lam Archives, Henry Ford Health System*, http://www.henryford.com/body_nologin.cfm?id=57254.
19. "The Visionary Who Built a Better Ford."
20. *Ibid.*
21. Nelson interview.
22. *Ibid.*
23. Dr. Bruce Steinhauer, interview by Jim TerMarsch, digital recording, 2013, Marsch Creative.
24. Nelson interview.
25. *Ibid.*
26. Patricia Scollard Painter, *Henry Ford Hospital: The First 75 Years* (Detroit: Henry Ford Health System, 1997), p. 134.
27. Dr. Oscar Carretero, interview by Jim TerMarsch, digital recording, 29 July 2013, Marsch Creative.
28. "Overview," *Ford Foundation*, http://www.fordfoundation.org/about-us/history.
29. Nelson interview.
30. *Henry Ford Hospital: The First 75 Years*, p. 129.
31. Nelson interview.
32. *Henry Ford Hospital: The First 75 Years*, p. 129.
33. *Henry Ford Hospital: The First 75 Years*, p. 129–130.
34. Dr. Oscar Carretero interview.

Chapter Seven Sidebar:
Nursing Integrates and Reorganizes

1. Theresa Jones, interview by Jim TerMarsch, digital recording, 17 October 2013, Marsch Creative.
2. *Ibid.*
3. *Ibid.*
4. *Ibid.*
5. *Ibid.*

Chapter Seven Sidebar:
Commitment to the Community

1. "The Great Expansion," *Henry Ford Health System*, http://www.henryford.com/body.cfm?id=47719.
2. "CHASS Center Opens $17 Million Facility to Expand Health Care Services for Southwest Detroit," Henry Ford Health System, press release, May 2, 2012.
3. *Ibid.*
4. Dr. Kimberlydawn Wisdom, interview by Jim TerMarsch, digital recording, 12 November 2012, Marsch Creative.
5. *Ibid.*

Chapter Seven Sidebar:
Let the Games Begin

1. Melanie Bazil, "Henry Ford Hospital Olympiad," *Lam Archives, Henry Ford Health System*, http://www.henryford.com/body_nologin.cfm?id=57633.
2. *Ibid.*
3. Randy Walker, interview by Jim TerMarsch, digital recording, 14 February 2013, Marsch Creative.

Chapter Eight

1. Dr. Bruce Steinhauer, interview by Jim TerMarsch, digital recording, 2013, Marsch Creative.
2. Dr. Melvin Block, interview by Jeffrey Rodengen, digital recording, 25 June 2013, Write Stuff Enterprises, LLC.

3. Dr. Roger Smith, interview by Jeffrey Rodengen, digital recording, 25 June 2013, Write Stuff Enterprises, LLC.
4. Patricia Scollard Painter, *Henry Ford Hospital: The First 75 Years* (Detroit: Henry Ford Health System, 1997), p. 132.
5. Smith interview.
6. Dr. Donald Ditmars, interview by Jeffrey Rodengen, digital recording, 21 March 2013, Write Stuff Enterprises, LLC.
7. Dr. Robert Chapman, interview by Jim TerMarsch, digital recording, 12 July 2013, Marsch Creative.
8. Dr. Daniel Reddy, interview by Jim TerMarsch, digital recording, 15 July 2013, Marsch Creative.
9. "History of the Division," *Endocrinology, Diabetes, & Metabolism Fellowship, Henry Ford Health System*, http://www.henryford.com/body_program.cfm?id=50691.
10. Capitol Words, online, "Honoring Dr. Richard D. Nichols, On His Retirement" speech.
11. Mlive, online, "Head of Hurley Bariatric Center, Dr. Farouck Obeid, Dies" article.
12. *Ibid.*
13. Dr. Kimberlydawn Wisdom, interview by Jim TerMarsch, digital recording, 12 November 2012, Marsch Creative.
14. *Ibid.*
15. Dr. John Popovich, interview by Jim TerMarsch, digital recording, 14 September 2012, Marsch Creative.
16. *Ibid.*
17. Dr. David Leach, interview by Jeffrey Rodengen, digital recording, 22 May 2013, Write Stuff Enterprises, LLC.
18. ARN Mortuaries, online, "Dr. Charles Eugene 'Gene' Jackson" obituary.
19. Chapman interview.
20. *Ibid.*
21. Melanie Bazil, "Dean LeSher, M.D.," *Lam Archives, Henry Ford Health System*, http://www.henryford.com/body_nologin.cfm?id=57435.
22. Dr. Sidney Goldstein, interview by Jeffrey Rodengen, 28 March 2013, Write Stuff Enterprises, LLC.

Chapter Eight Sidebar:
Ford Foundation Grant Provides
for the Long Term

1. Patricia Scollard Painter, *Henry Ford Hospital: The First 75 Years* (Detroit: Henry Ford Health System, 1997), p. 147.
2. *Ibid.*
3. Information provided from Henry Ford Health System via email, February 18, 2014.
4. *Ibid.*

Chapter Eight Sidebar:
Henry Ford II:
Behind the Scenes Supporter

1. Ted Thackery Jr., "Henry Ford II Dies; Led Auto Firm 35 Years," *Los Angeles Times*, September 30, 1987.

Chapter Eight Sidebar:
Eleanor Clay Ford and Benson Ford:
Decades of Support

1. Patricia Scollard Painter, *Henry Ford Hospital: The First 75 Years* (Detroit: Henry Ford Health System, 1997), p. 142.
2. "Death Claims Benson Ford," as reported by *Associated Press* and printed in *Rome News-Tribune*, July 27, 1978.
3. "A History of Giving," *Henry Ford Health System*, http://www.henryford.com/body.cfm?id=47762.
4. Benson Ford Jr., interview by Jim TerMarsch, digital recording, 9 August 2013, Marsch Creative.

Chapter Nine

1. Walter Douglas, interview by Jim TerMarsch, digital recording, 13 September 2012, Marsch Creative.
2. Jesse Nankin and Krista Kjellman Schmidt, "History of US Bailouts," *ProPublica*, updated April 15, 2009.

3. Patricia Scollard Painter, *Henry Ford Hospital: The First 75 Years* (Detroit: Henry Ford Health System, 1997), p. 149.
4. *Henry Ford Hospital: The First 75 Years*, p. 151.
5. Jane Muer, interview by Jim TerMarsch, digital recording, 12 September 2012, Marsch Creative.
6. Dr. Edward Coffey, interview by Jim TerMarsch, digital recording, 23 April 2013, Marsch Creative.
7. Benson Ford Jr., interview by Jim TerMarsch, digital recording, 9 August 2013, Marsch Creative.
8. Junior League Detroit, online, "Past Projects" timeline.
9. Bob Vlasic, interview by Jim TerMarsch, digital recording, 10 April 2013, Marsch Creative.
10. "About Henry Ford Wyandotte Hospital," *Henry Ford Health System*, http://www.henryford.com/body_wyandotte.cfm?id=40207.
11. Bill Alvin, interview by Jim TerMarsch, digital recording, 29 August 2013, Marsch Creative.
12. "History of Henry Ford Macomb Hospital, 1990-present," *Henry Ford Health System*, http://www.henryford.com/body.cfm?id=48501.
13. Vinod Sahney, interview by Jim TerMarsch, digital recording, 19 August 2013, Marsch Creative.
14. Christine Cole Johnson, interview by Jeffrey Rodengen, digital recording, 16 September 2013, Write Stuff Enterprises, LLC.
15. Steve Velick, interview by Jim TerMarsch, digital recording, 5 February 2013, Marsch Creative.
16. Stan Nelson, interview by Jim TerMarsch, digital recording, 2013, Marsch Creative.
17. "History of HAP," *Health Alliance Plan of Michigan*, http://www.hap.org/corporate/history.php.
18. Nelson interview.
19. Doug Peters, interview by Jeffrey Rodengen, digital recording, 20 February 2013, Write Stuff Enterprises, LLC.
20. John Polanski, interview by Jim TerMarsch, digital recording, 5 September 2013, Marsch Creative.
21. Greg Solecki, interview by Jeffrey Rodengen, digital recording, 20 May 2013, Write Stuff Enterprises, LLC.
22. *Ibid.*
23. Gail Warden, interview by Jim TerMarsch, digital recording, 2013, Marsch Creative.
24. Bill Alvin, interview by Jim TerMarsch, digital recording, 29 August 2013, Marsch Creative.
25. Ann Saphir, "The Visionary Who Built a Better Ford," *Modern Healthcare*, February 8, 1999.
26. Bob Vlasic interview.

Chapter Nine Sidebar:
Caring for the Patient
Wherever Needed

1. John Polanski, interview by Jim TerMarsch, digital recording, 5 September 2013, Marsch Creative.
2. *Ibid.*

Chapter Nine Sidebar:
Cottage Hospital:
A Long History, Poised for the Future

1. Grosse Pointe Historical Society, online, "A Brief History of Grosse Pointe" timeline.
2. John Polanski, interview by Jim TerMarsch, digital recording, 5 September 2013, Marsch Creative.
3. "Grosse Pointe's Cottage Hospital Joins Henry Ford Health System," Henry Ford Health System, press release, October 2, 2007.
4. Jay Greene, "Henry Ford to convert Cottage Hospital in Grosse Pointe to major outpatient center," *Crain's Detroit Business*, January 12, 2010.

Chapter Ten

1. Dr. Eric Scher, interview by Jim TerMarsch, digital recording, 9 April 2013, Marsch Creative.
2. "Internal Medicine Residency," *Henry Ford Health System*, http://www.henryford.com/body.cfm?id=49807.

3. Dr. John Popovich, interview by Jim TerMarsch, digital recording, 14 September 2012, Marsch Creative.
4. Patricia Scollard Painter, *Henry Ford Hospital: The First 75 Years* (Detroit: Henry Ford Health System, 1997), p. 79.
5. *Henry Ford Hospital: The First 75 Years*, p. 120.
6. Dr. Mark Kelley, interview by Jim TerMarsch, digital recording, 15 November 2012, Marsch Creative.
7. Dr. John Crissman, interview by Jeffrey Rodengen, digital recording, 23 August 2013, Write Stuff Enterprises, LLC.
8. Dr. Henry Lim, interview by Jim TerMarsch, digital recording, 23 June 2013, Marsch Creative.
9. Dr. Bruce Muma, interview by Jeffrey Rodengen, digital recording, 25 September 2013, Write Stuff Enterprises, LLC.
10. Muma interview.
11. Dr. Marwan Abouljoud, interview by Jim TerMarsch, digital recording, 27 March 2013, Marsch Creative.
12. *Ibid.*
13. Dr. Mani Menon, interview by Jim TerMarsch, digital recording, 14 November 2012, Marsch Creative.
14. Dr. Ted Parsons, interview by Jim TerMarsch, digital recording, 24 September 2013, Marsch Creative.
15. Dr. Stanton Elias, interview by Jeffrey Rodengen, digital recording, 21 March 2013, Write Stuff Enterprises, LLC.
16. Dr. Mark Rosenblum, interview by Jim TerMarsch, digital recording, 15 November 2012, Marsch Creative.
17. Gail Warden, interview by Jim TerMarsch, digital recording, 2013, Marsch Creative.
18. Dr. Dennis Lemanski, interview by Jim TerMarsch, digital recording, 2 October 2013, Marsch Creative.
19. *Ibid.*
20. Dr. Joanna Pease, interview by Jim TerMarsch, digital recording, 22 November 2013, Marsch Creative.
21. Dr. Susan Schooley, interview by Jim TerMarsch, digital recording, 4 September 2013, Marsch Creative.
22. Teresa Wehrwein, interview by Jeffrey Rodengen, digital recording, 10 September 2013, Write Stuff Enterprises, LLC.
23. "Nursing Research," *Henry Ford Careers, Henry Ford Health System*, http://www.henryford.com/body_careers.cfm?id=47798.

Chapter Ten Sidebar:
Film Work in Medical Education

1. Melanie Bazil, "Historical Collections," *Lam Archives, Henry Ford Health System*, http://www.henryford.com/body_nologin.cfm?id=39481#Kroll,%20John%20Audio-Visual%20Collection.
2. Melanie Bazil, "From the Conrad R. Lam Archives," *Sladen Library News* 2, no. 1 (2009): 6.
3. Council on International Nontheatrical Events, online, "About" tab.
4. "TV's Minds of Medicine – Fall Schedule," *Henry Ford Health System*, http://www.henryford.com/body.cfm?id=46335&action=detail&ref=1150.

Chapter Ten Sidebar:
Henry Ford Macomb Hospital

1. "History of Henry Ford Macomb Hospital 1899-1909," *Henry Ford Health System*, http://www.henryford.com/body.cfm?id=48495.

Chapter Ten Sidebar:
Henry Ford Wyandotte Hospital

1. Bill Alvin, interview by Jim TerMarsch, digital recording, 29 August 2013, Marsch Creative.
2. Dr. Dennis Lemanski, interview by Jim TerMarsch, digital recording, 2 October 2013, Marsch Creative.

Chapter Eleven

1. Dottie Deremo, interview by Jeffrey Rodengen, interview, 25 June 2013, Write Stuff Enterprises, LLC.

2. Centers for Disease Control (CDC), "Epidemiologic Notes and Reports Acquired Immunodeficiency Syndrome (AIDS) among Blacks and Hispanics – United States," *MMWR Morbidity and Mortality Weekly Report* 35, no. 42 (1986).
3. Dr. Evelyn Fisher and Dr. Norman Markowitz, interview by Jim TerMarsch, digital recording, 24 March 2013, Marsch Creative.
   David Benfer, interview by Jeffrey Rodengen, digital recording, 2 April 2013, Write Stuff Enterprises, LLC.
4. *Ibid.*
5. Dr. Richard Smith, interview by Jim TerMarsch, digital recording, 11 September 2013, Marsch Creative.
6. *Ibid.*
7. *Ibid.*
8. *Ibid.*
9. Dennis Archer, interview by Jim TerMarsch, digital recording, 17 July 2013, Marsch Creative.
10. *Ibid.*
11. Patricia Scollard Painter, *Henry Ford Hospital: The First 75 Years* (Detroit: Henry Ford Health System, 1997), p. 179.
12. Gary Valade, interview by Jim TerMarsch, digital recording, 21 November 2013, Marsch Creative.
13. David McCammon, interview by Jim TerMarsch, digital recording, 13 November 2013, Marsch Creative.
14. Vinod Sahney, interview by Jim TerMarsch, digital recording, 19 August 2013, Marsch Creative.
15. *Ibid.*
16. *Ibid.*
17. "Gail Warden, In First Person: An Oral History," interview by Diane M. Howard, American Hospital Association Center for Hospital and Healthcare Administration History and Health Research & Educational Trust, 2010.
18. Melanie Bazil, "Henry Ford Innovative Milestones," *Lam Archives, Henry Ford Health System*, http://www.henryford.com/body_nologin.cfm?id=39485.
19. Melanie Bazil, "Milestones of Henry Ford Hospital," *Henry Ford Health System*, http://www.henryford.com/body.cfm?id=47720.
20. Steve Velick, interview by Jim TerMarsch, digital recording, 5 February 2013, Marsch Creative.
21. *Ibid.*
22. Dr. W. Douglas Weaver, interview by Jim TerMarsch, digital recording, 8 April 2013, Marsch Creative.

Chapter Eleven Sidebar:
Henry Ford Health System Influences National Health Care Quality

1. Vinod Sahney, interview by Jim Termarsh, digital recording, 19 August 2013, Marsch Creative.
2. Institute for Healthcare Improvement, online, "Overview" section.
3. Health Research & Educational Trust, online, "Gail Warden" bio.
4. "Gail Warden, In First Person: An Oral History," interview by Diane M. Howard, American Hospital Association Center for Hospital and Healthcare Administration History and Health Research & Educational Trust, 2010.
5. "Nancy-Ann DeParle, White House Office Of Health Reform," *Huffington Post*, May 25, 2011.
6. "Gail Warden, In Person: An Oral History."

Chapter Twelve

1. Dr. Michael Chopp, interview by Jim TerMarsch, digital recording, 17 September 2013, Marsch Creative.
2. Dr. Benjamin Movsas, interview by Jim TerMarsch, digital recording, 24 October 2013, Marsch Creative.
3. Dr. Scott Dulchavsky, interview by Jim TerMarsch, digital recording, 14 November 2012, Marsch Creative.
4. Dr. Mark Kelley, interview by Jeffrey Rodengen, digital recording, 12 September 2012, Write Stuff Enterprises, LLC.
5. Margot LaPointe, interview by Jeffrey Rodengen, digital recording, 22 May 2013, Write Stuff Enterprises, LLC.

6. National Diabetes Information Clearinghouse, online, "What is DCCT" section.
7. Dr. Fred Whitehouse, interview by Jim TerMarsch, digital recording, 2013, Marsch Creative.
8. *Ibid.*
9. *Ibid.*
10. Joslin Center, online, "Milestones in Joslin Care and Education" timeline.
11. "History of the Division," *Endocrinology, Diabetes, and Metabolism Fellowship, Henry Ford Health System*, http://www.henryford.com/body.cfm?id=50691.
12. University of Texas Medical School at Houston, online, "t-PA paper named among NEJM's Top 9" press release.
13. Dr. K. M. A. Welch, interview by Jeffrey Rodengen, digital recording, 22 May 2013, Write Stuff Enterprises, LLC.
14. Chopp interview.
15. *Ibid.*
16. "Neuroregeneration Research," *Neuroscience Institute, Henry Ford Health System*, http://www.henryford.com/body.cfm?id=49054.
17. Dr. Mark Rosenblum, interview by Jim TerMarsch, digital recording, 15 November 2012, Marsch Creative.
18. "Research and Clinical Trials," *Hermelin Brain Tumor Center, Henry Ford Health System*, http://www.henryford.com/body.cfm?id=54571.
19. Patricia Anstett, "Researchers at Detroit Center Seek Solutions to Brain Tumors," *Chicago Tribune*, April 25, 2000.
20. Rosenblum interview.
21. *Ibid.*
22. "History of the Vattikuti Urology Institute," *Vattikuti Urology Institute, Henry Ford Health System*, http://www.henryford.com/body.cfm?id=38735.
23. Dr. Mani Menon, interview by Jim TerMarsch, digital recording, 14 November 2012, Marsch Creative.
24. Dr. Robert Chapman, interview by Jim TerMarsch, digital recording, 12 July 2013, Marsch Creative.
25. "Cancer Tumor Boards," *Josephine Ford Cancer Institute, Henry Ford Health System*, http://www.henryford.com/body.cfm?id=50998.

Chapter Thirteen

1. Tony Armada, interview by Jeffrey Rodengen, digital recording, 18 March 2013, Write Stuff Enterprises, LLC.
2. Nancy Schlichting, interview by Jim TerMarsch, digital recording, 22 October 2013, Marsch Creative.
3. *Ibid.*
4. *Ibid.*
5. *Ibid.*
6. *Ibid.*
7. Armada interview.
8. Robert Riney, interview by Jim TerMarsch, digital recording, 13 September 2012, Marsch Creative.
9. Schlichting interview.
10. Riney interview.
11. Dave Bing, interview by Jim TerMarsch, digital recording, 15 October 2013, Marsch Creative.
12. William Schramm, interview by Jeffrey Rodengen, digital recording, 19 March 2013, Write Stuff Enterprises, LLC.
13. Armada interview.
14. Darlene Burgess, interview by Jeffrey Rodengen, digital recording, 25 March 2013, Write Stuff Enterprises, LLC.
15. *Ibid.*
16. Dr. Richard Zarbo, interview by Jeffrey Rodengen, digital recording, 29 March 2013, Write Stuff Enterprises, LLC.
17. *Ibid.*
18. *Ibid.*
19. Connie Cronin, interview by Jim TerMarsch, digital recording, 3 December 2013, Marsch Creative.
20. *Ibid.*
21. Veronica (Ronnie) Hall, interview by Jim TerMarsch, digital recording, 30 October 2013, Marsch Creative.
22. Edith Eisenmann, interview by Jeffrey Rodengen, digital recording, 19 March 2013, Write Stuff Enterprises, LLC.

23. Dr. John Popovich, interview by Jim TerMarsch, digital recording, 14 September 2012, Marsch Creative.

24. Dr Charles Kelly, interview by Jim TerMarsch, digital recording, 18 September 2013, Marsch Creative.

25. *Ibid.*

26. Dr. C. Edward Coffey, interview by Jim TerMarsch, digital recording, 23 April 2013, Marsch Creative.

27. *Ibid.*

28. *Ibid.*

29. *Ibid.*

30. *Ibid.*

31. Henry Ford Health System, online, "Depression Care Program Eliminates Suicide" press release.

32. Coffey interview.

33. Henry Ford Health System, online, "Henry Ford to Receive National Patient Safety & Quality Award" press release.

34. Gary Valade, interview by Jim TerMarsch, digital recording, 21 November 2013, Marsch Creative.

35. Patricia Stoltz, interview by Jeffrey Rodengen, digital recording, 12 September 2013, Write Stuff Enterprises, LLC.

36. Schlichting interview.

37. *Ibid.*

38. *Ibid.*

39. Dr. Bill Conway, interview by Jim TerMarsch, digital recording, 7 August 2013, Marsch Creative.

40. Armada interview.

41. Schlichting interview.

Chapter Thirteen Sidebar:
Focused on Wellness

1. Dr. Kimberlydawn Wisdom, interview by Jim TerMarsch, digital recording, 12 November 2012, Marsch Creative.

2. *Ibid.*

Chapter Thirteen Sidebar:
First, Do No Harm

1. Dr. Bill Conway, interview by Jim TerMarsch, digital recording, 7 August 2013, Marsch Creative.

2. *Ibid.*

3. "No Harm Campaign Progress Report – May 2012," *Quality and Safety, Henry Ford Health System*, p.17, http://www.henryford.com/documents/Quality/No%20Harm%20Annual%20Report%202012%20FINAL%2052312.pdf.

Chapter Fourteen

1. Robert Riney, interview by Jim TerMarsch, digital recording, 13 September 2012, Marsch Creative.

2. Tony Armada, interview by Jeffrey Rodengen, digital recording, 18 March 2013, Write Stuff Enterprises, LLC.

3. Gerard van Grinsven, interview by Jim TerMarsch, digital recording, 12 April 2013, Marsch Creative.

4. Allan Gilmour, interview by Jim TerMarsch, digital recording, 12 April 2013, Marsch Creative.

5. van Grinsven interview.

6. *Ibid.*

7. Nancy Schlichting, interview by Jim TerMarsch, digital recording, 22 October 2013, Marsch Creative.

8. "Departing Henry Ford Medical Group CEO Mark Kelley looks back," *Crain's Business Detroit*, December 4, 2012.

9. Dr. Michael Benninger, interview by Jeffrey Rodengen, digital recording, 25 March 2013, Write Stuff Enterprises, LLC.

10. *Ibid.*

11. Dr. Kathleen Yaremchuk, interview by Jim TerMarsch, digital recording, 25 November 2013, Marsch Creative.

12. Dr. Felix Valbueno, interview by Jeffrey Rodengen, digital recording, 16 August 2013, Write Stuff Enterprises, LLC.

13. Dr. Emanuel Rivers, interview by Jim TerMarsch, digital recording, 22 October 2013, Marsch Creative.

14. *Ibid.*

15. Dr. Bill O'Neill, interview by Jim TerMarsch, digital recording, 11 October 2013, Marsch Creative.

16. Denise Brooks-Williams, interview by Jim TerMarsch, digital recording, 29 October 2013, Marsch Creative.

17. "Departing Henry Ford Medical Group CEO Mark Kelley looks back," *Crain's Business Detroit*, December 4, 2012.

18. "Residential Incentive Program, 'Live Midtown,' Launched," Henry Ford Health System, press release, January 13, 2011.

19. Matt Roush, "Henry Ford Health System Announces $1 Billion Development," CBS Detroit, May 30, 2012.

20. Kresge Foundation, online, "Grant Highlights" section.

21. Dave Bing, interview by Jim TerMarsch, digital recording, 15 October 2013, Marsch Creative.

22. "$35 Million Henry Ford II Pavilion Expansion to Open," Henry Ford Health System, press release, December 8, 2008.

23. Schlichting interview.

Chapter Fourteen Sidebar:
Henry Ford West Bloomfield:
Serving the Whole Body

1. "Welcome to a Hospital Designed to Keep You Well," *Henry Ford West Bloomfield Overview Brochure*, Henry Ford Health System, http://www.henryford.com/documents/westbloomfieldhospital/Henry%20Ford%20West%20Bloomfield%20Overview%20Guide.pdf.

2. Gerard van Grinsven, interview by Jim TerMarsch, digital recording, 12 April 2013, Marsch Creative.

3. "Creating the Hospital of the Future," Henry Ford Health System, press release, April 8, 2010.

4. "Happy Birthday, Henry Ford West Bloomfield," Henry Ford Health System, press release, March 15, 2010.

Chapter Fourteen Sidebar:
Improving Lives a World Away

1. Dr. Scott Dulchavsky, interview by Jim TerMarsch, digital recording, 14 November 2012, Marsch Creative.

2. *Ibid.*

3. *Ibid.*

Chapter Fiftteen

1. Nancy Schlichting, interview by Jim TerMarsch, digital recording, 22 October 2013, Marsch Creative.

2. Denise Brooks-Williams, interview by Jim TerMarsch, digital recording, 29 October 2013, Marsch Creative.

3. Thomas Nantais, interview by Jeffrey Rodengen, digital recording, 28 March 2013, Write Stuff Enterprise, LLC.

4. Schlichting interview.

5. Barbara Rossmann, interview by Jim TerMarsch, digital recording, 23 April 2013, Marsch Creative.

6. Dave Bing, interview by Jim TerMarsch, digital recording, 15 October 2013, Marsch Creative.

7. Dr. Bill Conway, interview by Jim TerMarsch, digital recording, 7 August 2013, Marsch Creative.

8. Schlichting interview.

9. "Henry Ford Facts and Statistics," *Henry Ford Health System*, http://www.henryford.com/body.cfm?id=38768.

10. Robert Riney, interview by Jim TerMarsch, digital recording, 13 September 2012, Marsch Creative.

11. *Ibid.*

INDEX

Page numbers in italics indicate photographs and illustrations.